TAKE OFF

ALL ABOUT RADIO CONTROLLED MODEL AIRCRAFT

TAKE OFF

ALL ABOUT RADIO CONTROLLED MODEL AIRCRAFT

ALEX WEISS

CARTOONS BY
BOB GRAHAM

Special Interest Model Books

This book is for Richard who, like my father, does not share my passion for aviation

Special Interest Model Books Ltd.
P.O. Box 327
Poole
Dorset
BH15 2RG
England

First published by Nexus Special Interest Ltd. 1998

This edition published by Special Interest Model Books Ltd. 2004
Reprinted 2007

ISBN 978-1-85486-166-5

www.specialinterestmodelbooks.co.uk

Printed and bound in Great Britain by Biddles Ltd, King's Lynn, Norfolk

Cover pictures: Biplane - Mike Sullivan, MiG 29 - Jim Fox.

Contents

Acknowledgements

This book has only been made possible by the help of many people in providing suitable photographs and information. The source of the former is acknowledged in each caption.

Balsacraft International supplied me with drawings and instructions for their Hi-boy trainer, many of which are reproduced in Chapter 12.

Terry Pattinson, Richard Smart and the staff of Flair were so helpful when I visited their works. They gave me the run of their facilities and enabled me to take many of the photographs in this book. They also allowed me to reproduce words and illustrations from their Cub instructions.

Kevin Crozier of MacGregor Industries Ltd. kindly loaned me the radio equipment to photograph and much useful information for Chapter 7.

Malcolm Corbin and others of Weston UK provided several photographs and allowed me to take pictures of their new jet engine.

Mr M.D. Hodge, the owner of Chart Hobby Distributors Ltd. has kindly allowed me to reproduce many of the excellent illustrations from his company's catalogue.

Jim Morley gave a lot of his time and helped me photograph several of his helicopters at the airfield where his company is located. In addition, he kindly read and commented constructively on Chapter 18.

Howard Metcalfe prepared a number of his models for photography and provided background information on them

Chris Moynihan of BARCS came and saw me and left some excellent pictures. Mike Sullivan supplied me with a number of examples of his superb photography, particularly some of the flying shots.

The members of the West London and Slough Radio Control clubs patiently let me take pictures of them and their models, not always at the most convenient time.

Many of the companies, listed in Appendix A, provided photographs or sent me hardware for photography. If there is anyone that I have not mentioned, please forgive my forgetfulness.

Alex Weiss with a fun scale Saab Viggen, his first model published as a plan. (Photo courtesy Ron Dawes.)

Chapter 1 Introduction

So you've decided that you want to start building radio controlled (R/C) model aircraft and then, of course, you are going to learn how to fly them. Reading and thoroughly understanding this book provides a first step. It will not, however, teach you everything.

In the early stages of learning to fly, an instructor is invaluable in avoiding accidents and speeding the learning process. However, if you have understood the contents of this book, you are well on the way to your first solo. Once you have learned to fly, then this book shows how you can continue to increase your abilities and broaden your interests as an R/C modeller.

This is a hobby equally well suited to the young and old, male and female, rich and poor.

It is fun, it is demanding and it is rewarding. It requires some indoor work, usually done alone, at home and in the winter. It mostly involves the gregarious activity of flying out of doors. Whilst the outdoor part of the activity is weather dependent, the fact that there is always building or repair work to carry out means that wind and rain do not prevent you enjoying the hobby.

It requires the development of several skills. You have to build and complete the aircraft in your chosen colour scheme. You then have to learn to fly it. Routine maintenance will be necessary to keep the model serviceable and, from time to time, you will have to undertake repairs. If you think that your major interest is going to be in flying rather than building, you

Figure 1.1 John Carpenter's beautiful scale Hawker Tempest with retracts and a five blade propeller is the latest in his line of competitive models. In the background an equally attractive de Havilland Dragon Rapide taxies across the strip. (Photo courtesy Mike Sullivan.)

1

Figure 1.2 The classic lines of a tail dragger basic trainer. The Ezee Pzee from Paper Aviation is larger than most basic trainers. It is easy to see and it appears to fly slowly. (Photo courtesy Paper Aviation.)

can always go the ARTF or 'Almost ready to fly' route, accepting that it is a rather more expensive approach to the hobby.

Something you will have to come to terms with is the fact that you will have crashes. The best brains in the world, supported by one of the largest industries, are unable to stop the occasional airliner from plunging to earth. What chance do you have?

You will undertake a building programme without any formal quality control qualifications. You will be a student pilot who will not undergo a formal course of flying training and you will act as an unqualified maintenance engineer looking after the aircraft.

Despite all these factors, success is a highly likely outcome. Model flying has roughly reached the stage that full size aviation did in the 1920s. Most aircraft flew successfully most of the time. A great step forward from the time of the Wright brothers at Kittyhawk.

It can be difficult mentally to cope with the fact that hours of work lie in a mangled pile of balsa wood, not to mention the financial loss. It is, fortunately, rare to destroy an engine or radio. The knowledge that you will crash can help, as can the construction of a second model, as soon as the first is finished, to act as a spare.

Why radio control rather than, for example free flight or control line? The answer is simple. It is only with radio control that you can fully replicate all the controls and manoeuvres used by a pilot in a full size aircraft.

Before going any further, it is useful if you can decide where you fit into each of the three categories opposite. The first group indicates

---

Tip

Don't launch into a new hobby if you have just:

- Moved house
- Got married or formed a permanent relationship
- Had a child

Wait until things have settled down and you have some more spare time! You will then have a greater chance of success.

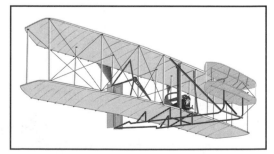

Figure 1.3 The Wright Flyer was the first powered heavier-than-air craft to achieve sustained flight.

Level of knowledge

No knowledge of aviation, internal combustion
 engines or electronics
Avid aviation enthusiast
Understand basic aerodynamics
Good knowledge of internal combustion
 engines
Good knowledge of radio control and/or
 electronics
Good knowledge of woodwork or other
 modelling activity
Experienced with R/C cars but want to try
 aircraft
Experienced with free flight or control line
 aircraft but want to try R/C
Have flown R/C aircraft but still not flown solo
Competent R/C flier
Expert R/C flier

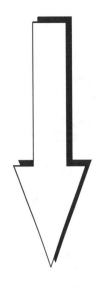

Increasing
relevant
experience

Disposable income and available time

At school
Unemployed with family
Unemployed with partner
Unemployed and single
Disabled
At college
Retired
Working with family
Working with partner
Working but single

Increasing
disposable
income

Building facilities – will work:

With new tools which I will acquire
With some new tools but some existing hand
 tools
With existing hand tools
With existing hand/power tools

On the kitchen table
From a box or cupboard in the living room or
 kitchen
In the loft
In a spare room
In the garage
In my workshop

Better
building
conditions

BUT I CAN'T DO MORE THAN THREE THINGS AT ONCE!

how much you will have to learn, the second how much available cash and time you may have, and the third group where you will carry out your hobby and what basic equipment you may need to purchase. This self-assessment will help you to understand your limitations, both personal and financial, and allow you to set the level of your expectations accordingly.

This book makes the premise that you will want to start by flying conventional powered models rather than gliders and that you will not be starting with a helicopter. Gliders make good trainers as they fly slowly. They do, however, require either some sort of launching gear such as a tow line or a suitable slope soaring site. Chapter 17 examines their main characteristics in some detail, while the following chapter summarises the field of rotating wing aircraft, both autogyros and helicopters.

Learning to fly R/C models is not easy. As a beginner you will need any help you can get. If

at all possible, join a club and get assistance from experienced model fliers. This is the quickest and cheapest road to success.

As a beginner you may feel frightened of looking stupid and clumsy. Remember all model fliers have experienced these feelings. They know learning is not easy and are normally sympathetic. You may, however, lose sympathy if you become big-headed, ignore club rules or forget to be polite to other club members.

This book divides into six main sections:
- Getting started.
- The basic materials.
- Model construction.
- Choosing and building your model.
- Learning to fly.
- Advanced manoeuvres and other types of models.

A bibliography, list of useful addresses and a glossary of terms are included at the end of the book.

Chapter 2 Getting started

It is an almost natural reaction on taking up this hobby that you will want your first model to be a Spitfire, Lancaster or other aircraft which you find charismatic. To commence with such a model is like putting a learner driver into a Formula 1 racing car. It is vital that you start by building and learning to fly a suitable trainer if you are to be successful and progress to your dream model. I know it's hard to restrain yourself, but many, including myself, made the wrong choice at the beginning and wasted a lot of time and money. You don't want to do that, I'm sure. So, let's start by looking at some of the terminology used in the hobby.

What makes a model

Many people starting R/C modelling will already be familiar with the various parts of a model, but to ensure that all readers are starting from the same baseline, Figures 2.2, 2.3 and 2.4 overleaf show the principal parts of a monoplane, a biplane and a tailless aircraft. You can use the glossary at the back of this book at any time if you find an unfamiliar term.

Radio controlled models come in all shapes and sizes from around 300mm (1ft) to 8 metres (26 feet) wing span. The majority of models, however, lie in the 1 – 2.5 metre (3 – 7½ feet) range, the smaller end being defined by difficulties of control and visibility, while the larger end is usually restricted by transportation problems. Most powered models use a small two stroke internal combustion (I/C) engine, though four stroke engines and electric flight have a major following. Gliders are also popular for those who enjoy a rather more tranquil approach to the hobby.

There is a theme which will occur throughout this book. Weight is the enemy of flight. At

Figure 2.1 Looking at this Avro Lancaster airborne at dusk, it is hard to believe that it is powered by a single 10cc (0.61 cu in) two stroke engine in the nose. (Photo courtesy Mike Sullivan.)

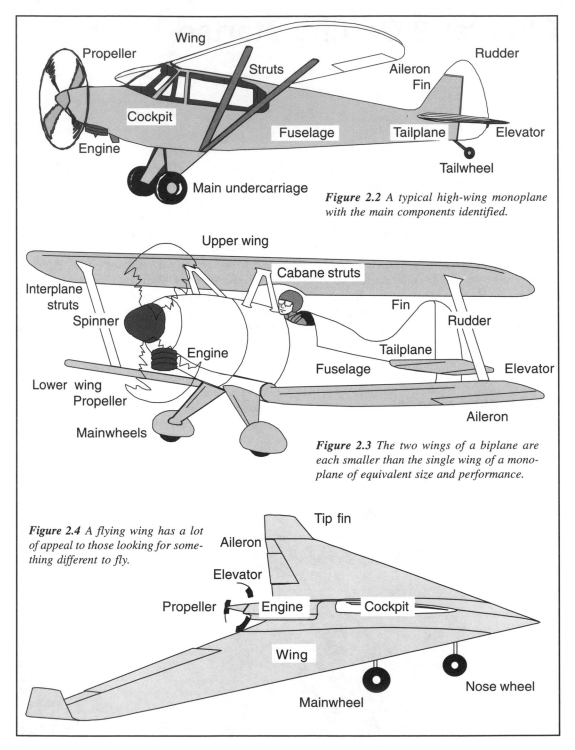

Figure 2.2 *A typical high-wing monoplane with the main components identified.*

Figure 2.3 *The two wings of a biplane are each smaller than the single wing of a monoplane of equivalent size and performance.*

Figure 2.4 *A flying wing has a lot of appeal to those looking for something different to fly.*

Figure 2.5 The Buccaneer is a classic vintage design, with plenty of construction work for the builder.

any and every stage of building a model, your key priority should be to build in lightness.

Fine weather models

Powered gliders are relatively cheap to build and operate because they require only a basic radio and a small motor. Their relatively large wings demand accurate building and they are not ideal for a first construction project.

Gliders fly slowly and you can operate them from rough flying fields but some of their flight characteristics need careful handling. A 1½ – 2 metre (5 – 6½') span glider will require two channel radio operating elevator and rudder, and a small glow or diesel engine of around 0.06 cu in (1cc) capacity. You will learn a lot about gliders and how to control a model using radio. However, you will not learn much about powered flying, particularly how to fly in less than perfect weather.

Vintage models are designs from around fifty or more years ago. They are comparatively complex to build and repair but they will be lightweight for their size, low powered, slow and stable in flight. Two or three radio channels are needed for elevator, rudder and optional throttle. Generally, they have similar flight characteristics to powered gliders, but can be taken off and landed on their wheels and are more closely matched in looks to the standard trainer.

Basic trainers

The classic high-wing three channel trainer has provided the route to success for more R/C modellers than any other type. Some offer an aileron wing conversion, using a fourth channel, once you have reached an initial degree of competence. The classic type provides a reasonable degree of speed allied to positive handling. Construction is straightforward, often with sheet fuselage and tail surface allied to a foam wing. The result will be a medium weight, medium powered model that is robust and practical. It will be easy to build, maintain and repair. When compared with more advanced models you may see at the flying field, it will be comparatively lightweight, stable and slow flying.

High-wing aileron models

Some people think it is better to learn to fly a model with four channel control, avoiding the need to convert later to aileron control. However, few aileron models retain the safe characteristics of a three channel model with its significant amount of dihedral.

To make perfect balanced turns requires the use of both rudder and ailerons. Model pilots tend to use one or the other unless they have chosen to couple their ailerons and rudder. The result will be either a slip into the turn or a skid out of it.

Figure 2.6 There is little doubt that the Balsacraft International Hi-boy is Britain's most popular trainer. It is available in three and four channel versions.

As a novice you should not try to learn how to co-ordinate ailerons and rudder during the initial learning phase. Furthermore, the use of ailerons to try to pick up a wing on take off or landing can easily cartwheel the model into the ground. Directional trimming becomes more complex and, all other things being equal, a four channel model will be a little heavier, fly faster and be less stable. For these reasons, the best start comes with a three channel model.

Some trainers have an aileron wing conversion, which you can add once you have reached an adequate standard. The conversion is ideal as it will only require a new wing, retrimming and rebalancing of the model.

Mid- and low-wing models

A high wing places the centre of lift above the centre of gravity and the engine thrust line. This helps to produce a stable model. Lowering the wing reduces this stability so that ailerons become essential for positive roll control. Mid-wing models require a more complex wing/

> **Tip**
> Make your first model:
> - A high-wing trainer
> - Requiring three channel radio
> - Powered by a 0.25 - 0.40 cu in two stroke glow motor

fuselage interface while low-wing models tend to be very responsive and demand continuous control inputs from the pilot to keep them airborne. This is why the latter are so popular for aerobatic models and rarely found as trainers. However, although it is difficult to make a low-wing model stable and easy to fly, it is not impossible.

Biplanes

It is rare to find biplanes used as trainers, even though they have some desirable characteristics. They are relatively slow flying and manoeuvrable, while being significantly smaller than the equivalent monoplane. On the negative side, they have poor gliding characteristics, there are two wings to build, and the structure supporting the upper wing adds to the complexity. Most people who regularly fly biplanes do so because the look of the model evokes aircraft built during the first thirty years of aviation in the period from 1903 until the start of the Second World War.

Electric flight

Electric flight models are not ideal for beginners despite the attractions of a clean motor which is elementary to start. The need for lightweight construction makes them fragile, while the battery pack makes them heavy. Duration is limited and there is rarely sufficient power for

Figure 2.7 A biplane has a smaller wing span, flies more slowly and is more manoeuvrable than an equivalent monoplane. (Photo courtesy Mike Sullivan.)

more than one missed approach. These characteristics make them far from the perfect model for the learner.

The situation is, however, always changing as battery performance continues to improve. Having said all this, there are a number of electric flight trainers on the market and environmental factors may force their use by those of you who cannot find a flying site where the noise of internal combustion engines is acceptable.

Unorthodox layouts

If you are attracted by the unusual, learn to fly first and then have a go at an unorthodox model.

Deltas and flying wings are typical of the breed. They are capable of very fast flight and high rates of roll. Canards which fly tail first will not stall in the conventional sense, but orientation is difficult. Such models are lots of fun, but definitely not for the beginner.

Some years ago, I was flying both a delta and an old timer biplane. The delta needed a high nose attitude when on the final approach to landing. Out of habit I attempted the same thing with the biplane, only to stall and hit the ground quite heavily. Unorthodox models often require a somewhat different approach to flying. which is why they are unsuitable for learners.

Figure 2.8 Of all electric flight models, powered gliders, such as this Flair Volture, are the most popular.

9

Figure 2.9 The speed performance of a delta is exceptional. It is always an exciting model to fly.

About radio control

Radio control has been about since the 1920s and used by hobbyists since the Second World War. Its real popularity, however, dates from the 1970s when affordable and reliable lightweight four channel proportional radio control became readily available. The phrase 'proportional' means that the primary aircraft controls can all be operated in a manner where the amount of control input fed in by the pilot on the ground is exactly matched by the control deflection on the model in the air. A modern R/C system comprises an ergonomically designed hand-held transmitter which is used in conjunction with a

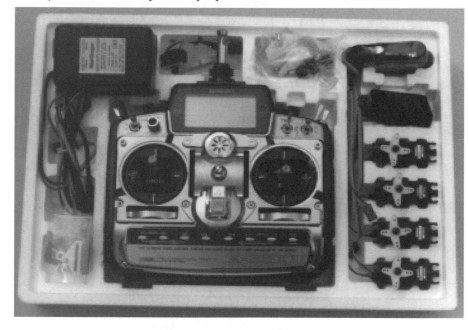

Figure 2.10 The MacGregor/JR X3810 is an eight channel computer radio, supplied complete with four servos

compact receiver and four servos powered by a small battery fitted with a switch and charging socket. Such a system costs upwards of £150 but this figure may initially be reduced slightly by purchasing only three servos. You should avoid the use of dry batteries, offered as an option by some manufacturers, as it reduces reliability and is likely to prove just as expensive in the long term. Choosing the right radio for your present and future needs, as well as your pocket, is covered in Chapter 7.

The operating frequencies used in the UK are in the 35MHz band. That compares with CB (Citizens band) radio at 27Mhz and FM radio broadcasts in the range 88MHz to 106MHz. The band divides into 26 discrete frequencies, allowing several models to fly at the same time, provided they are not operating on the same frequency. These frequencies are controlled by pairs of interchangeable crystals fitted to the transmitter and receiver.

What you need and what it will cost

It is important for most of you to understand how much it will cost you to first get airborne. The figures below are typical for an internal combustion engined powered training model and its accessories. The figures, which total some £500,

No	Item	Comments	Price
1	Kit	Basic trainer	£50
2	Glue	For construction of model (not all used)	£6
3	Covering material	Assumes use of Solarfilm	£10
4	Iron and heat gun	.	£50
5	Fuel proofer	For engine bay	£3
6	Building board	12mm MDF medium density fibreboard	£5
7	Razor knife and blades	1 knife, 5 blades	£5
8	Screwdrivers and spanners	For installing engine/prop and servos	£10
9	Sandpaper	For finishing model	£1
10	Engine	Low cost 0.40cu in/6cc two stroke	£50
11	Propeller	1 plus a spare	£5
12	Radio	Basic 4 channel nicad system + charger	£150·
13	Flight box	Save money by making your own	£20
14	Starter	Better than a chicken finger	£25
15	Power panel	No separate glow battery needed	£20
16	Plug lead		£6
17	Plug spanner		£3
18	Battery	12 volt rechargeable gel battery	£18
19	Battery charger	12 volt battery charger	£15
20	Fuel pump	12 volt or mechanical	£15
21	Flight insurance	Essential	£12
22	BMFA subscription	Much recommended	£10
23	Club subscription/joining fee	Much recommended. Prices vary a lot	£20/£15
24	Fuel	Straight castor per 4½ litres (1 gallon)	£7
25	Glow plug	One plus a spare	£5
	Total	**Items 1-3, 5-23**	**£537**

are only a guideline as items like a flight box you can make more cheaply and you may already own a selection of hand tools. On the other hand, it does provide a baseline if you have been wondering about the financial implications of taking up this new hobby. Day-to-day running costs are mainly the expense of fuel. Your consumption will depend on the size and thirst of your engine, how often you fly and the duration of your flights. You will need the odd replacement glow plug and propeller and, from time to time, a new model. Kit prices vary from as low as £30 to several hundred pounds and you can purchase new engines for similar figures. All the prices are current in the UK in the middle of 1997.

Should you decide to go along the electric flight route, then you will not require items 14 – 17 or 20 and instead of an engine, you will need a 540 electric motor, battery and charger. The cost of these three items is from £50 upwards, depending on the performance you choose. You may already own all these items if you have been into R/C cars. However, your radio, two channels

> **Tip**
> Accept that you should purchase a radio set with the following features:
> - Four channels
> - 35 MHz frequency band
> - Nicad batteries for transmitter and flight pack
> - Cost about £150

operating in the 27MHz band, is not suitable for flying an aircraft. Your running costs will be miserly, but you will still have to pay for club membership and insurance each year.

You will also need somewhere to build your models. This can be anything from the proverbial kitchen table to a custom built workshop. The options are discussed in detail in Chapter 5.

Gathering information

Model shops and mail order
Model shops can vary from the 'haven for the beginner' to the 'take as much money from you

AT LAST! MY QUARTER SCALE SPITFIRE HAS ARRIVED!

as possible and never mind the consequences' attitude. Fortunately, the former are in the vast majority. Friendly advice from the shopkeeper, preferably approached when the shop is not too busy, can result in information about local clubs and flying facilities, recommendations for suitable trainers and suggestions for engines and radios for which the shop holds spares.

In addition, a local model shop can supply all those essential ancillary items you need to get started. The main advantage of model shops over mail order is that you can actually see the item before you part with your hard earned cash. Even a small purchase of a few pence does not attract any packing and postage costs and you can buy items such as fuel, which cannot be posted.

Not that mail order is to be decried, and it is often cheaper for major purchases, such as a radio or engine. However, it is worth bearing in mind that getting an item serviced or repaired may not be quite as simple and that if you only buy small items from your model shop, it may soon go out of business and that certainly won't help you. Mail order companies advertise in the hobby's magazines, giving details and prices of a wide range of kits, radios, engines and ancillary equipment. They may be your only salvation if you live in a remote area.

Books, magazines and videos

One basic way of learning is to read books on the subject. Presumably that is why you are reading this book. In the bibliography, on page 243, you will find a list of other books which contain a wealth of useful information about various aspects of R/C modelling.

Magazines like *RCM&E* or *Radio Modeller* are essential reading matter to keep abreast of what is happening in the hobby, and again the bibliography contains a list of suitable journals. Increasingly, specialised sections of the hobby

Figure 2.11 Many companies produce comprehensive catalogues, which provide an excellent reference to what is available and include helpful tips.

are covered by specialist magazines dealing with gliders, electric flight, scale models and model jet aircraft.

The use of videos is a growing and popular way of learning. More and more titles are becoming available. Some are particularly useful for those wishing to learn to fly and are a useful addition to books and magazines.

Exhibitions, shows, clubs and club meetings

To see what is happening in the hobby, there is no better way than to visit an exhibition or show. These range from the major flying shows which

---

Tip
Support your local model shop if you want it to continue to exist.

Tip
A subscription to a magazine such as *RCM&E* or *Radio Modeller* will help you to learn the ins and outs of R/C modelling.

Figure 2.12 This Bill Kits stand at a summer flying display is crammed with a variety of models, all of which can be bought on the spot in kit form.

are held at locations across the country during the summer months to local club flying events. The show season usually starts at Easter and ends in October. Locations and timings are given in the modelling press.

Most shows include ready-built models that you can examine, as well as flights by trainers and sports aircraft, scale and large scale aircraft. These provide an excellent opportunity to see what is going on at first hand. Trade stands offer everything from kits to balsa wood or nuts and bolts. You can purchase almost any item at a competitive if not bargain price. However, it is worth thinking about the problem of returning

any goods which are faulty if the supplier is located at the other end of the country.

The other important way of gathering information is to join a club. A few questions at your local model shop will usually result in details of any clubs in the area as may an enquiry at your nearest public library. It is important to recognise that in congested urban areas there may be a waiting list as well as a joining fee.

However, once accepted, any club provides a source of like-minded people who should be happy to swap information and provide tuition both during the building phase and when learning to fly. Many clubs hold monthly meeting with speakers from a wide field, some working in the trade and describing their wares, others talking about their personal aviation experiences. You can acquire many good tips, not to mention bargain items at such evenings.

Figure 2.13 Club meetings are opportunities to learn about the hobby and make new friends.

Tip

Join a local model club, remembering to:
- Thank those who help you or give encouragement
- Do your fair share of club chores such as mowing the strip
- Return anything you have borrowed
- Help anywhere you have special skills

Tip
Your membership of the BMFA will help
to:
• Support the hobby nation wide
• Keep you abreast of new developments
• Provide recognised low cost third party insurance

BMFA

The British Model Flying Association (BMFA) is the UK organisation which deals directly with the FAI, the international governing body for aviation. It handles all UK model flying activities at the international level, including the selection of teams to compete in the various events. It organises national competitions and also discusses proposed new legislation which may affect model flying with the UK Civil Aviation Authority. It also helps clubs with difficulties in retaining their flying sites.

The Association produces the *BMFA News* five times a year, which is mailed to all members (approaching 30,000) as well as a comprehensive code of practice for model fliers. The BMFA public liability insurance scheme provides £5M

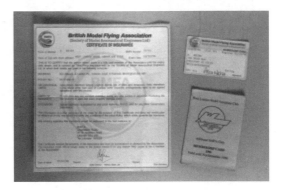

Figure 2.14 The BMFA provide a credit card size membership card and a certificate of insurance. Also shown is a typical club membership card.

cover for fliers in the UK, including those who fly on Ministry of Defence property.

The BMFA runs a basic ability grading system based on straightforward tests which can normally be taken at your club. The 'A' certificate is a basic indication of competence to fly, whilst the 'B' certificate indicates an advance capability, including the ability to fly at shows with public attendance. Most clubs have their own examiners so taking the test is relatively straightforward and encouraged as a goal for the beginner.

Figure 2.15 Is this model your ultimate aim? Powered by the Scorpion gas turbine, the Weston UK T-JET is fast, sleek, and attractive as well as highly manoeuvrable.

Chapter 3 What you need to know

The law

As with other activities, R/C flying is subject to the law. Two items affect modellers. No doubt you are already groaning having got this far but remember, you are legally responsible for any flight you make, so read on. You must comply with the Air Navigation Order and noise pollution guidelines.

No-one suggests that you immediately get hold of copies of these documents and learn them by heart. Instead, a summary follows of the main points, at the time of publication. Significant changes are widely reported in the modelling press.

Air Navigation Order

This law applies to all R/C aircraft, but how does it apply to the vast majority of models that weigh less than 7kg (15lb)?

The key rule for models, regardless of size is: A person – that's you – shall not recklessly or negligently cause or permit an aircraft – that's your model – to endanger any person or property. It's pretty much of a catch all.

This implies that you should only fly:

1. At an unobstructed site in suitable weather.
2. A safe distance from other people, vehicles, structures, and boats if you fly near water.
3. With due consideration for other people and their property.
4. Within the restrictions of local bye-laws.

It sounds pure common sense but there is more to come:

A person – you – shall not cause or permit any article or animal – your pet cat! – (whether or not attached to a parachute) to be dropped from a small aircraft – your model again – so as to endanger any person or property. This includes dropping bombs, sweets, parachutists or whatever from your model.

Additional restrictions only apply if your model weighs more than 7kg.

Noise

Noise regulations are increasingly important as local authorities are given muscle to deal with those who create noise. Most clubs set stringent rules to keep within government guidelines – 82 dB at 7 metres. If you decide to purchase your own noise meter, remember that these instruments are far from precisely accurate, particularly those more economically priced.

Insurance

In today's climate in which anyone will sue for the slightest reason, insurance against injuring

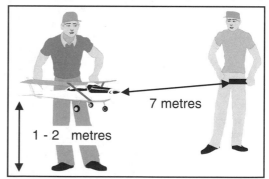

Figure 3.1 Noise checks involve holding the model, with its engine at full power, 7 metres from the noise meter. Measurements are made with the model pointing at the meter, directly away from it and from both sides. No reading may exceed 82dB.

YOUR HONOUR! MY CLIENT REQUESTS AN ADJOURNMENT NOW IT HAS STOPPED RAINING .. SO HE CAN GO AND FLY HIS MODEL AEROPLANE !! . . . . .

anyone else or damaging their property is absolutely essential. At the time of writing, £5,000,000 of third party cover is available for as little as £12 per year. It will give peace of mind against most imaginable accidents. Typical is an out of control aircraft hitting a car, building or even worse, a person. Membership of the BMFA normally includes insurance cover.

You should always carry your insurance certificate with you as most clubs and flying sites require proof of insurance before you are allowed to fly. It is possible, with some insurance

companies, to get model flying added to normal household third party liability, but not all companies will do this. Some will put limitations on the cover provided and, in general, it is a less than satisfactory approach. Having said all this, insurance cover is no excuse for dangerous flying. There is, unfortunately, no insurance cover for damage or destruction of your own model in a crash and, if there was, it would probably be prohibitively expensive.

Safety

Talk of insurance conveniently brings us to the subject of safety. This is considered by many to be a real bore, but is essential if you and other modellers are to fly with minimum risk of damaging yourself or someone else, your model or someone else's. A sports model, flying at 100 kph (60 mph) has roughly the same amount of energy as a rifle bullet. The consequences of being hit by such a model can be as lethal as by a bullet fired in anger.

Tip

Never even think about flying without suitable insurance cover.

Keep to the law. Remember, ignorance of the law is no excuse.

Fit a silencer so you do not exceed recommended noise limitations.

Always fly safely.

The word airmanship implies taking a safe and sensible approach to all areas of R/C flying. Remember Murphy's Law, familiar to all full size pilots: "If something can go wrong, sooner or later, somewhere, it will." The chief designer of Avro, Roy Chadwick, who designed the Lancaster, died in the prototype Avro Tudor airliner which had its ailerons connected up back to front. This should have been impossible, but the fact that the threads in the connectors to the left and right ailerons were the same meant that Murphy just had to play a fatal waiting game.

There is more to safety than just the items covered here. What are mentioned are most of the items which are special to radio modelling. As an example of a topic not fully covered, it is always dangerous dealing with mains electrical voltages.

Further information about flight safety is given in Chapters 13 and 14.

Construction

Modelling involves using materials and tools which can be lethal in the hands of children. You should take precautions to ensure that they can never gain access to such items. However, you can also hurt yourself and a little forethought can prevent unnecessary injury. Many materials such as glues, fillers and paints include safety instructions on the container. Do read them.

Glues and paints

Jokes continue to abound about the misuse of cyano instant glues, but care is necessary to avoid gluing fingers or other parts of the body during construction. Other glues and paints can also have unpleasant side effects, particularly if you tend to have dermatitis or other allergies. A barrier cream or thin disposable plastic gloves provide good protection, so try to ensure that the glue does not come into contact with your skin.

Sanding and spraying

When sanding some fillers, glass fibre components or even balsa wood, a simple face mask is necessary to avoid inhaling the dust. The same is true when spraying most paints.

Razor knives

It is only too easy to cut your fingers with a razor knife, many of which are identical to the scalpels used by surgeons. Recognise the dangers, dispose of old blades safely, and keep a box of plasters or a first aid kit handy.

Power tools

Even a power drill can be dangerous in the wrong hands, while power saws require great care if they are only to cut wood, as opposed to fingers. Many power tools are fitted with safety guards, but these can only minimise dangers, never eliminate them. There are also risks from the mains electricity they use.

Avoid leaving trailing cables across your working area and never use a tool with a frayed or worn cable. Ensure the correct fuse is fitted and if using an extension lead, make sure that it is fully unwound from its drum to avoid overheating.

Fuel

Fuel contains highly inflammable chemicals; methanol in the case of glow fuel. Think carefully about a suitable storage place to minimise fire risks and avoid invalidating your household insurance. Fuel is also poisonous and must be kept away from young children. Ready-mixed fuel is supplied in containers with childproof lids.

How an aircraft flies

You need to know very little about aerodynamics to fly R/C models, but it does help to have some understanding of the basic principles of flight. This knowledge will also help to turn you into a better pilot. What follows is kept to the simplest language and avoids all mathematics.

There are three basic requirements which must to be met if any R/C aircraft is to fly successfully. It must be able to generate sufficient lift, it must be stable in flight and it must have effective controls. In addition, it needs sufficient power to get it into the air and overcome the drag it generates in flight. A glider uses, instead, one or a combination of gravity, thermal or orographically rising air.

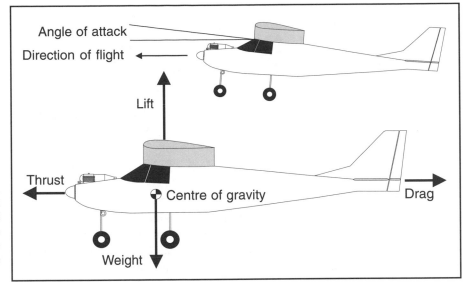

Figure 3.2 A model flying in straight and level flight experiences forces which balance out.

At this point, five simple definitions may help your understanding:

1. Lift is the upward force produced by a wing which supports a model and balances its weight in straight and level flight.
2. Drag is the total retarding force opposing the flight of a model through the air.
3. Thrust is the force generated by the engine/propeller combination fitted to a powered model. (Advanced models may use a ducted fan, turbojet or even a rocket motor.)
4. Centre of Gravity (C of G.) The balance point of a model or the point through which the total weight of the model acts.
5. Angle of Attack, the angle between the wing and the airflow.

How lift is generated

Lift results from air flowing over the wing of a model. A curved aerofoil shape is the most effective producer of lift, and this can easily be demonstrated by holding a piece of paper and blowing over it. As the air passes over the curved surface, it speeds up, and this speed increase produces a pressure reduction (otherwise we would be getting something for nothing). Two-thirds of the lift is generated by the air flowing over the top of the wing, and one-third by the air pressing up under the wing. The generation of lift causes an unfortunate penalty. It results in the generation of drag.

Any model will use one of three main types of aerofoil section; flat bottomed which are easy

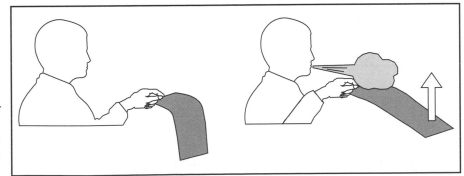

Figure 3.3 Simply blowing over a curved sheet of paper generates lift which raises the free end of the paper.

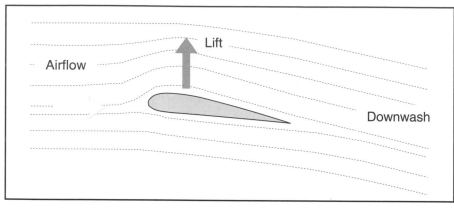

Figure 3.4 A wing produces lift by deflecting the airflow over and under the curved surfaces of the aerofoil.

to build, symmetrical or semi symmetrical which give an excellent aerobatic performance and undercambered which are found on scale models from the World War I era.

Stability

Stability is the term used to define an object's ability to return to its original position. This is easily shown by looking at the ball in Figure 3.5. There are three possible consequences if the ball is deflected from its position.

- Positively stable – the ball returns to its original position
- Neutrally stable – the ball remains in its new position.
- Unstable – the ball continues to move away from its original position.

A basic trainer should be stable to fly. Positive stability means it will return to straight and level flight once the controls are released. This state of affairs is ideal in the pitching plane but less so in the rolling plane, as it means that you must hold on continuous aileron during a turn.

It is recognised that neutral stability in the rolling plane is the best solution, and this is what is found on most trainers. Once you have entered the turn, you can return the aileron stick to neutral until you want to exit from the turn.

The only reason a normally designed model can become unstable is if its centre of gravity is located too far back. You have been warned!

Centre of gravity location

The location of the centre of gravity of an R/C model in the correct position is absolutely essential if the model is to fly safely. The centre of gravity is the position on the model from which, if suspended, the model will balance slightly nose down in pitch and level in roll. The fore and aft position is the one marked on the plan with one of two symbols; either an ⇧ or a ◐ .

While the designer will try to ensure that the C of G turns out in the correct place, this will depend on the engine/prop/silencer combination used, the radio gear and the final covering and paint decor. Thus you must try to position the components of the radio to achieve the correct position. You **must** correct any out of balance by putting lead weight in the nose or tail.

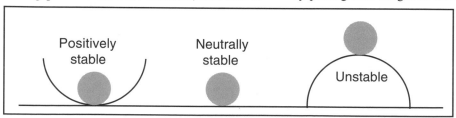

Figure 3.5 The three different types of stability.

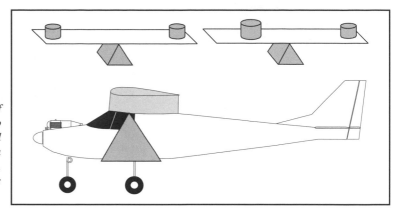

Figure 3.6 Top left, a pair of equal weights on a balance. Top right, a light weight on one end of the balance matched by a heavier weight nearer the pivot. Bottom, a model balanced at its centre of gravity.

On some plans, the C of G is shown as a range of positions, which may vary by as much as 25 mm (1"). In such cases, you should always make the first flight with the C of G located at or near the forward most position.

The lateral balance point is on the centre line of the fuselage and you can achieve this with either a screw or small piece of lead firmly attached to the lighter wing tip.

Primary controls and their functions

There are three primary controls surfaces; elevator, aileron and rudder. The elevator is fitted to the trailing edge of the tailplane and pitches the nose of the aircraft up and down. The ailerons are a pair of controls either fitted to the outer half of the wings, when they are known as inset ailerons, or full span. When one aileron moves up, the other moves down rolling the aircraft about its fore and aft axis. The rudder yaws the aircraft about its vertical axis and is fitted to the trailing edge of the fin.

Secondary controls

A number of additional controls, such as flaps and airbrakes, are fitted to some aircraft, though rarely to trainers. Their functions are not essential to basic flight control, but they can

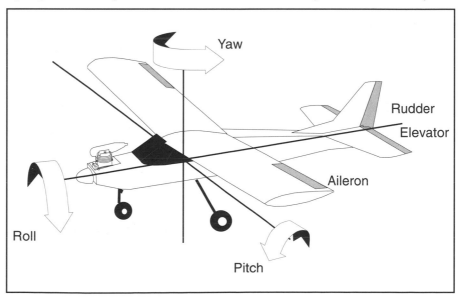

Figure 3.7 The primary controls are elevator, aileron and rudder. They control the movement of the model in pitch, roll and yaw, respectively.

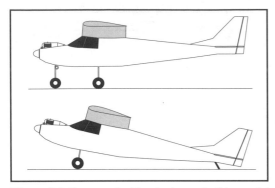

Figure 3.8 *You must decide whether to build a model with a noseleg or tailwheel.*

improve performance and add additional pleasure when flying a model.

Undercarriage issues

Although not strictly a control surface, the choice of undercarriage layout does affect the ground handling of a model. The question of whether to fly a model with a tricycle undercarriage or a tail dragger might seem initially to be a simple matter of aesthetics and personal choice. In fact there are a number of performance issues that you should understand before making an informed choice, though most trainers plump for a nose wheel.

A noseleg is heavily stressed during take off from all but the smoothest strip and often has to take the initial thump of landing, particularly during the early stages of flying training. This means that it must be securely attached to the fuselage, implying increased weight.

However, a noseleg does inherently keep the aircraft straight on take off and landing. This stable characteristic is a worthwhile advantage for any beginner.

A tailwheel, on the other hand, provides a lighter solution, though care must be taken not to let weight build up at the rear of the model. However, keeping straight on the ground is harder as a tailwheel configuration is inherently unstable. To start with, you may find the dreaded ground loop, where the model performs a spiral turn of reducing diameter, often digging in a wing tip, or the nose-over quite a handful.

Chapter 4 The basic materials

Wood

Traditionally, model aircraft were built largely from balsa and plywood. These materials are pleasant to work with and straightforward to cut and shape. While sanding them produces a lot of dust, they are otherwise clean and simple to glue. For those who enjoy carpentry in miniature, wood is the perfect material for building an airframe.

Balsa

Balsa is one of the materials used almost from the start by aeromodellers. It is lightweight, easy to cut and sand, and stronger than steel for a component of a given weight. It is widely used for fuselage formers and wing ribs as well as tail surfaces and sheeting wings and fuselages. Strips of the wood are found as wing spars, leading and trailing edges as well as fuselage longerons.

Balsa wood is cut at the sawmill to provide straight grain and cross grain wood. Straight grain material is used in most applications, but formers and wing ribs should be made from cross grained wood, which is better able to resist splitting. It is important to learn to recognise the differences even when building from a kit, where several sheets of balsa may be provided, and is essential when building from a plan. The speckled nature of cross grained material makes it easy to identify, though some sheets – to be avoided – are a mixture of both.

Balsa wood is supplied in a wide range of densities and your kit supplier should have selected the right grade for each task. If you are building from a plan, you will have to make the correct choice of wood yourself. With experience, you will be able to pick up a piece of wood and gauge its density. This is vital because the heaviest balsa of a given size in a model shop will weigh twice as much as the lightest. To assist in this learning process, a pair of scales and Table 4.1 overleaf will help. The table shows how much the weight of balsa wood can vary. It is easy to double the weight of wood in a model by selecting the wrong grade when building a model from plans.

The typical applications of the various grades of balsa will help you to find the right wood for each particular job.

* Very soft – cowls, wing tips and other parts from balsa block.

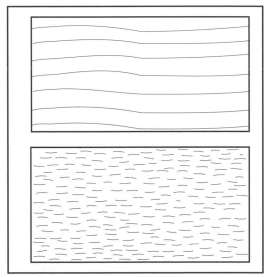

Figure 4.1 *Straight grained balsa (top) shows the grain running its length, while cross grained wood (bottom) has a speckled appearance.*

Grade	Thickness	Weight	Thickness	Weight	Thickness	Weight
Soft		14g/0.5oz		28g/1oz		56g/2oz
Medium	1.5mm/1/16"	21g/0.75oz	3mm/1/8"	42g/1.5oz	6mm/1/4"	85g/3oz
Hard		28g/1oz		56g/2oz		112g/4oz

Table 4.1 *The weight of 0.9 metre x 75 mm (36" x 3") lengths balsa wood of varying densities and thicknesses highlights the importance of selecting the right grade.*

- Soft – sheet tail surfaces, fuselage top decking, wing sheeting.
- Medium – wing ribs, trailing edges, sheet fuselages sides, formers and sheet wings.
- Medium hard – wing spars and longerons, fuselage doublers.
- Very hard – main spars and leading edges.

Balsa is available in a number of different cross sections, shown in Figure 4.2, and several of these are likely to be found in any kit. You can cut square and rectangular strip from balsa sheet, but the other specialist shapes can save considerable time during construction, particularly the shaped leading and trailing edges. Be careful, however, as the shaped sections have a great tendency to warp. You may need to replace them with straight pieces before wing construction commences to avoid a warped structure which will cause all sorts of problems when it comes to flying the model.

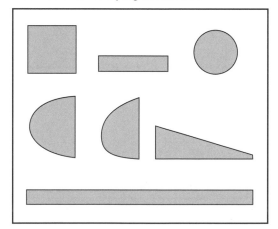

Figure 4.2 *There is a wide range of different balsa sections on the market.*

If you build from a plan rather than a kit and have to purchase your own wood, your model shop may help you select the right grades. Take special care if you need matching pairs of items such as fuselage sides, wing sheeting, spars, leading or trailing or edges. If you are lucky, you may find sheets cut from the same balsa log: usually every other one if the pile has not been disturbed. These will have similar grain patterns.

Obechi

About the same weight as very hard balsa, obechi is a fairly coarse textured soft wood. It is widely used as the veneer for covering foam wings. At this stage, you are only likely to see it on ready covered wing cores. If, later, you start cutting your own foam cores, then the application of 0.8mm (1/32") obechi veneer will become second nature.

Liteply

Liteply is a very lightweight form of plywood and is increasingly found in kits and specified on plans (not those designed before the 1990s). It has many of the characteristics of normal plywood, is quite resistant to warping, but is weaker and, of course, lighter. The most important use of liteply is for fuselage formers, but complete fuselage sides, fins, tailplanes and wing ribs are often made from this versatile material.

Another form of 'lightply' is home made from layers of balsa, with the grain of alternate layers at right angles, glued together with contact adhesive to avoid the warping caused by water-based glues. This lightply is even lighter than the commercial product and is sometimes

Thickness	
mm	**inches**
0.4	1/64
0.8	1/32
1.0	1/24
1.5	1/16
3.0	1/8
6.0	1/4

Table 4.2 Although plywood is only available in metric sizes in the UK, it readily converts to the imperial sizes found on many plans.

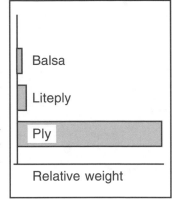

Figure 4.3 The comparative weights of balsa, liteply and plywood show just how heavy ply is compared with the other two materials.

specified on plans. A sandwich of balsa between two layers of thin conventional ply, or a sandwich of the ply between two layers of balsa are both variations on the theme and their use indicated on some plans.

Ply

There are two different sorts of plywood sold today and those looking for materials when building from plans need to choose the right one. DIY quality ply is far from ideal for model aircraft. Good quality birch ply, sold for marine or aeromodelling purposes, has a more uniform strength and quality. Plywood comes in a wide range of sizes, popular thicknesses ranging from 0.4mm to 6mm. The thickness of ply available in the UK is always metric, but Table 4.2 shows imperial equivalents.

Plywood is ideal for highly stressed formers around the engine and undercarriage. It is commonly used to make engine firewalls, undercarriage mounting plates and dihedral braces. To reduce weight, lightening holes are common, and the material is always used sparingly at the rear end of any model. It is an excellent material, though care is required when sawing

Figure 4.4 No need to ask what it's made of. This FU2 with transparent covering reveals all. (Photo courtesy Parc-Amber.)

Figure 4.5 Kit balsa and ply parts are usually pre-cut to shape. These parts are laser rather than die cut.

Figure 4.6 Typical vacuum formed pilots and cockpit interiors are lightweight and easy to paint to provide convincing replicas.

across the grain. A sharp Stanley knife run along the cutting line on each side should prevent splintering. It is readily cut with a fret saw, coping saw or small tenon saw, as well as almost any powered saw. Any component you have cut out will need its edges sanding smooth.

Spruce

Spruce strip is used for longerons or wing spars to provide greater strength than balsa of the same size. It is regularly found as spars on high aspect ratio wings and as longerons on open structure fuselages. A range of standard metric and imperial sizes is available from model shops for use when building from plans, but it is important to choose straight grained unwarped pieces.

Beech

Beech is a hard, close grained wood, widely employed for engine bearers and undercarriage mounting blocks. In kits the bearers will be cut to length. When obtaining materials for plan building, 300mm or 450mm (12" or 18") lengths are the norm in a range of cross sectional sizes from 6mm to 18mm (¼" to ¾") square or rectangular. Small offcuts make useful attachment points if you to wish to retain a hatch with screws.

Plastics

The range of different plastics which have been developed during the second half of the

twentieth century has transformed the materials used in the construction of many radio controlled models. Some kits contain more plastic items than wooden ones.

Plastic fuselages, GRP cowls, foam wings and tail surfaces, covered with heat-shrink self-coloured plastic covering materials mean that a model can be finished with virtually no wood in it at all. Whether this type of construction suits you, or you prefer to build from wood, is an entirely personal choice.

Expanded polystyrene

A very lightweight material in this form, expanded polystyrene is best cut to shape with a hot wire, though you can employ a sharp serrated knife or razor saw. The most popular use of foam or expanded polystyrene is as cores for wings. White foam is normal for this purpose, cut with a hot wire bow.

The foam can be obtained from builders' merchants in sheets 50mm (2") thick. Blue foam is a slightly different variant of expanded polystyrene, white being roughly half the weight of blue and also rather less expensive. Blue foam's strength is an asset in high aspect ratio wings and is also more resistant to knocks and dents.

Thin balsa sheet or obechi veneer are the normal coverings for foam wings, but brown paper, thin cardboard and even heat-shrink film have been used with success provided there are leading and trailing edge spars to take the flight

Figure 4.7 There is a lot of working in making a mould suitable for vacuum forming. This one is for a cowl enclosing a radial engine. (Photo courtesy Vortex Plastics.)

loads. Such an approach can result in a lightweight solution which is useful for electric models. Additional lightening holes can also be cut out of the foam.

Not only wings but turtle decks and other parts of fuselages are sometimes made from the material, not to mention fins, tailplanes and ancillary items. Foam core coverings, in order of increasing strength, weight and cost, are heat-shrink film (not necessarily the cheapest), brown paper (attached with wallpaper paste), cardboard, balsa wood and obechi veneer. Most coverings are applied with contact adhesive, such as Copydex, but a check must be made that the glue will not dissolve the foam.

Foam board

Foam board is an artist's material consisting of a layer of expanded polystyrene sandwiched between two sheets of thin white card. It can be obtained from artist supply shops in sheets of quite substantial size, nominally 3mm or 5mm thick.

It is easily cut to shape and, as well as being ideal for wing ribs and formers, can be used to build almost a complete airframe. Exposed edges can have strips of thin balsa, ply or card glued to them for protection.

Plastics and vacuum forming

Many of the modern plastics are used to make most of the small components for R/C models including such items as wing bolts, hinges, horns, clevises and engine mounts. They are particularly resistant to fuels and oils but sometimes difficult to glue. However, the aim here is to examine those plastics which lend themselves to vacuum forming.

Cockpit canopies are almost invariably formed over a wooden pattern as are many of the components found in kits such as cowls, spats and hatch covers. Furthermore, many household and food containers can be cut to provide useful pre-formed components. A good example is the use of part of a one litre lemonade bottle for a cockpit canopy.

You can make a simple vacuum forming machine from a wooden box and an electric heating element with a vacuum cleaner providing the vacuum. Alternatively, many schools are equipped with such machines and are happy to provide the required part for the cost of the materials and a small contribution to school funds.

More to the point, as often as not just heating the material and pulling it over a form will suffice, providing the form is not too deep. Mould design

I DIDN'T THINK YOU'D BE THAT INTERESTED IN MY NEW VACUUM FORMING MACHINE!

is important in terms of avoiding reverse curves which make it impossible to remove the finished component from the form. Gluing requires some care in the choice of adhesive and, in particular, careful degreasing of the plastic. The key plastics are:

ABS
ABS is often used for awkwardly shaped parts in R/C model aircraft kits. It is reasonably impact resistant and straightforward to form, but its main asset is its very low cost.

Acetate
Most commercial canopies are moulded from transparent acetate which is widely available and reasonably inexpensive. It is easy to mould and resulting canopies have good optical properties.

Acrylic
The most widely known is perspex, but there are many other forms which are popular for moulding stiff forms. You can easily obtain clear, translucent and opaque types.

Polycarbonate
This is the strongest mouldable plastic but also the hardest to form. It is also the most expensive. It withstands the highest temperatures (120°C)

and is widely used for R/C helicopter canopies and R/C car bodies. It is a clear material that you can paint with polycarbonate paints. It is widely available from shops stocking R/C cars.

PVC
Clear corrugated PVC sheet is an excellent material for moulding DIY canopies. It can be shaped by simply being heated and pulled over a form. Its low cost and wide availability make it a good choice.

Styrene
This is the material used for making small plastic aircraft kits. It is usually sold in white sheets and is cheap to buy, strong, gives excellent mould detail and is readily available in sheets of varying thickness.

Plastic coverings
The other main application of plastic is in the manufacture of iron-on, heat-shrink covering materials. Some of the more commonly used plastics are described below.

Polyester
Available in a variety of forms, polyester is popular as a resin for use in GRP work, which

may be clear or coloured. It is also produced in sheet form and is the basis of many iron-on covering materials, as well as being the material used for blow-moulded bottles.

Polycarbonate

This plastic is very tough and flexible. It is used to manufacture many commercial and domestic items including hinges. Solarfilm is made from it, in sheet form.

Composite materials

Increasingly, the materials used in the construction of full size aircraft are composite materials rather than the more traditional aluminium alloys. For model aircraft, composites are likewise popular for cowls, fuselages of gliders and scale models of jet aircraft.

Glass reinforced plastic

GRP or fibreglass offers a number of features which make it attractive to use in R/C models:

- High strength/resilience and low weight.
- Dimensional stability.
- Weatherproof and resistant to fuels.
- Transparent to radio signals.
- Simple to colour.
- Easy to make with inexpensive equipment.

When using GRP there are three types of glass reinforcement:

1. Chopped strand mat – random direction, non-woven fibres, used for making items like cowls, wheel spats and fuselages
2. Rovings – fibres orientated in a single direction, mainly used to reinforce spars on high aspect ratio wings.
3. Plain weave fabric – fibres woven in two directions at right angles. As glass fibre tape, this is ideal for joining wings.

You can make GRP with either of the two main types of resin; polyester or epoxy based. Polyester is easier, but very smelly. Epoxy has virtually no odour, but is harder to use.

You can use GRP to make small components such as cowls and spats or to make whole fuselages or even complete airframes. You can use it to join wing panels together or to add strength

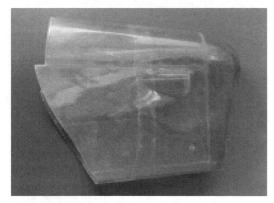

Figure 4.8 This beautifully moulded cowl comes with the kit for the Flair Tiger Moth and completely encloses the engine.

around highly stressed areas like engine bays and undercarriage mounts.

Strength

The strength of GRP laminate depends on the type of reinforcement and the resin/glass ratio. Rovings provide the maximum strength in a single direction. Woven fabrics provide strength in two directions at right angles. Least strong, but by far the easiest to form into three dimensional shapes is chopped strand mat, which is why it is used to make most components. Figure 4.9 compares the strength of these various materials with steel.

The GRP mouldings used in R/C models are quite thin but in spite of this you can easily achieve adequate stiffness and rigidity. This is usually provided in the form of the moulding

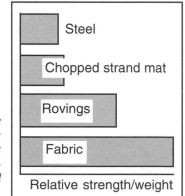

Figure 4.9 The relative strength/weight of GRP materials compared with steel.

Steel

Chopped strand mat

Rovings

Fabric

Relative strength/weight

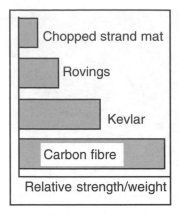

Figure 4.10 Kevlar and carbon fibre both provide marked strength improvements for a given weight of laminate.

itself. A semi-circular, oval or curved cross section is inherently stiff along its length.

You can provide a local increase in stiffness by adding additional layers of material, together with resin, where more strength is needed. Any increase in cross section should be progressive to avoid weakness at the point where the section changes.

Moulds and producing components

Should you decide to make a new or replacement component for a model yourself, you will need to think about how to make the mould. The easiest method is to carve a plug from balsa or pine, and then provide a smooth hard surface layer. The plug must be marginally smaller than the final component to allow for the thickness of the component itself.

The finish of the plug is all important, and a couple of coats of epoxy resin, smoothed down with increasingly fine wet and dry emery paper and finished off with an abrasive polish, such as Brasso, will ensure a near perfect result.

Having made the plug, you must then make a female GRP mould, which you will use to produce the final component for your aircraft.

One of the keys to success in working with GRP is to use an effective release agent. Though wax polishes are often recommended, the safest solution is to use paint on PVA release agent, normally coloured bright blue so that you can see where you have applied it. You should follow the manufacturer's instructions exactly and

leave the GRP item in the mould for 24 hours to harden.

Assuming you are using a female mould, start with a layer of gel coat to give the component a shiny exterior finish, then a coat of resin followed by one or more layers of glass fibre, pushed into place with a short stiff brush using a stippling motion.

You will need a coat of resin between each layer of glass, and you must apply each new coat when the previous layer is just tacky. Take care not to use too much resin as this is where excessive weight can build up.

Exotic materials

Figure 4.10 shows the strength to weight ratio, using the same resin, of GRP chopped strand mat, rovings, kevlar and carbon fibre. The superiority of both kevlar and carbon fibre is clear. However, the significantly higher price of these two materials means you will rarely find them specified and where they are, they are likely to be used sparingly to provide the greatest possible strength in highly stressed areas. A typical example is the reinforcement of the spars of a glider wing.

Cardboard and paper

The main attraction of card is that it can often be salvaged, free of charge from old boxes. Cartridge paper, a thin strong card, is available from graphic design and office supply shops. It is suitable for covering foam wings. A few kits employ double-sided card with internal corrugations to make virtually a complete model.

You can use brown wrapping paper to cover foam components. It is economic and easy to use, particularly if you have any experience of wallpapering. Wallpaper glue is ideal for sticking panels of paper in place, matt surface down.

Metal

There are many metals found in R/C trainers and other more advanced models. Engines are almost entirely fabricated from metal and radio

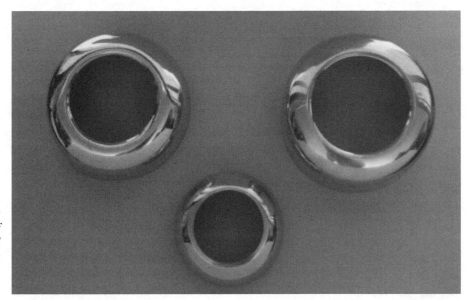

Figure 4.11 You will find many different sizes of spun polished aluminium cowls are available on the market.

equipment also contains a lot of it. For the remaining parts of a model, although heavy, metal is used for thin, highly stressed items. However, be careful not to use too much of this material in your R/C models as it is much heavier than wood.

As most R/C modellers have limited metal working facilities, designs requiring much more than bending piano wire or cutting and forming an aluminium undercarriage mount are rare. For the scale modeller, lithoplate can be glued to finished structures to give a realistic metal finish.

Steel

While steel has numerous applications in aeromodelling, it is mainly used during model building in the form of piano wire for undercarriages and cabane struts. It will, of course, also be found in the screws, nuts and bolts you will need for mounting the engine, clevises and various parts for connecting servos to control surfaces.

Piano wire

This material is the first choice for undercarriage legs. It is strong and springy, the latter being of particular importance. It is available in a wide range of diameters. When joining two pieces of piano wire you should avoid silver soldering as the process removes the springy temper from the wire. A design of joint which is wrapped with thin wire and then soft soldered will not impair the strength of this excellent material. Piano wire is also widely used for making elevator joiners and aileron torque rods.

Aluminium alloy

Aluminium alloy is the traditional material of the full size aircraft industry. This is not surprising in view of its remarkable strength to weight ratio.

It is often employed for making engine mounting plates and undercarriage legs. Circular aluminium cowls are an attractive feature of some designs and some cowls are even made from converted teapots or saucepans!

Aluminium alloy is most commonly used in sheet form. It is readily cut and bent to shape. You can produce more complex forms if you first heat soften the material to anneal it before trying to bend it.

The alloy is also available in the form of lithoplate, usually obtained in A4 sized sheets as scrap from printers. This material is so thin that you can cut it with scissors.

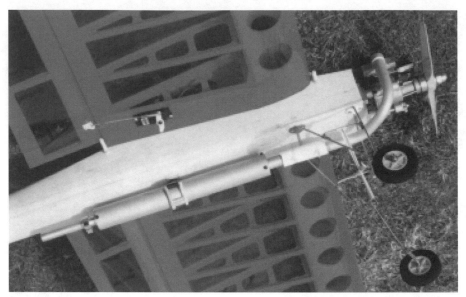

Figure 4.12 An FU3 showing off its metal parts including piano wire undercarriage, aileron servo push rod, resilient engine mount and in-line tuned pipe. (Photo courtesy Parc-Amber.)

Brass

The sizes of brass tube available are such that each size is a sliding fit into the size above, making the material ideal for telescopic undercarriage legs. The tube is useful for passing fuel though sealed bulkheads, making control hinges and torque rods. The material is also supplied in rectangular tube section and as thin sheet; the latter useful for making metal fuel tanks as brass is particularly easy to solder.

Lead

Lead is a very dense material used to adjust the centre of gravity of a model to its correct position once it has been built. Lead can be obtained from builders' merchants (not church roofs!) as lengths of thin strip or from tyre centres in the form of lead wheel balance weights, each of which is stamped with its actual weight. The self-adhesive weights which attach to alloy wheels are ideal for balancing a model.

Holding it together

There are a number of ways of joining two parts together. Primarily, the method chosen will depend on whether the joint is to be permanent, occasionally has to be undone or is just to hold the parts together temporarily while you make a permanent joint. There is a variety of adhesives available on the market which will join most materials together. Nuts and bolts are the normal way of attaching engines to their mounts, while screws are used for installing servos. Wings are usually held on with elastic bands or wing bolts.

During construction, you often need to hold materials or parts together while you are gluing them. Perhaps the most popular method with balsa parts is simply to pin them. Weights can be a good substitute as you do not have to make holes in the wood. Lumps of metal, particularly lead are excellent, but you can press pieces of hardwood or even books into service. You will find that there is a wide range of small G clamps and other moulded plastic clamps that you can purchase relatively cheaply, which will prove invaluable when you are building a model. Some of these are shown in Figure 5.10 on page 41.

Adhesives

The range of glues available is quite bewildering and hardly a day seems to pass without some new and specialist adhesive appearing on the market. However, many are not required in the early stages of R/C modelling. A brief examination of the main groups of adhesives indicates their strengths and weaknesses, and highlights their main uses. Remember it may take some time for a joint to reach its maximum strength after the glue has finally set. Furthermore, many adhesives depend for their adhesion on perfectly clean surfaces.

This can be a particular problem with metals and plastics, where even the oils from your skin can prevent a successful joint. From the modeller's point of view, the key factors are strength, weight and cost. These are shown in Table 4.3 for the basic glues on the market in 1997. Table 4.4 shows the materials these glues will join.

Having examined the properties of the various adhesives, the question is, which ones should we use, and where, when building a model.

Contact

The traditional way of attaching joiners to the fuselage sides is to use a contact glue, which you have to apply to both surfaces and leave to dry for about 10 minutes before bringing the two parts together. The positioning must be correct first time as there is only the slightest allowance for movement once you have formed the joint.

Cyano

Certainly the quickest and lightest way to build a model is to use cyano. This glue does require accurately cut joints and some people find it difficult to use. Basically, the technique is to hold the parts together and then apply a single drop of glue, which will enter the joint by capillary action. Cyano has little or no gap filling capability and dries in seconds rather than minutes. Thus you can hold the joints together by hand while the cyano sets, but there is little time for adjustment. There are gap filling additives specially formulated for use with cyano, not to mention relatively slow drying variants.

	Contact	Cyano	Epoxy	PVA
Drying speed	Med	V fast	Med./slow	Slow
Weight	Med	V low	High	Med
Penetration	V poor	V good	Poor	Med
Gap filling	Poor	Poor	Good	Med
Strength	High	Med	V high	Med
Cost	Med	High	High	Low

Table 4.3 The main characteristics of the four most popular adhesives. They will glue most materials used by modellers

	Contact	Cyano	Epoxy	PVA
Paper/fabric	X	X		X
Balsa	X	X		X
Hardwood	X	X	X	X
GRP			X	
Acetate		X		
Metals		X	X	
Foam			X	X
Veneers	X			
Canopies		X		X

Table 4.4 The various materials which the popular adhesives will join.

Epoxy

Epoxy's main use is in the engine bay area where its strength in holding firewalls and engine bearers together is its greatest asset. The rapid setting variety takes only around five minutes to set, while the 24 hour variant takes a whole day. The longer setting varieties produce much stronger joints than the quick setting ones. You can speed up the setting process up by the application of heat from a hot air gun, hair drier, radiator or airing cupboard. Heating the adhesive makes it much more runny, allowing it to really

IT'S NO GOOD.... HE'S STUCK FAST.......
..I GUESS HE'LL JUST HAVE TO BE THE PILOT!

flow into joints. Its gap filling qualities are excellent.

PVA

This wood-working glue is the other most popular adhesive for assembling airframes, but does require you to fix the joint securely with pins or clamps while the glue dries. Depending on the brand, it takes about half to one hour before clamps can be removed. It is ideal for sheeting as well as general construction. It is an especially thick, gap filling glue, and comes in a container with a long spout. This makes getting into the corners much easier. Some brands are a bit rubbery when it comes to sanding joints.

Other adhesives

Table 4.5 details other glues which may find their way into some models and gives some pointers on their applications. New adhesives are being created all the time and it is worth experimenting with a range of adhesives to learn their advantages and limitations.

The purpose of tissue paste and balsa cement should be apparent from their names. The former is used for attaching tissue covering to open frameworks such as wings and the latter for gluing pieces of balsa together. In fact, PVA white glue is probably a better choice for building balsa wood structures.

Finally, mention should be made of wallpaper glue, which is ideal for attaching paper skins to foam cores, the various forms of Loctite, used for securing nuts to bolts, instant gasket which is perfect for stopping leaks between exhaust manifolds and silencers, and last of all, chemical metal and epoxy putties like Milliput, which both might better be described as fillers rather than glues.

Nuts, bolts and screws

Many parts of R/C models, such as engines, engine mounts, control horns and servos are bolted or screwed into place, rather than glued.

You will need a selection of small metric or BA nuts and bolts, not forgetting the washers and locking washers, together with some reasonably short thin self-tapping screws for the finishing stages of most models.

- Metric bolts 1.5, 2.0, 2.5 and 3.0 mm diameter – 15 and 25mm long.
- 10, 8, 6 and 4BA bolts – ½" and 1" long.
- Self-tapping screws ½" x 4" and ½" x 6".

Elastic bands

The use of elastic bands to hold on wings and other parts of the model is very common. A wide range of widths and lengths is available and it is important to select the right size for the job. Also important is to remember that bands deteriorate with age and that exposure to fuels and exhaust products speeds this process. However, some bands are designed to resist these characteristics and should be used on your R/C models. Thus the regular replacement of all elastic bands is essential. Furthermore, an absolute minimum of four broad 6mm (¼") bands is essential to hold on a key component like a wing.

Wing bolts

The wings are often attached to the fuselage with a pair of plastic bolts. It is a clean and convenient method of attachment, but not very

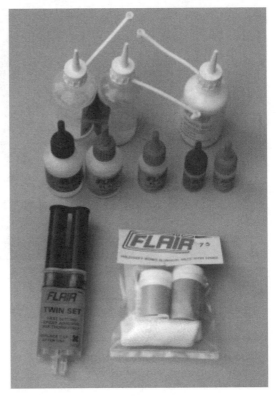

Figure 4.13 Some of the more popular adhesives on the market today. From the top, a pair of bottles containing two part epoxy, a white glue, two types of cyano available in three different sizes, a handy epoxy syringe container and a glass fibre wing joining kit.

Table 4.5 More specialist adhesives may prove useful for specialist applications demanding a strong joint.

	Acrylic	Ali-phatic	Balsa cement	Hot glue	Latex	Loctite	Polyester resin	Solvent weld	Tissue paste
Paper/fabric		X	X		X				X
Balsa		X	X				X		X
Hardwood	X	X		X			X		
GRP	X			X			X		
Plastics	X			X			X	X	
Metals	X			X		X	X		
Foam		X			X				
Veneers					X				
Canopies		X							

Figure 4.14 The owner of this fun flier has taken great care to hold the wing securely in place.

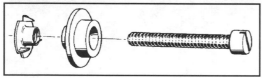

Figure 4.15 Wing bolts are made from plastic, with a washer to prevent the bolt cutting into the wing. They screw into captive nuts and are designed to snap in a serious accident. (Picture courtesy Chart.)

forgiving in the case of a poor landing where a wing tip digs in.

Made of plastic, they come with specially shaped washers and metal captive nuts. The two popular sizes available are M5 and ¼" Whitworth, both 50mm (2") long. They are supplied in pairs with a spare bolt in case of damage. Plastic bolts may also be used to hold items such as the main undercarriage mounting in place.

Chapter 5 Building your model

A place to build your model

Where you end up building your model depends very much on where and how you live. Some fortunate people own large houses with plenty of spare space while others occupy a small flat or bedsitter. Many people have no permanent work space and rely on the use of a kitchen table or a desk in their bedroom. This is fine to start with, but a suitable permanent base will become necessary as more and more models are built.

You can set up a modelling den in a spare room, loft or garage, or you can even purchase and erect a wooden shed in the garden. It is worth considering each option in turn and understanding the advantages and snags.

The kitchen table

For some of you, a table in the kitchen is the only flat working space you will have available. A building board, placed on the table will protect its surface and allow you to remove all the modelling work when the table is required for its primary purpose, food preparation and/or eating a meal.

SORRY DEAR! I CAN'T CLEAR THE TABLE UNTIL THE GLUE'S DRY!

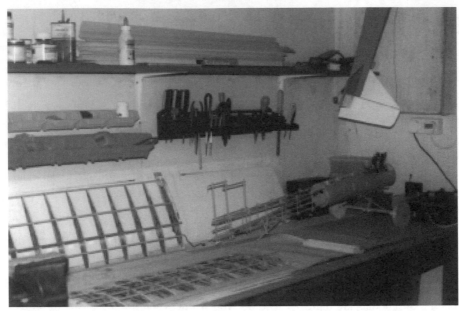

Figure 5.1 A typical work area layout with balsa, glue, paint and iron-on covering on the top shelf, tools and storage bins below and a new model under construction on the work bench.

Provided the building board is no more than 70cm (2ft 4in) wide, it will pass through any normal door frame. Such a portable building board will have an affect on the size of model which you can readily construct. Furthermore, the annoyance of having to share the work space will soon make you search for a more permanent solution.

The spare room

Any spare room, bedroom or otherwise, is an excellent option for use as a modelling den. It reduces disruption both to you and anyone else who shares your accommodation. You can convert the room into a permanent modelling den or use it in a temporary way, with just a building board placed on a bed or other piece of furniture.

The loft

Your loft can often provide just the space you need for a reasonably spacious modelling den, particularly if it is already fitted with a permanent chipboard floor. You will probably have to undertake some conversion work. The main requirements for such an approach are:

- A good folding loft ladder.
- Permanent flooring.
- A good source of lighting.
- Preferably some roof insulation to reduce summer heat and winter cold.

The garage

Many people park their car on the road, in the drive or under a carport, rather than in their garage. This gives the opportunity to turn the garage into a suitable working area. Usually fitted with light and electrical power, a garage can provide almost ideal working conditions.

A shed in the garden

The last possibility is a wooden shed connected to electricity and provided with heating and security. Again many modellers use this solution and find it the simplest for a permanent workshop.

The work area

Whichever option you choose, there is a range of fixtures and fittings which you can use. The number and complexity of these depend on the permanence of the solution, the amount of time

Figure 5.2 The ceiling provides excellent storage for complete and partially complete models.

and how much money you want to invest in the project.

It is a truism that more models get damaged during their construction than at the flying field. While this may be an exaggeration, hanger rash is a real issue. An easy access to the work area will help to reduce this problem.

Work bench

A solid work bench is a great luxury. Many people build their own from scrap wood – old pallets and packing cases provide a good source. Metal benches are also available at a fairly modest cost. The advantage of a bench is that it allows you to cut, drill and glue on a really firm base.

Storage containers

It is possible to purchase boxes of storage drawers to house small items, but you can also use empty food boxes, tobacco tins and for small items, 35mm film containers. You can keep larger items, such as lengths of balsa and rolls of iron-on covering, on shelving. DIY stores offer economy shelf units at reasonably afford-able prices.

Model storage

The single most important factor when storing a model is to find a dry place, as damp will quickly warp almost any model and, in extreme cases cause the veneer to become detached from foam wings. Damp is also the enemy of all electronic equipment and exposure to such conditions will lead to premature failure.

Think carefully about where you store your precious equipment. Models can easily be hung from the ceiling or the wall to keep them out of the way of your building activities. Remember that your modest start with a training model will, in all probability, lead to a stable of half a dozen models or more. You will need to find storage space for all of them.

The tools you need

Balsa knife

Undoubtedly the most basic of modelling tools is the balsa knife or scalpel. Invest in a good one and it will last you a lifetime. You will need a selection of replaceable blades and if you are that way inclined, a sharpening stone will considerable extend the life of the blades.

Cutting mat

A self-healing cutting mat will protect any surface underneath and prevent premature blunting of your knife blades. Although they may seem an unnecessary luxury, the investment is well worthwhile if you can afford it. The alternative is to use a piece of spare hardboard, ply or other

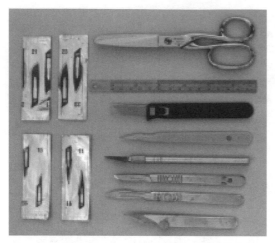

Figure 5.3 There is a wide choice of balsa knives and blades; essential when working with balsa wood.

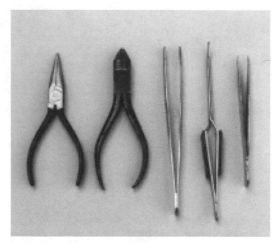

Figure 5.4 Pliers, side cutters and tweezers are a vital adjunct when building more advanced models.

wooden sheet material, any of which you will need to replace from time to time.

Metal straight edge

A metal ruler provides not only a means of making measurements, but also of cutting straight edges in balsa wood. A 300mm (12") rule is ideal, with 500mm (18") and 1000mm (36") rules being an optional addition. A strip of self-adhesive baize or other non-slip material stuck to the back of the straight edge can prevent your cut diverging from the desired line.

Razor saw

Replaceable Exacto razor saw blades with a heavy duty handle are useful for cutting thick balsa. A fine and a coarse blade make a good

starting point. The handle will also take knife blades for really heavy duty cutting.

Razor plane

A razor plane is the ideal tool for rapidly removing balsa wood either from blocks or thick sheet. Fitted with a conventional razor blade as the cutting edge, it makes a far better job of balsa removal than a balsa knife.

Sanding blocks

The ability to produce a smooth surface on the wood of any model is an essential, and there are many sanding tools from the humble sanding block with a piece of sandpaper folded around it to the more sophisticated, long lasting and, in truth,

Figure 5.5 A razor plane is incomparable for the rapid removal of balsa wood when shaping a nose or wing tip block.

Figure 5.6 Special sanding tools, such as these shaped Perma-Grit sanding blocks, last far longer than sandpaper. (Photo courtesy Perma-Grit.)

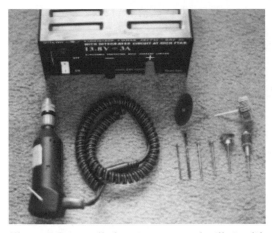

Figure 5.7 A small electric power tool will simplify many tasks including drilling holes.

more cost effective metal-based sanding tools. These latter come in a variety of shapes which can be most helpful when sanding awkward corners.

Pins

You might think that a pin is a pin, but there are at least four types of pin. Two are ideal for holding pieces of balsa together and two are far less well suited. In the former category are those with folded metal triangular tops and those with coloured plastic heads, either of which allow you to push the pin easily into wood. Normal dress-making pins and those with coloured glass heads are far more likely to damage your fingers when you push hard.

Clamps

As an aid to construction 'Handiclamps' are incredibly useful. They are the sort of item that once used, you wonder how you got on without

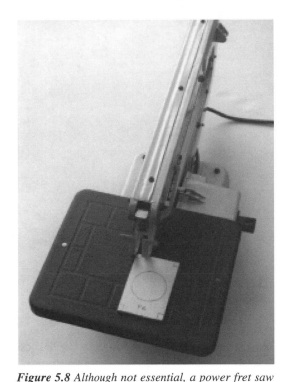

Figure 5.8 Although not essential, a power fret saw is worth its weight in gold when cutting out ply parts.

them. They come in two sizes and are available from most model shops. Plastic G clamps are also widely sold as is a range of other types of clamp. You can see many of these in your local model shop, or on the trade stands at modelling exhibitions and flying displays.

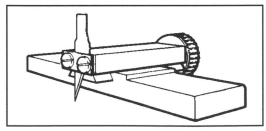

Figure 5.9 A tool for cutting strips of consistent quality from sheet balsa. (Picture courtesy Chart.)

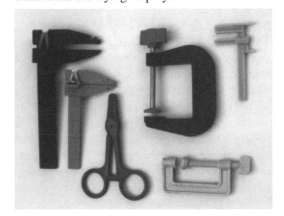

Figure 5.10 Several clamps, including Handiclamps (left) which hold parts together during construction.

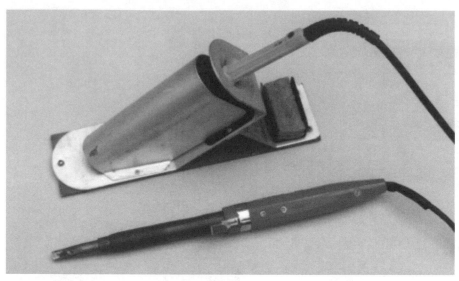

Figure 5.11 In front a 75 watt iron suitable for heavy metalwork. Behind the 15 watt iron in its stand is ideal for electrical and electronic work.

Weights

Weights are ideal for holding two pieces of wood together while the glue sets. Probably you will end up using books or old batteries, but the best answer is cast lumps of lead. These are compact in size for any given weight and you can shape them to suit the required purpose.

Soldering

Soldering is a method of bonding metal together using a molten metal alloy. Success in soldering requires cleanliness above all other things, the right flux and sufficient heat. There are two basic types of soldering:

Soft soldering

The art of soft soldering is one that you will find you need almost from your start in the hobby of radio modelling. It uses a lead/tin alloy which melts at around 200°C and involves the use of a soldering iron to heat the items you are joining and a suitable flux. It is ideal for making up lightly stressed components such as metal fuel tanks and you can also use it for joining undercarriage or cabane components, providing you first bind them with thin steel wire to give the finished joint adequate strength. In addition, you may wish to do electrical work such as soldering wires to switches, plugs and sockets.

For those who have never mastered the art, soft soldering seems a very difficult skill to acquire. In fact, there are only four basic rules:

1. All the parts you are going to solder must be perfectly clean. Use emery paper to clean all surfaces until they gleam.
2. Always use plenty of flux on the parts you are joining.
3. Use a large enough iron to heat the parts you are soldering together.
4. Apply the solder to the heated joint.

You will eventually need two different sizes of soldering iron.

- A 15 watt iron, to attach wire to switches and connectors.
- A 75 watt iron for soldering undercarriage wires and cabane struts.

A stand will stop the hot iron damaging any work surface and prevent it from overheating. The stand will also provide a space for a damp sponge, used for cleaning the tip of the iron.

You will have to tin the tip of any iron before use. Once it is hot, wipe it on a damp sponge and apply resin cored solder or dip in flux and apply solder until the tip is shiny with a coat of fresh solder. Avoid scraping the tip with a file or the like as you will remove the protective layer applied by the manufacturer.

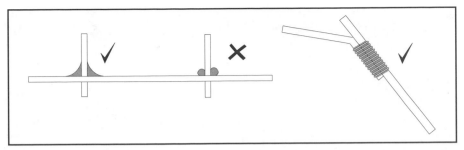

Figure 5.12 The right way to produce soft soldered joints is to ensure cleanliness, sufficient heat and support for any stressed joints.

There are two types of flux that you can use. The first is Bakers fluid, a clear, slightly acidic liquid. Its use means that you will have to wash the completed component in water after you have finished soldering. It is totally unsuitable for electronic work.

The other is a paste which is non-corrosive and suitable for all types of work. There are even two basic types of solder; resin cored solder for electrical and electronic work and solid bars of plumber's solder. You can use the former for all radio modelling jobs and a reel of 1.2 – 1.5mm cored solder is ideal. Do not think, however, that because there is flux within the solder that you can get away without fluxing the component parts.

Any non-electronic task requires you to secure the components so that they cannot move, and to apply a little flux to the joint. Heat up the iron and tin the tip. Apply the iron to the joint, give it a few seconds to warm up and then apply the solder until it melts and flows into the joint.

Remove the iron and as soon as the solder has set, wipe away any excess flux. Any solder that sits in globules on top of the joint is indicative of a dry joint, usually caused by lack of cleanliness, occasionally by too little flux or an iron so hot it has burned the flux away.

Tip

For success when soldering
- Always use a sufficiently large iron
- Make sure all parts are really clean
- Coat the parts with flux
- Apply heat and then solder

You will have to use resin cored flux for electronic work and definitely not apply flux to the joint before soldering it. You will also have to work quickly, taking care not to overheat the joint and damage the delicate components.

Silver soldering or brazing

Silver soldering requires you to heat the metal to a temperature of 600°C to 800°C, which is red hot, using a brazing torch. Safety is a major issue as the materials can quickly burn you and there is also a fire risk.

It is not a technique that you have to learn, but you may find its use an advantage as your building skills increase. It provides a much stronger joint than soft soldering, but has the disadvantage that it removes the temper from piano wire.

Aluminium brazing

It is possible to fabricate aluminium silencers using a special aluminium solder and a wire brush. The technique again requires you to heat the components you are joining close to the melting point of the metal, so great care is needed to avoid ending up with a large blob of molten metal. Like silver soldering, it is not a technique you will need in the normal course of radio modelling. It has particular application in the making and repair of silencers.

Boards and jigs

The right building board is essential if you are to construct accurate warp-free models. A composite material such as MDF, block board or chipboard is an ideal base, but you should cover one side with a material which will accept pins, such as insulation board or cork tiles.

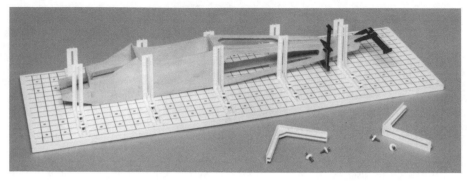

Figure 5.13 A building jig is one the best ways of avoiding building banana shaped fuselages. (Photo courtesy Balsacraft International.)

The size of the board will depend on the space you have available for building and your ambitions in terms of the size of the model. For most people, a board one metre by ½ metre (40" x 18") allows you to construct models with two-piece wings up to 2 metre (78") wing span. If you are going to build big, increase the size proportionately. A building jig such as the one shown in Figure 5.13 makes it much easier to build true fuselages.

DIY tools

Many people own a selection of spanners and screwdrivers, the smaller sizes all being useful for modelling. A hammer, hand, hack and fret saws will also prove invaluable. A good vice fitted to a work bench, or a Black & Decker Workmate enables you to hold materials securely while you work on them.

Power tools

The ubiquitous power hand drill has many applications, but is not quite as useful as a pillar drill which allows you to drill vertical holes with much greater accuracy. A power fret saw is invaluable for cutting out plywood parts, while a band saw is very practical for cutting out balsa parts, several at a time if the parts are identical.

Model construction

Basic fuselages

The fuselage of a conventional model houses the radio, provides a mount for the engine/fuel tank and locates the wings and tail surfaces in position. You must build any fuselage true, without warps or curves which should not be there. Probably the most common error is to end up with a banana shaped fuselage when viewed from above.

There are many ways of building a fuselage, most of which use formers to determine their cross section. You will often have to build directly over a plan. You should protect this either with a sheet of thin transparent polythene, or by

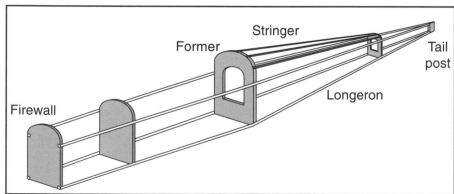

Figure 5.14 The basic components used in fuselage construction.

rubbing candle wax over the places where glued joints occur to stop them sticking to the plan. First, a few useful definitions.

- A longeron is a strip of wood which runs most or all of the length of the fuselage.
- A former is a fuselage cross sectional member.
- A stringer is a secondary longitudinal member which runs along the length or part of the length of the fuselage.
- A firewall is the former located just behind the engine.

Formers

Formers support the outer skin of the fuselage. Their location along the fuselage determines the material used. Engine bay formers are usually made of plywood. Those supporting the wing and undercarriage may also be ply, liteply or thick balsa.

Those near the tail end of the fuselage are normally thin balsa. Sometimes formers are made from strips of wood, particularly those aft of the servos which require openings for control runs, as well as low weight.

Whatever type of formers you are using you must cut them out accurately, if the kit manufacturer has not already done this. It is usually easier to drill holes for fuel pipes and control runs while you can place the formers flat, rather than waiting until they are built in and difficult to access.

Simple boxes

The simplest fuselage to build is the profile one. It leaves the problem of where to house the radio, particularly for internal combustion engined models where the exhaust oil may damage the radio. Perhaps the most popular is

Figure 5.15 Formers can take a variety of shapes and may have hollow centres to reduce weight or to allow control rods to pass through.

the rectangular box cross section. It is quick to build but is almost always less attractive than a more curvaceous shape.

All-sheet

All-sheet fuselages are very popular as they are so easy and quick to build. The resulting shape is usually rather dull. Many are given a more rounded effect by fitting strips of triangular balsa to the corners of the fuselage enabling you to sand it to an oval shape. A doubler of ply, cross grained balsa or liteply is almost invariably used to increase strength in the engine bay and wing area. You must carefully glue these doublers in place, preferably with contact adhesive, making sure that you end up with a pair of sides and not two identical ones.

A thin grade of wood is sometimes used for the fuselage sides and reinforced with balsa strip longerons and vertical members glued to the inside. As with doublers, you will need to glue

Figure 5.16 An all-sheet fuselage is the quickest and easiest to build.

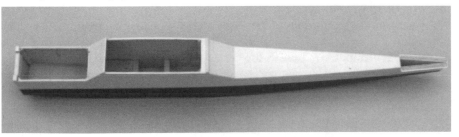

Figure 5.17 An open frame fuselage requires a lot of careful building.

these longerons and other parts in place, using pins or weights to hold them in place and again making sure you end up with a pair of sides.

Then glue the central formers in place and after they have dried, add the front and rear ones. This is the point where twists can accidentally get incorporated. Either use your eye looking the length of the fuselage to check it is true before it dries or, even better, use a building jig.

Open frame

The traditional open frame layout provides exceptional strength to weight. However you must cut the joints accurately before you glue them in place. You will need to practise this to acquire the necessary skill.

The structure is inherently strong, even in its uncovered state, though covering adds rigidity. The structure may be built from balsa or spruce strip depending on the preference of the kit manufacturer or plan designer, the size of the model and the dimensions of the individual longerons.

Often additional strength in the joints is achieved with a thin plywood plate over each joint or balsa gussets fitted in each corner.

The open frame may join onto a sheet forward section or the front of the frame may have sheet in-fill around the engine and radio bays. Either of these solutions puts strength and weight where they are required.

This type of fuselage is also built flat, and sometimes the second side is built over the first to ensure identical dimensions. Cut each piece of wood and sand it carefully to size, dry fit it and then glue and pin it in place.

Advanced fuselages

So far, the fuselages described are fairly easy to build, but may be less than perfect from an artistic point of view. You can readily construct more complex shapes but the techniques are really only suitable if you have already built one or two models, or have gathered building experience from allied hobbies such as model boats or free flight aircraft.

As well as being harder to build and taking more time, the following fuselages, which are oval or circular in cross section, are also harder and more time consuming to repair, making them less suitable if you are still a student pilot and more prone to crashing your models.

There are several methods of building double curvature fuselages from wood, each of which will produce a pleasing shape.

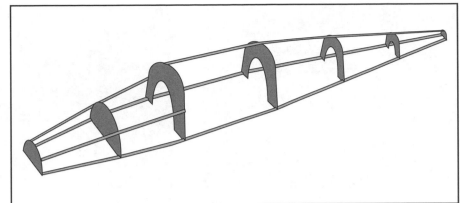

Figure 5.18 The use of a vertical crutch allows you to build a complex fuselage shape on a strip balsa outline, using symmetrical formers.

Horizontal and vertical crutches

A crutch is a frame on which formers locate and to which you add the fuselage skin. Figure 5.18 shows a fuselage divided vertically (it can also divide horizontally) with formers added to a basic strip wood outline. It is essential that you mount these formers at right angles to the crutch.

The crutch may have stringers attached to provide basic strength and support the covering, or may be planked with strips of balsa to give a rigid monocoque. This can take quite a time to complete. Once you have completed the two halves, you can glue them both together to provide a complete fuselage.

The resulting structure will be both light and strong. If you have used planking, you can cut the necessary access hatches out of the completed fuselage.

47

Figure 5.19 *This fun scale Lockheed Hercules uses stringers which run the whole length of the fuselage apart from the nose block.*

Figure 5.20 *Both the cowl and the area immediately behind the cockpit use planking to achieve the right shape.*

Stringers

Some R/C designs, particularly old timers, employ a fully stringered fuselage. It is also common to find part of a rear fuselage built up with stringers, as, for example, where a rear turtle deck is used as part of the structure.

This construction method is straightforward, if time consuming, and should be carried out two stringers at a time, glued in place on opposite sides of the fuselage to avoid building in a twist. The final result is lightweight, with much of its strength resulting from the covering.

Sheeted

Sheeting is an excellent way to achieve a smoothly curved finish, but double curves are impossible. Dampening the balsa on one side will curve the wood before you glue it to the formers. Use a slow setting adhesive such as PVA, together with plenty of pins, to hold the sheeting in place.

For severe curves, a touch of cyano along one edge can hold it in place while the remainder of the sheeting is pinned. If you sand the finished sheeting too much, you easily produce a 'starved' look, particularly on models with few formers and thin sheeting.

Planked

You can build more exotic fuselage cross sections by planking over formers. This technique enables you to construct models with double curvatures. The resultant monocoque is immensely strong. It is also the only practical answer for a wooden fuselage where the curvature is too great for sheeting. There is quite a skill to learn if you are to end up with a satisfactory planked fuselage. Quite thick material is used for the planking to allow for sanding to a smooth finish. As with stringers, gluing planks in a pair at a time helps avoid warps.

Figure 5.21 *This forward part of a sheet fuselage will have slightly curved sheeting on top to provide a more interesting shape.*

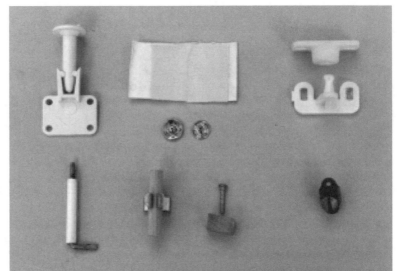

Figure 5.22 Kits and plans are often deficient in terms of detailing hatch catches. Working clockwise from top left, a commercial turn and twist catch, self-adhesive Velcro with a pair of press studs below, a kitchen cupboard catch, a Dzus turn and twist fastener, a small screw and block, a dowel and Terry clip, and finally a spring loaded rod and tube.

Tubes

Pod and boom models as well as twin boomed ones often use a simple tube for the rear fuselage. Suitable materials include balsa sheet, thin ply, glass fibre, carbon fibre, or even standard commercial items such as a length of fishing rod or an arrow shaft. Such construction is unusual in trainers but is often found in more advanced sports models.

Pre-formed fuselages

Quite a number of kits contain ready formed fuselages moulded from plastic such as ABS or made from GRP. These fuselages save a lot of building work and are ideal for avoiding warps or incorrect wing/tailplane incidence angles.

Hatches

The opening where the wing attaches to the fuselage provides the access to the radio equipment on most models. There are, however, several

Figure 5.23 This fun flier is typical of the layout of a pod and boom model.

reasons why a model built from a kit or a plan may involve you in the construction of one or more hatches. You will need access to the fuel tank and the engine.

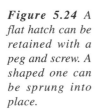

Figure 5.24 A flat hatch can be retained with a peg and screw. A shaped one can be sprung into place.

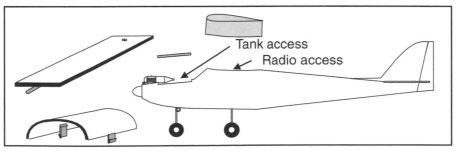

Tank access
Radio access

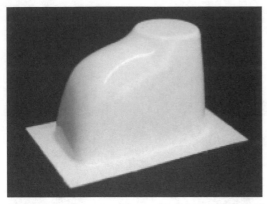

Figure 5.25 *This superbly moulded ABS cowl should completely enclose a four stroke engine. (Photo courtesy Vortex Plastics.)*

Once you are beyond the initial training stage, you may decide to build a one piece model or the layout of the model may not result in the radio being sited below the wing.

Figure 5.26 *A parallel chord wing has the advantage that all the ribs are the same and at right angles to the spars, leading and trailing edges.*

Hatches always seem to provide awkward problems. Lightweight, easy to operate catches provide an interesting challenge and are not always included in kits or detailed on plans.

A hatch made from a single thickness of balsa sheet will tend to warp. Most kits and plans specify balsa cross pieces to avoid this problem. Do not leave them out. Think about hatches and equipment access before you rush ahead with the construction of any model.

Cowls

Built-up cowls feature a mixture of balsa and ply while pre-formed ones are usually made from ABS, GRP or metal. These latter materials are almost perfect for engine cowls. They are strong, lightweight and totally fuel resistant, though ABS does tend to tear along fixing holes.

When building a model with a GRP cowl from a plan, you have to make a mould first. In kits, these materials allow complex and attractive shapes to be achieved and demand little work by the builder. Some care is needed with the selection of the adhesives to join these materials or to glue wooden formers in place. Always follow the recommendations of the kit supplier, or failing these, refer to Chapter 4.

Always carefully follow the designer's advice about engine cooling. The path for the air flow must be as unobstructed as possible. Conventional wisdom advises an air outlet twice the inlet area. This is fine unless the inlet area is large. Perhaps a better guideline is to ensure that the outlet area is at least the size of the top of the cylinder head, and that the inlet area is at least two-thirds of this size. Although four stroke engines run hotter than two strokes, if the silencer of the latter is included within the cowl, there is little difference in the total heat.

Wings

The wing is the most important part of any aeroplane. This is not unexpected as the wing overcomes the weight of the model in the air and has a major influence on its flight performance. A wing is most heavily stressed at its roots and

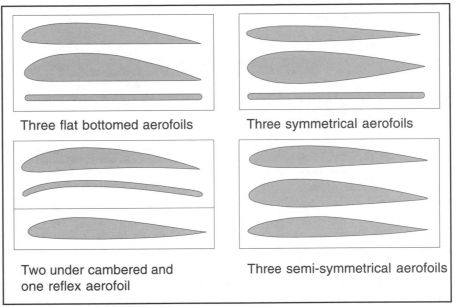

Figure 5.27 The main categories of aerofoil all show an almost infinite number of variations depending on the designer's search for high lift, gentle stall, low drag, structural strength, ease of construction or small movement of the centre of lift as angle of attack changes.

Three flat bottomed aerofoils

Three symmetrical aerofoils

Two under cambered and one reflex aerofoil

Three semi-symmetrical aerofoils

most lightly at its tips. Because of this, you must take care when joining a pair of wing panels to ensure that the joint is well made. There are many choices when it comes to producing a wing; its planform, aerofoil section, method of construction and the way it attaches to the fuselage. These will be specified in any kit or on the plan, but it is worth understanding the various options.

Aerofoils

A designer will choose a wing aerofoil for a number of reasons, the outcome usually being something of a compromise. The following paragraphs should help you to decide the relative merits from constructional and flying points of view and help in the selection of a model to build. It is worth noting that sometimes the aerofoil changes from root to tip. It is also important to know that fat aerofoils fly more slowly than thin ones because they produce more lift at slow speeds and more drag at high ones.

Flat bottomed aerofoils

Flat bottomed aerofoils, like the widely used Clark Y, are very straightforward to construct. Having a flat underside, they are easily assembled on a flat building board which is why they are

so popular. They are found on many trainers. Their shortcomings include a tendency to balloon when rolling out of a turn and a lack of smoothness in flight, particularly in windy conditions. These must be offset against their ease of construction. Furthermore, if building from a plan, most pre-shaped leading and trailing edges are designed to fit these type of aerofoils.

Symmetrical/semi-symmetrical aerofoils

The fact that these aerofoils are not flat bottomed is the basis of their construction problems. Often a tab is built into each rib, so that you can build the wing on a flat board and then remove the tabs.

However, the difficulties may not end here if you are building from a plan. Many pre-shaped leading or trailing edges are not symmetrical in shape and thus other solutions, such as square or rectangular strip may be necessary for the leading edge, with a pair of strips of sheet wood for the trailing edge.

Any model with a symmetrical or semi-symmetrical wing tends to fly slightly faster than one with a flat bottom aerofoil. For the best aerobatic performance, this type of aerofoil is essential.

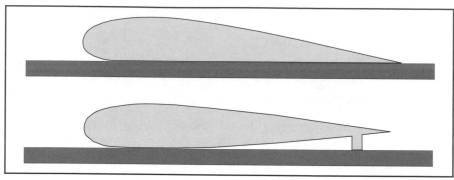

Figure 5.28 The Clark Y shape (top) is easy to build because of its flat underside. Tabs on symmetrical ribs help solve the building problem.

Under cambered aerofoils

These aerofoils present quite a few constructional problems and should be avoided by beginners. The leading and trailing edge strips almost always need wedging at an angle on the building board. The real difficulty is attaching the covering material to the concave under surface. This is because the tautening effect, when shrinking the material in place, tries to pull it away from the ribs.

Under cambered ribs are generally only found on old timers and scale models of pre-1940 aircraft. Their flight characteristics can also cause difficulties, even to experienced pilots. While they produce lots of lift, they are prone to a very sudden stall, often allied to a wing drop and tendency to enter a spin.

The wing shape or planform

The term aspect ratio compares the length of a wing to its width, when viewed from above. The higher the aspect ratio, the more efficiently the wing will produce lift and the more difficult you will find it to construct.

High aspect ratios in the modelling world are almost entirely limited to gliders and electric flight, where aerodynamic efficiency is so important. High aspect ratio wings also have a nasty habit of tip stalling, which can lead to a fatal spin near the ground.

Washout

A primary method of reducing tip stalling is to employ washout. It is used on many R/C aircraft and you must include it as specified when building a new model. Figure 5.30 shows the relative incidences of the wing root and wing tip.

Effective washout requires only a few degrees, somewhere between one and three degrees is common, otherwise the outer portion of the wing will provide insufficient lift.

Building in washout is easy with foam wings and is built in if you purchase the cores. For

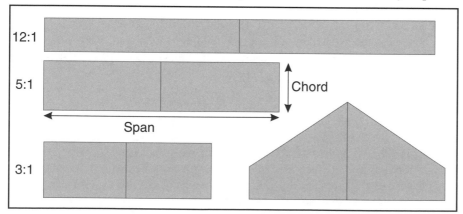

Figure 5.29 The three rectangular wings have very different aspect ratios and are compared with a typical low aspect ratio delta wing. The figure also shows the terms wing span and chord.

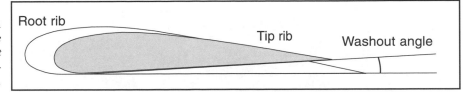

Figure 5.30 A negative angle between the root and tip ribs reduces tip stalling.

Root rib

Tip rib

Washout angle

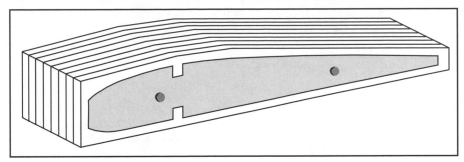

Figure 5.31 You can use bread and butter construction to make identical ribs or those needed for a tapered wing.

home cutting, you should carefully attach the root and tip master ribs to the foam at the appropriate angles. Built-up wings require propping up the trailing edge with a tapered strip prior to starting wing construction. Take care to ensure that both wings have the same amount of washout

Parallel chord

Undoubtedly, parallel chord wings are the easiest and quickest to build. The benefit of identical wing ribs is attractive from a constructional view point and the use of washout is unusual as the chances of tip stalling are slight. For many, the problem with parallel chord wings is their utilitarian looks, though the shape of the wing tips may help to improve the basic appearance.

While most parallel chord wings are straight from one tip to the other, a small amount of sweepback can improve their looks immensely. However, the joining together of such wings, if they are of the built-up kind, can cause added complexity.

Tapered

Tapered wings are slightly more difficult to construct than parallel chord ones, but not significantly so. In the case of built-up construction, each rib is different, but unless the taper is severe, you can form the ribs from master root and tip ribs using the bread and butter technique. For a foam wing, the taper makes little difference when the core is cut. Since tapered wings are more prone to tip stalling than parallel chord

Figure 5.32 This Extra aerobatic model shows off a well tapered wing.

Figure 5.33 The Spitfire has the classic elliptical wing shape, which makes it a difficult model both to build and to fly.

ones, designers usually specify some washout which you must build in during construction.

Elliptical

Eventually, most people are tempted to build a Spitfire. Because of its elliptical wing, you will have to accept the constructional problems and build in plenty of washout to help minimise tip stalling.

Some designs use a straight leading and trailing edge giving a close approximation of an elliptical wing and simpler construction. Because of the awkward construction, this planform is never used on trainers.

Wing tips

There many varieties of wing tip shape and models will use a particular shape because of attractiveness, ease of construction, strength, lack of vulnerability to damage and aerodynamic performance. A study of the photographs in this book will show the wide range found.

Figure 5.34 Most people either love or hate biplanes. Their flight characteristics make them easy to fly and highly manoeuvrable.

Figure 5.35 A tri-plane like this Flair Baronnette is for those who enjoy building wings. (Photo courtesy Flair.)

Despite the wide choice, square or almost square wing tips are undoubtedly the most popular due to their ease of construction. Square tips either use a strong tip rib, thicker balsa or ply, or balsa block.

The latter is also used for slightly curved tips. A semi-circular tip, uncommon on training models, is more complex and usually built up from pieces of balsa sheet or laminated from strips of balsa or thin ply.

Biplanes and tri-planes

The wings used in multi-wing models are different from those used in monoplanes. All things being equal, they are smaller, of lower aspect ratio and usually provided with struts, sometimes bracing wires, which can help to take the loads imposed on them. This does allow the use of lighter wings on such aircraft, which is a good thing bearing in mind that two or three wings are likely to be heavier than a single one

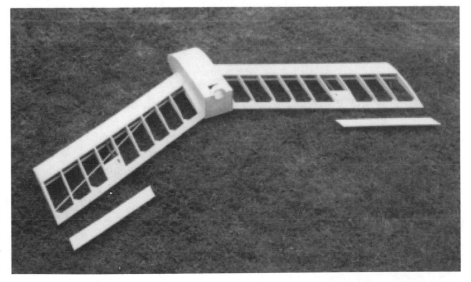

Figure 5.36 The swept wing of this tailless model has no taper, but a fairly complex joint at its centre.

55

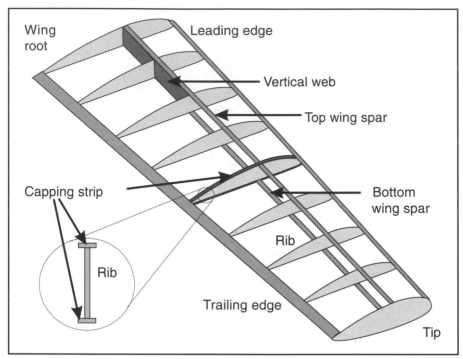

Wing root

Leading edge

Vertical web

Top wing spar

Capping strip

Bottom wing spar

Rib

Rib

Trailing edge

Tip

Figure 5.37 The names of the main parts of a built-up wing are clearly identified.

of the same area. Even worse, the interaction between closely mounted wings means that for an equivalent monoplane area, a biplane needs 1.3 times the total wing area. In construction terms, there is twice or even three times as much building to do. Trainers are invariably monoplanes, but a biplane as a second or third model is a good idea if the layout appeals to you.

Sweptback wings

Deltas and flying wings, neither of which are recommended for the beginner, are classic examples of the use of sweepback. Reasons for

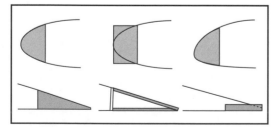

Figure 5.38 There many of ways of building wing leading and trailing edges.

their unsuitability in the early stages of flying training include their high speeds and exceptional rates of roll allied to orientation difficulties.

Their construction can also require additional care with built-up wing construction to ensure that all the slots for spars, leading and trailing edges are cut at the correct angle. Of course this is not a problem if you are building from foam. Sweptback wings rarely use dihedral so the construction and joining of both wings on a flat building board is usually a practical proposition.

Built-up wings

Before attempting to construct a built-up wing, it is important to understand the various parts used in their construction.

1. A spar is a major component which lies along the span of a wing.
2. An aerofoil is the cross sectional shape of a wing.
3. A rib is a component, usually at right angles to the spar, the outline of which helps to define the aerofoil section of a wing.

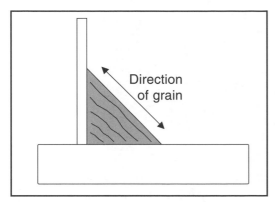

Figure 5.39 *The direction of the wood grain on a reinforcing gusset is important.*

4. The leading edge is a spar at the front edge of the wing, shaped to match the front of the aerofoil section of the wing.

5. The trailing edge is the rear edge of the wing. It is usually a spar but may be formed from sheet.

6. A web is a vertical component joining two spars, one above the other, to increase strength.

7. A capping strip is a length of wood glued along the length of the top and bottom of a rib to provide additional strength and to give support to the covering material.

Leading and trailing edges

Generally, it is easiest if the kit includes, or the designer of the plan has specified the use of specially shaped balsa strip for these tasks. A number of standard sizes and shapes are available, and some of these are shown in Figure 5.38. Their use saves significant time which you must otherwise spend planing and sanding square or rectangular wood to shape.

Sometimes for leading edges, square or rectangular balsa strip has been chosen, a common reason being the requirement for some vertical wing taper. However, such wings are much harder to build and are usually found only on relatively advanced models.

Trailing edges are commonly made from custom shaped stock, though sometimes they are built from pairs of strips of balsa sheet with the

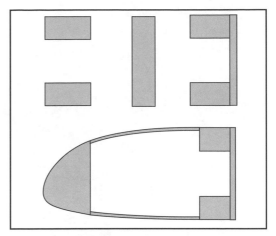

Figure 5.40 *Starting top left, a pair of spars top and bottom, a single vertical spar, a pair of spars with a web, and a D section spar/leading edge combination.*

bottom one sanded to a taper. You must add vertical webbing, if specified, as it will add considerably to the strength of this method of construction. The overall strength of a wing is often increased by the use of strategically placed gussets glued into vulnerable corners. Never omit these and, when cutting them from scrap balsa, ensure the grain direction is diagonally across the gusset.

Spars

Normal practice is for a pair of main spars, located at the top and bottom of the wing ribs. The use of webs to join the spars adds significantly to their strength in the vertical plane. Never leave them out when building a wing, even though fitting them can be a tedious task. This strength has to resist the upward lift of the model in flight and the downward load on landing.

The spar does not provide all the strength of a wing. The leading and trailing edges, the wing ribs and the covering all contribute to the strength of the wing in the vertical direction. The choice of actual wing spar configuration will depend on the views of the designer when deciding on wing planform, depth of chord, strength requirement and constructional complexity. Figure 5.40 shows various popular spar configurations.

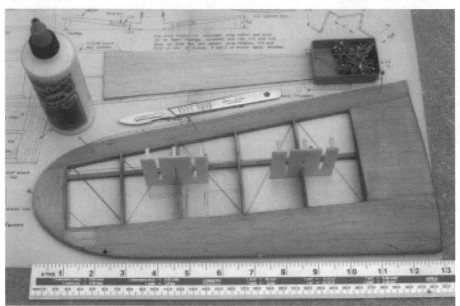

Figure 5.41 A built-up wing still on the building board. This one uses the classic D box leading edge and conventional pre-formed trailing edge.

On any normal wing, regardless of planform, the stress is greatest at the root and reduces to zero at the tip. For this reason, more advanced models commonly use a tapered spar to reduce wing weight without compromising strength.

The D box spar is a particularly strong solution, spreading the load between the leading edge and the main spar. This is why sheeting between the leading edge and the main spar is so popular. It is also the area of greatest curvature of the wing and the sheeting helps maintain the accuracy of the aerofoil.

Ribs

Wing ribs hold the various spars in position and give the surface of the wing the required aerodynamic curvature. For rectangular wings, all ribs are identical. For built-up tapered wings, either every wing rib is drawn separately or the sandwich method is used requiring only a master root and tip rib. While kits provide the ribs ready cut out, working from plans requires the production of an accurate set of ribs for each wing.

For more exotic wing planforms, every rib is different. Geodetic wing construction has diagonal wing ribs of the original aerofoil section, but stretched along the chord axis only. The structure itself is immensely strong for a given weight and warp resistant.

Rib thickness and spacing

Ribs are normally made from cross grained balsa, the spacing between ribs depending on their ability to support the wing surface material. Clearly ribs will be closer together for a wing covered with film or fabric than for a balsa sheeted one and the spacing is likely to be wider for larger wings.

Occasionally, particularly on scale models, half ribs may be added in front of the main spar between full ribs to help to support the wing covering in the area where the curvature is at a maximum.

Capping strips

Capping strips serve two roles. They improve the vertical strength of the rib, in a similar manner to main spar webs, and they provide a wider surface to support the wing covering. Capping strips are also found on foam wings to make them look like built-up ones after they are covered.

Never leave out capping strips which are specified in a kit or a plan, despite the fact that they may take some time to cut to length and glue in place.

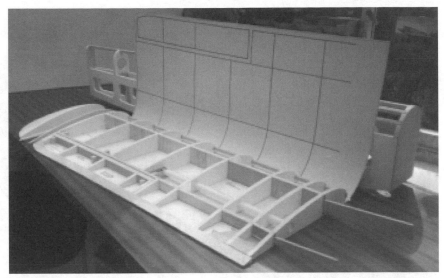

Figure 5.42 This wing, made from a mixture of wood and foam board, is ready for the top skin of thin card to be fixed in place. (Photo Courtesy Paper Aviation.)

Sheeting

For a built-up wing, sheeting over the whole of a wing's upper and lower surfaces to provide a double skin results in an excellent surface which accurately reproduces the aerofoil section. The sheeting acts as a monocoque, stiffens the wing and helps to resist any puncturing of the covering. As already mentioned, sheeting between the leading edge and main spar provides many of the advantages of full sheeting but at lower weight and reduced cost.

Constructing a built-up wing

As with the fuselage, most wings are built over a plan which you should protect. Usually, the bottom spar or spars are carefully pinned in place on the plan, together with the leading or trailing edge. A flat building board is essential if you want a warp-free pair of wings. If the wing features washout, you may have to prop up the outboard end of the trailing edge before adding the ribs which are then glued in place, taking care to keep them vertical using a small set square or plastic jig (see Figure 5.41).

You may need to build in the dihedral angle when placing the root ribs and a template for this is provided in some kits or you can transfer it to a piece of card from the plan. Often balsa gussets are specified in the corners of the wing to increase strength. Again, you must carefully cut these out with the grain running parallel to the diagonal side and glue them in place.

With the top spars added, you can then fix any sheeting in place using the technique indicated on page 48. It is a good idea to leave the wing in place overnight while the glued joints harden.

Foam wings

Foam wings are regularly supplied in trainer kits and the ease with which they are converted to the finished article is one reason for their popularity. Other factors include their resistance to warping and their ability to reproduce aerofoil sections with ease and accuracy. Home-made foam cores are quick and simple to cut out with the right tools if the shape is a straightforward one. For most, all that is needed is the root and tip ribs and the degree of washout. Normally, leading and trailing edge spars are added to the core to provide strength. Cores are obviously provided in many kits, but when building from plans you have two choices. Either you can cut your own or you can approach one of the companies which will do the whole job for you, including veneering the cores.

Figure 5.43 A foam wing provides a really accurate reproduction of the designer's chosen aerofoil and is not prone to warps. This one is complete with leading and trailing edges as well as a substantial vertical main spar.

If you cut your own cores, the two popular veneers for coverings are obechi and balsa. Obechi is stronger and more resistant to dings. Both are applied with a latex contact adhesive such as Copydex. Plans sometimes specify cores covered with brown wrapping paper or cardboard, the latter providing the more substantial surface finish. Regardless of the veneer used, the end result can be covered and painted as usual, GRP resin providing a long lasting finish but requiring plenty of elbow grease with wet and dry emery paper to get the perfect finish. On some small wings the bare foam is covered only with iron-on film or fabric.

Cut-outs in foam wings

If you are using a ready-made wing, you will probably find the snakes, if required, are already in place together with cut-outs for the aileron servo and undercarriage mounts. If you cut out your own cores, and on some kit wings, you will have to make your own cut-outs. As these weaken the wing, plywood or balsa inserts are normally specified to provide strengthening.

You can make any cut-outs you require with a balsa knife or by melting the foam with the tip of a soldering iron.

Cutting out foam wings

Making your own foam wings from scratch is not a difficult task provided you equip yourself with the correct tools. You will need a hot wire bow and power supply. You can buy both from a model shop, or make your own bow and use a car battery charger to power it. You will find much more information on this subject in David Thomas' comprehensive book **Radio Control Foam Modelling** (see page 243.)

You will also need a clear flat surface to work on. First cut a block of foam slightly larger than the size of the required wing panel. Attach the rib profiles, cut from ply with a short lead in at the leading and trailing edges, to each end of the foam with pins. You must hold the blocks firmly in place with weights, as shown in Figure 5.45.

Now you will need a helper. Feed the hot wire into the foam just above the top of the trailing edge of the rib at each end with a slow continuous movement, ease the wire right through the foam block, keeping the wire pressed to the rib outline. The hot wire cuts by melting the foam. Try to keep the speed of movement constant, not so fast as to cause dragging of the centre of

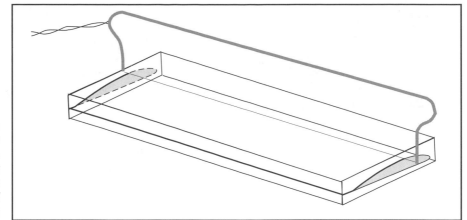

Figure 5.44 A foam cutting bow and power supply. The use of a hot wire cutter calls for practice and a reliable helper.

the wire, not so slow as to cause a rough surface to the cut. Relax, and turn over the block, keeping the piece of foam you have cut off as a jig to support the top profile of the wing core. Repeat the cutting process on the bottom of the block starting from the leading edge. It is best if you retain the offcuts to protect the wings until you have fully assembled them.

Veneering foam cores

To veneer the wing, first cut out the covering panels. If made from sheet balsa, join the sheets along their edges by running masking tape over one side of the joint, turning them over,

opening the joint and running a bead of glue into the crack. Close the join, wipe off any excess glue and put down to dry on a flat surface, masking tape upwards with weights on top.

When ready to skin the cores, lightly sand them and brush off the dust. Then cover the wing surface and the veneer panel with a latex glue. With a sheet of transparent polythene, such as the removable backing from iron-on wing covering material, on top of the wing's glued surface, place the veneer on the wing. Carefully position it and then slide out the polythene. Rub the whole surface thoroughly with a rag to make sure the

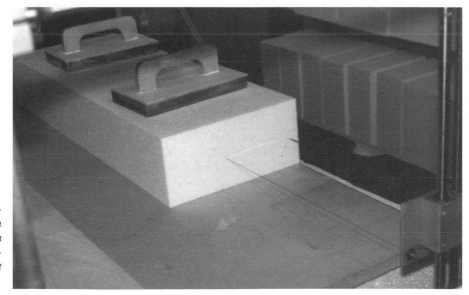

Figure 5.45 Cutting out a foam core using a computer controlled cutter at the Flair works

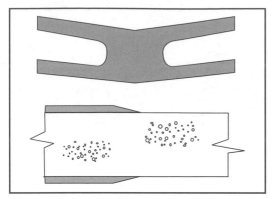

Figure 5.46 Top, a typical ply dihedral brace. Bottom, take care when joining foam wings with GRP to taper the resin to avoid a stress build up where it ends.

covering is firmly glued in place. Repeat for the under surface and then add the leading and trailing edges.

Joining wing panels

Dihedral braces are the traditional way of joining built-up wings. You should glue them carefully into place as they are heavily loaded in flight. They are generally made from plywood and found at the leading edge, main spar and trailing edge.

You can join foam wings with a bandage and some GRP resin across the centre section, extending just beyond the sides of the fuselage. More recently, long dihedral braces epoxied into the foam have provided a much neater solution.

Attaching wings to the fuselage

There are two popular methods that allow you to remove the wings quickly from a model. The advantages of removal include ease of transportation and access to the interior of the fuselage and radio. The first method uses a pair of dowels through the fuselage, together with elastic bands. The second involves a pair of dowels in the leading edge, forward pointing, with a pair of wing bolts at the trailing edge. More common on gliders than powered models are plug-in wings employing metal rods and tubes, or metal or wooden strips and slots. Finally the tongue and groove system has retained its following, offering an easy knock off solution without damage.

Cabane struts

Monoplanes with a parasol layout, biplanes and tri-planes all use cabane struts to support the upper wing clear of the fuselage. These are made from piano wire, metal strip or tubing. The better kits provide these already bent to shape, and if you are unsure about your metal working ability, it is best to select a kit which does this for you.

If you work from a plan, think carefully about the shape in three dimensions before you start to bend or cut the material. The accuracy of your construction and attachment of these parts to the model is critical if you are to maintain the correct wing incidence. Occasionally, cabane struts are made from hardwood, but the same care is essential during their assembly.

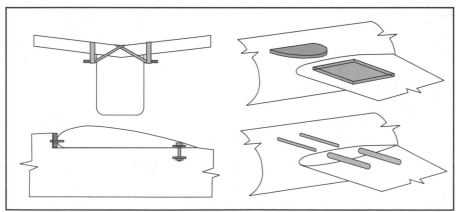

Figure 5.47 The two main ways of attaching wings to fuselages are by elastic bands and wing bolts, shown left. Slide on wings, right, are more popular on gliders.

Figure 5.48 *This Flair Puppeteer biplane is a mass of struts, replicating the original Sopwith Pup. (Photo courtesy Geoff Lamb.)*

Wing struts and rigging.

Many biplanes and a few scale monoplanes use wing struts and the construction of these requires similar care to cabane struts. Some struts are just for show, others carry loads in flight, or on landing for that matter.

The choice of material for any strut depends on the loading it is likely to have to withstand. Decorative struts are built from balsa, but load carrying ones are made from hardwood, ply or metal. If made from wood, care is needed with the end attachment. You can epoxy metal strip, wire or a clevis into the end of the strut to produce a neat attachment.

Rigging wires may be functional and use nylon covered fishing trace, which consists of a number of twisted steel wires with a rustproof nylon covering. It is available in a wide range of

Figure 5.49 *Wire cabane struts are usually bound or clamped to formers. Metal strip can be screwed. If the model has engine bearers, you can screw the struts to them. Interplane strut attachments may use a hole in the strut itself, a metal plate epoxied into the strut, a clevis and rod or a press stud.*

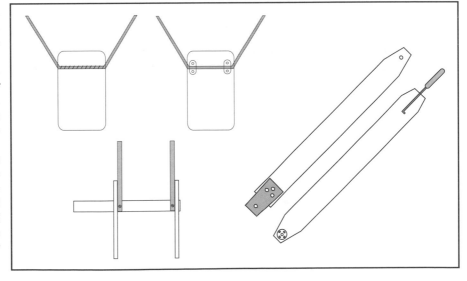

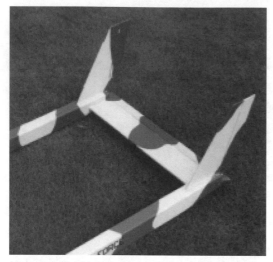

Figure 5.50 *This all-sheet tailplane spans the gap between a pair of twin booms.*

Figure 5.51 *The classic built-up structure of this model ensures the tail end is as light as possible.*

strengths from a few to many tens of kilograms (pounds).

Decorative rigging is usually shirring elastic, a monofilament elastic covered with a cotton sheath and available from drapery stores. In both case, fittings are located to attach the rigging wires to the wing and fuselage. These are found ready-made in kits but can also be made from small pieces of ply or metal sheet, cut to the appropriate shape and drilled. Alternatively, you can purchase small metal screw eyes.

Tailplanes and fins

Fins and tailplanes are generally placed a long way aft of the centre of gravity, so their construction needs to be lightweight. They must also be warp resistant and securely attached to the fuselage, normally at right angles to each other

with the elevator and rudder at their trailing edges. The tail surfaces usually glue directly to the fuselage often with additional support in the form of triangular balsa strip. An alternative utilises slots in the fuselage to give the surfaces greater support.

It is important to think about the way the you will attach the control surfaces to the tailplane and fin. Many hinging systems, when used with built-up surfaces, require you to glue balsa blocks in front of the spar to house the hinges. In fact, the construction method may well influence your choice of hinges.

All sheet

Undoubtedly the most popular form of tailplane or fin is all-balsa sheet. As such a solution is prone to warp, tips with the balsa grain across are the norm, as shown in Figure 5.52. Holes

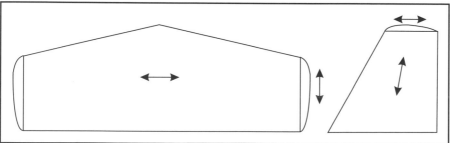

Figure 5.52 When building all-sheet surfaces, it is essential to fit the cross grain pieces to avoid the tendency for warps.

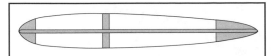

Figure 5.53 A central core of 1.5mm (1/16") balsa provides a rigid tail surface.

are occasionally cut in the sheet to reduce the overall weight. This also gives an attractive effect if you decide to cover the surface with a translucent material.

Built up

To build even lighter surfaces, a balsa framework provides a better solution. A tailplane constructed entirely from balsa strip is not hard to put together provided the lengths of strip are accurately cut to size.

You may have to cut out ribs if an aerofoil section is specified. The tips, if shaped, are cut from pieces of balsa sheet or even formed in the same way as wing tips.

Sheet cored

For a lightweight structure with each rib clearly apparent, a thin balsa sheet core sandwiched between two frameworks is a popular solution. Aerofoil sections are often incorporated by cutting each shaped rib in half longitudinally prior to assembly.

Foam

Sheet covered foam cores provide a rapid building solution but, due to their weight, are less ideal from a balance point of view if the model has a long fuselage. However, if constructed with lightening holes and a lightweight skinning, they can provide a rapid and low cost solution. There are many ARTF kits which feature this type of construction.

Figure 5.54 Avoid holding the tailplane in place with elastic bands. Glue it securely to the fuselage.

Attachment to the fuselage

The main reason for even considering attachment of the tailplane to the fuselage is the paramount requirement for accuracy relative to the fuselage datum line or, more importantly, to the angle of incidence of the wing. All the work of the designer of the model in this area may be lost if you do not maintain constructional accuracy. It is also crucial that the fin is mounted truly at right angles to the tailplane and you must check this carefully when you glue the fin in place. You will mostly find the tail on the top surface of fuselage, or on the underside as these provide the easiest options from a constructional point of view. A tailplane mid-mounted in the fuselage, halfway up or on the top of the fin is more difficult and you should avoid models with this layout until you have gained some constructional experience. In the case of a fin mounted

Figure 5.55 The positioning of the wing and tail at the correct angles in relation to the fuselage is absolutely vital. They are exaggerated in this illustration.

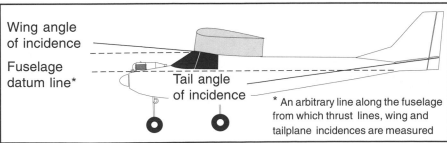

Wing angle of incidence

Fuselage datum line*

Tail angle of incidence

* An arbitrary line along the fuselage from which thrust lines, wing and tailplane incidences are measured

Figure 5.56 The V configuration of the Stiletto keeps the tailplane well clear of the ground on landing. (Photo courtesy Phoenix Model Products.)

tailplane, you will also not find it easy to fit the control runs to the elevator.

The past practice of attaching the tailplane to the fuselage by rubber bands is not a good one, since any movement of this surface will affect the neutral of the elevator due to an increase or reduction in the length of the control run from the servo arm.

All-moving tailplanes produce a different set of problems. They need a pivot point through the fuselage or fin and a slack-free control

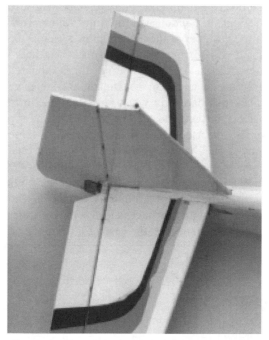

Figure 5.57 Perhaps the commonest way of avoiding elevator/rudder fouling is to have a two part elevator with angled inner edges.

connection if you are to avoid the fatal effects of flutter.

V or butterfly tails

A few more advanced and unusual kits employ a V or butterfly tail. These tails incorporate the functions of tailplane and fin in two surfaces, usually set at an angle of 120°, instead of three set at right angles. They are built in exactly the same way as conventional tailplanes except for mounting the two surfaces at an angle to each other and the fuselage. This may involve the use of lightweight dihedral braces and a V groove in the top of the fuselage, or just the provision of suitably angled slots in the fuselage sides.

The primary controls

Any conventional four channel model will use three primary controls, elevator, ailerons and rudder, to control the model in pitch, roll and yaw. Some models, including many trainers, will employ only elevator and rudder, the latter providing control both in roll and yaw.

Elevators

Elevators are normally hinged to the rear of the tailplane and provide control in the pitching plane. The angular movement of the elevator necessary to obtain a given change of attitude varies with speed. A low speed model will require a larger movement than a high speed one. This is a natural phenomenon arising from the increased effectiveness of any deflected surface as speed increases.

Elevators are normally cut to the required shape from sheet balsa, though they are sometimes built up from balsa strip and sheet. Often, separate

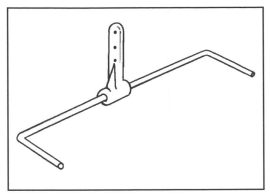

Figure 5.58 A commercially available elevator joiner provides a simple yet strong way of joining two halves of an elevator to a single servo. (Picture courtesy Chart.)

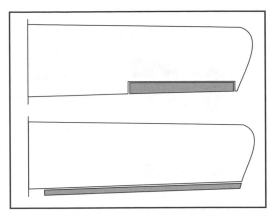

Figure 5.59 Inset ailerons, top, are harder to build and connect up than strip ones, bottom.

elevator halves offer an attractive solution and joining them together requires care. Depending on the design, the two halves may be connected by a bifurcated elevator push rod from the servo, or with a strip of plywood, spruce or dowel. Metal joiners provide a secure method but do increase tail weight.

The rudder

Rudders need to be light as they are invariably fitted at the rear of the aircraft. They are a simple control and usually made from balsa sheet or a built-up balsa framework, although you may find any of the methods used for building elevators.

Elevator/rudder fouling

Different kit and plan designers employ different methods of ensuring that elevators and rudders do not touch each other when they are deflected. They may:

- Locate the rudder in front of the elevator.
- Divide the elevator in two with a joiner through the fuselage, fin or rudder.
- Cut off the areas of the rudders and elevator where they foul.

What is important is that you build in the way specified and check that the controls do not touch at full deflection of both surfaces. If they do foul, then you will have to take remedial action. The most common causes are setting up the controls with more than the specified deflections and incorrect construction. The former is easy to remedy, the latter will frequently demand the use of the balsa knife. What is essential is to remove the problem since surfaces which touch will overload the servos and quickly flatten the flight battery.

Ailerons

Two types of ailerons are commonly used, the inset type where the aileron is part of the outboard wing and the strip aileron which is hinged to the whole or almost all of the trailing edge. Both are most often made from strips of trailing edge section, although inset ailerons are sometimes built-up structures similar to those used in wings. Differential movement helps to make the control more effective and you can easily achieve it using any of the methods shown in Chapter 8.

Undercarriages

The only reason that a model is fitted with an undercarriage is to enable it to take off and land from the ground. During flight, it produces weight and drag, neither of which help flight performance. As your flying improves, flying off snow or water is a real option which produces enormous satisfaction.

You may, therefore, fit floats or skis to your model to enable you to try them for yourself. These usually produce even more drag and weight than wheels. In Chapter 16, there is some

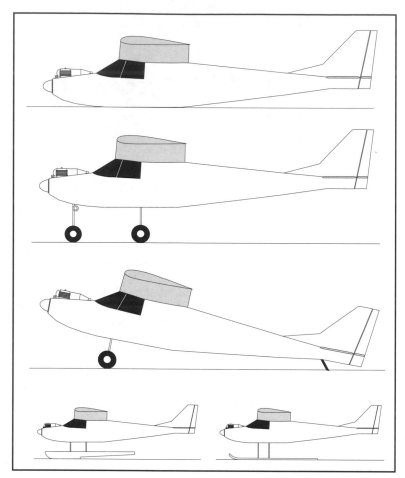

Figure 5.60 *There are many alternatives when it comes to landing gear for an R/C model. From top to bottom, no undercarriage, noseleg tricycle, tail dragger, floats and skis.*

information about floats and hulls for water planes as well as skis.

The simplest solution for a model is to land on its belly or a skid. A ply under surface, or strip of spruce in the case of a skid, are easy to construct and may be reinforced with GRP if the landing area is rough. However, you have to hand launch the model and you will miss out on the joys of take offs and proper landings.

A fixed undercarriage should be as light as possible and is usually made from piano wire, sometimes from aluminium alloy or composite materials. Streamlined struts and spatted wheels reduce drag, although the latter can cause problems when operating off rough grass. Piano wire and composites such as carbon fibre provide a fair degree of built-in springiness to help absorb the impact of imperfect landings. Many fixed undercarriages rely on the springing of the leg material, but noselegs usually have coil springs, and torsion bar springing is common on mainlegs.

Scale models may use coil springs, housed in telescopic tubes to simulate oleo operation. The extra constructional effort of a working system becomes worthwhile when you are finally able to watch the vertical movement of the undercarriage struts on take off and landing.

Noselegs

The majority of R/C trainers use a noseleg configuration because of its advantages. Steerable nosewheels provide excellent control on the

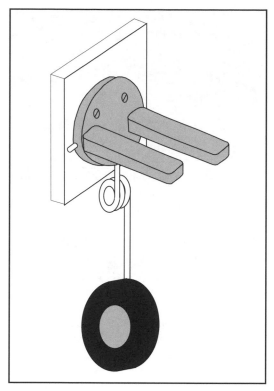

Figure 5.61 The noseleg can be trapped behind a purpose designed commercial engine mount.

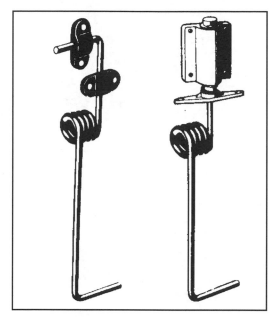

Figure 5.62 On the left is a fixed noseleg, on the right a steerable one with a built-in horn allowing the control link to connect on either side. (Pictures courtesy Chart.)

ground, particularly when taxying at low speeds. A snake is a convenient way of running the connection down from the rudder servo to the noseleg and can provide a degree of bump protection for the rudder servo (or aileron servo if rudder control is not fitted).

Noselegs are normally attached to the engine firewall. Many commercial engine mounts include facilities to trap the leg between the mount and the firewall. The best alternative is to fix the leg to the firewall with saddle clamps as shown in Figure 5.62.

Tail draggers

A tailwheel configuration provides a lighter weight, lower drag form of undercarriage. Once you have managed to master the difficulties of managing to keep straight on take off, you may find you actually prefer it to a noseleg. Clearly a simple skid can be employed at the rear in a tail

dragger configuration, made from wood or piano wire. In either case some springing is possible. The next stage up is a tailwheel. This may be fixed, or a steerable unit connected either to the

Figure 5.63 This tailwheel connects to the rudder enabling you to steer the model on the ground. (Picture courtesy Chart.)

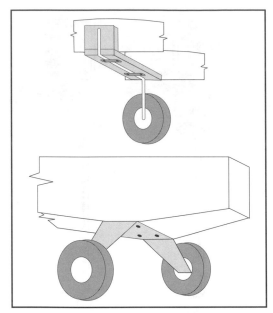

Figure 5.65 The classic trainer undercarriage consists of a coil sprung nosewheel and torsion bar mainlegs.

Figure 5.64 Two popular ways of mounting mainlegs are in grooves in the wing and bolted to the underside of the fuselage.

rudder or directly to a separate servo to provide the ultimate solution for ground steering.

Free castoring tailwheels can cause problems in ground handling, with a particular propensity for ground looping if you open the throttle too fast. All tailwheels attach to a substantial tail post or rear former, but great care is needed to avoid a build up of weight in this area.

Mainlegs

Mainwheels normally sit on, or in a groove in, hardwood blocks built into the wing, and are attached with saddle clamps. Drilled vertical blocks are used to anchor the end of the torque rod. These blocks attach to wing ribs, which are often reinforced with plywood. In the case of foam wings, the blocks are glued into suitable cut-outs.

Figure 5.66 A selection of the many shapes and sizes of wheels commercially available.

Equally common are fuselage mounted mainlegs. These are installed in the same way as the wing mounted ones, except that it is usual to place one torque rod behind the other.

When the mainwheels are fitted to an aluminium mount or piano wire frame, there are a number of ways of fixing the mount to the fuselage of a model. It can be held on with elastic bands and dowels, clamped at the rear with bands and a dowel at the front, screwed in place, or even plugged in. The choice depends on the design of your particular model, your landing skill, the roughness of your flying field and your desire to build in a degree of bouncability.

Regardless of the method of installation, you should understand that the greater the distance between the mainwheels the better the lateral stability on the ground and, if a tailwheel model, the greater the tendency to ground loop.

Wheels

Having looked at the undercarriage layout, it is important to consider the wheels themselves. Many kits still exclude wheels from their contents. If you are building from a plan, only the wheel diameters are likely to be specified.

There are however, other factors you need to think about. The smoother the take-off strip, the smaller the acceptable diameter of wheel and, of course, with smaller size comes a weight and drag reduction. Obviously, the larger the wheels, the better they will be able to cope with the bumpiness and grass tussocks found on the average club strip.

Select your wheels to suit the model from the wide range of commercially available items. The key factors to bear in mind are as follows:

- The size of the model.
- The weight of the model.
- The type of model.
- The surface of the flying strip.
- Whether a main, nose or tailwheel.

Securing wheels in place is often done using collets, but these have an unfortunate habit of coming undone at the worst possible moment,

Figure 5.67 Well banded on, the undercarriage mount is aluminium while the spats are from ABS plastic.

usually resulting in the loss of both wheel and collet. The use of a proprietary locking material, such as Loctite is a good idea.

A more permanent solution results if you solder the wheel to the undercarriage leg using a suitably sized washer with a strip of paper or thin card behind the washer while it is being soldered. Removing the paper after the job is complete should allow the wheel to rotate freely. Wheels may be attached to a bent aluminium mount using nuts and bolts, but again remember to use a locking material.

Make sure the wheels are parallel and that the model tracks straight. For tail draggers, there is a slight advantage in pointing both mainwheels in slightly to reduce the chances of ground looping.

Spats

Wheel spats can look attractive and reduce the drag caused by the wheels when in the air. Some are built from ply and balsa wood, others are pre-formed from plastic or GRP. They are not a good idea for beginners as they are easily damaged in a less than perfect take off or landing.

You should consider their durability in relation to the roughness of the strip from which you fly your model. More important is their method of attachment to the undercarriage legs and the ease with which you can remove them for repairs. A good solution is to build a small framework of metal wire into the spat and then solder it to the undercarriage leg.

Chapter 6 Finishing the model

Getting the right shape

Basically, there are three ways of getting the final model to exactly the right shape. You can carve it, you can use a plane or you may sand the required part of the airframe to the correct outline.

Where balsa block is used, for example with wing tips, a razor plane will quickly remove material until approximately the final outline is reached. You can similarly approach more tricky shapes with a razor knife.

You should reach the final finish with sandpaper formed round an appropriately sized block, or use a Perma-Grit or similar metallic sanding tool. Sandpaper comes in a variety of grades, from 10, the roughest, to 1200, the finest. Working with balsa is best with papers in the range 200 – 600.

Fillers

It is also essential to have an unblemished finish to your model before you start to paint it. There are a number of lightweight proprietary fillers which dry reasonably quickly and you can sand as easily as balsa wood. DIY fillers, such as Polyfilla, work equally well but are somewhat heavier.

Smooth the filler over any dents, cracks or joins and leave it until it has hardened. A small palette knife or the edge of a phone card is ideal to avoid building up too thick a layer of filler. Then carefully sand the filler down until it melds perfectly into the surrounding area. Care is needed when filling balsa to avoid sanding a slight indentation into the surrounding wood.

Bare sheet balsa surfaces normally require a couple of coats of thinned sanding sealer, a cellulose dope with a powder in suspension, to fill the grain. However you should not use sanding sealer if you are going to cover these parts of the model with an iron-on covering.

A coat of filler will raise the grain of the wood and harden the surface. When dry, in a matter of minutes, you can sand the surface smooth and apply a second coat if necessary. You can obtain a better and stronger result if you cover balsa sheeting with tissue prior to the application of grain filler.

For working on sealed and filled surfaces, wet and dry emery paper, used with constant dipping into a bowl of water, will avoid any clogging of the paper.

Covering

The aims of the covering of a model are several and varied. First, you may want the material to make an open structure airtight. Second, it may be an aid to structural strength or to resist dings. Finally, it may form part or all of the final colour scheme and/or fuel proofer.

There is a large choice of covering systems available to today's modeller and thought should be given to the final choice of covering before making a purchase.

- What does the kit or plan suggest?
- Is it required to aid structural strength?
- Is smell a problem when applying the covering?
- Must it provide the final colouring?
- Must it be fuel proof. If so, to what fuels?
- How much strength must it add to the surfaces covered?
- Must it be relatively puncture proof?

	Tissue	Nylon	Ht-shrink film	Ht-shrink fabric	Glass skin
Structural strength	Low	High	Medium	High	High
Smell	High	High	Nil	Nil	Medium
Colour	Some	Some	Excellent	Excellent	None
Fuel proof	No	No	Excellent	Good	Excellent
Puncture resistance	Low	High	Medium	High	High
Weight	Low	Medium	Medium	Medium	Med/high
Initial Cost	Low	Medium	High	High	Medium

Table 6.1 The characteristics of the various different covering materials vary considerably. You should bear them in mind when choosing which one to use.

- What weight is acceptable?
- What will it cost?

Table 6.1 considers these characteristics for all the more popular covering systems.

Most modellers seem to find either a heat-shrink film or fabric is the best choice these days.

Although these materials may appear to be rather expensive, the price does effectively include the adhesive, covering material, final colouring and fuel proofer all within the single material. With a little practice, they become very straight-forward to apply.

I AGREE .... IT DOESN'T LOOK VERY ATTRACTIVE ....
.. BUT AT LEAST IT STOPS YOU COMPLAINING ABOUT THE SMELL !

Figure 6.1 All ready for covering, the choice of material depends on the structure of the model and the type of field where you will be flying.

Tissue

As a covering material, tissue may appear to have little place on modern R/C aircraft, but it does offer a cheap and well proven method of strengthening any part of a model which has an all-sheet finish. It is a good medium for covering fuselages and, where wings are covered with heat-shrink film, matching paint colours are available. On small models, it may even be the appropriate material for the whole structure, though the ease with which it is punctured makes it an unattractive covering for open structures.

Nylon

Nylon is much stronger than most other available fabrics or materials for covering a model, be it sheeted or an open structure. What you must bear in mind, however, is that nylon shrinks considerably and will distort or warp any inadequately strong structure. Furthermore, the material absorbs a great deal of clear dope (fortunately fairly light) and can also absorb a lot of coloured paint (not so light). However for longevity, it is only bettered by GRP. The skill in putting on nylon depends on wetting it first.

Heat-shrink fabric and film

By far the most popular coverings are the heat-shrink, usually self-adhesive, iron-on materials. Their weights and strengths vary considerably. The following information refers to the popular range made by Solarfilm. Similar materials are produced by other companies under other names. Table 6.2 compares Solarfilm's range with more traditional covering materials.

Note that where a range of weights is given, paler colours such as yellow and white are heavier than dark colours, with transparent colours the lightest of all.

For those iron-on materials which do not have an adhesive backing, Balsaloc may be painted over the airframe and then used as a heat-sensitive adhesive.

The art of covering

A vital point to remember is that the finish of any model is only as good as the surface on which you apply it. Before starting to cover a model, it is important mentally to divide the surface of the model into manageable sections. You can cut out panels from old newspapers and alter their

Name	Type	Self adhesive	Wt gsm	Wt oz/ sq yd
Modelspan	Light/medium/heavyweight tissue	No	12 - 21	½ - ¾
Silk	Silk	No	15	½
Nylon	Nylon	No	30	1
Airspan	Polyester tissue (needs a light coat of dope)	No	24	1
Litespan	Tough synthetic material to replace tissue and dope	No	30	1
Fibafilm	Super light, fibre reinforced polyester film	No	42	1⅓
Solarfilm	Iron-on plastic film with smooth glossy surface	Yes	55 - 70	2 - 2¾
Solarspan 2000	Multi layer, heavy duty iron-on film, 50% stronger than Solarfilm	Yes	65 - 75	2½ - 3
Solartex	Iron-on fabric	Yes	85 - 95	3½
Glosstex	Iron-on fabric with high gloss fuel-proof paint finish	Yes	120 - 130	4¾ - 5
Solarkote	Iron-on polyester film	Yes	70 - 80	2¾ - 3

Table 6.2 Weights of various covering materials, excluding the weight of any dope, paint or fuel proofer needed.

size and shape until they are correct before you use them as a pattern for cutting out the actual covering material. Whatever material you choose, you will need to make an allowance of about 25mm (1") for overlapping the covering.

Tissue, nylon and silk

When using tissue, it is sensible to lightly iron out any folds or creases. When covering an all-sheet structure, apply a coat of thinned dope or sanding sealer first and then lightly sand with 600 grade paper to smooth the raised grain.

Cut the tissue into handleable sized panels with an overlap all round. Float the paper over a bowl of clean water and carefully lay onto the surface you are covering. Gently pull out any wrinkles and dope all over,

trimming the edges as you go. Use a small pad of damp tissue to help smooth down the covering. When you have covered the whole model, apply a second coat of dope and you are then ready to put on some decoration.

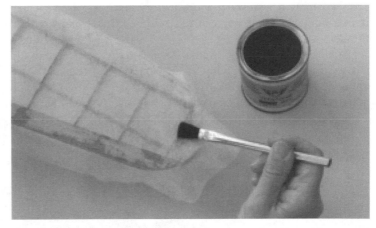

Figure 6.2 The tissue is applied damp and stuck to the airframe with clear, thinned dope.

Figure 6.3 Try to ensure the overlap does not face into the airflow. Cover the undersurface of a wing first.

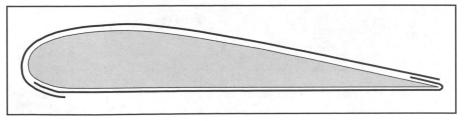

Figure 6.4 You really need a special tacking iron and hot air gun for successful heat-shrink covering.

Covering an open structure model with tissue can either be done in a similar way, using dope as a glue around the edges and when the lot is dry doping the whole surface.

The alternative is to attach the tissue dry with tissue paste, making sure you carefully pull the tissue tight. With the tissue firmly in place, you can then spray it with water and when dry give it two coats of clear dope mixed with 30% thinners.

You can use a similar technique for nylon or silk as you use when applying tissue. You may apply the material wet and use dope as the adhesive. Due to the large amount of shrinkage that can be induced, you should pin the material in place while the dope and water dry out.

Heat-shrink covering

Heat-shrink materials fall into two categories: those with a heat-sensitive backing, the vast majority, and those without. For the latter, you must paint a suitable adhesive around the surface you are covering.

Again, cut out panels and after removing the transparent protective backing, lay the covering on the surface of the model. Avoiding creases or excessive slackness, fix the edges of the covering with a tacking iron. Smooth down the edges with the iron, trimming with scissors and pulling the material where there is a curve to keep it taut.

Use a heat-shrink gun to direct heat, moving the gun rapidly about 100mm (4") above the material, until you see it tightened. You can use an iron for this task but it is not as easy and certainly not as fast. Avoid getting the gun too close to the surface or holding it stationary since either of these can result in a hole in the material.

A special thermometer is available to ensure that you set your iron to the correct temperature. Failing this, use a scrap of the material on the iron and adjust the heat until it just starts to curl up. At best, overheating will damage the tightening properties of the material, at worst it will burn a hole right through.

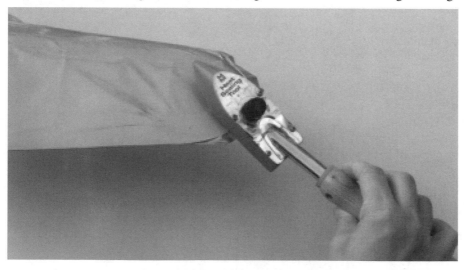

Figure 6.5 Start by tacking the film in place with an iron set to the correct heat. Try to keep the covering fairly tight during this process.

The aim is to get a smooth taut finish with the edges carefully sealed. Some materials shrink more than others but all require you to pull the material nice and tight during the tacking process. Try to avoid pulling unevenly during the tacking process as this has a tendency to build in warps.

When using materials with a shiny surface, such as Solarfilm, you can produce successful and secure overlaps of the material by first painting the overlap area with an etchant like Prymol. Allow it to dry before ironing on the overlapping material.

Some textured materials, such as Solartex, benefit from a coat of fuel proofer to help keep the material clean.

Glass skinning

One of the best ways of producing a perfect finish on a sheeted wing is to skin it with resin. There are a number of proprietary types but care is needed to avoid adding too much weight to a wing.

They do provide a really tough solution and, with a little elbow grease, probably the smoothest and glossiest one. The best way to apply them is to spread them on the surface of the wing using a plastic spreader such as an old phone card, until the wing is covered with a thin even coating

of the resin. Once this is hard, it is a matter of sanding the final surface with increasingly fine wet and dry paper until a final polish produces a gleaming surface.

Painting

The pigments used in any coloured paint are heavy. When the solvent has dried out, there is still a major weight penalty to consider. Thus the choice of covering of any model may largely be dominated by this single fact. Visibility in the air is also a factor, particularly with unusual configurations. Reds, oranges and yellows give the best contrast with the sky, and day glo colours are particularly visible.

The ability of fuels and exhaust oil to attack paint surfaces has led to a number of fuel-proof paints. Generally, these are harder to apply or less able to resist long term fuel attack than a finish that you treat with a two part fuel proofer. There are several types of paints which are popular. These include:

- Cellulose – dopes and car touch up cans.
- Enamels – Humbrol/Airfix tinlets and many household paints.
- Acrylics – single and two part paints used by the car industry.
- Epoxies – two part fuel-proof paints.

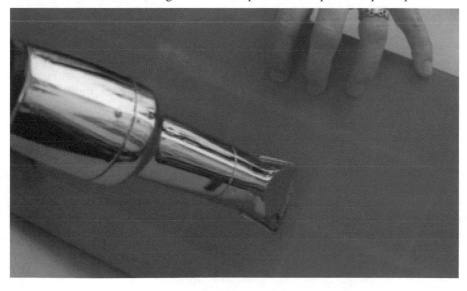

Figure 6.6 The easiest way to tighten the material is with a heat gun, kept moving some 100mm (4") from the covering.

Figure 6.7 A large and small brush, a selection of tinlets of enamel paint, a jar of Solarlac fuel resistant paint and a 2oz (50g) tin of enamel. This last item is inverted to seal the lid after use to avoid a skin forming in the tin.

One major difficulty is that not all paints are compatible and given the wrong combination, paint bubbling will ruin the surface and require a complete strip down and restart. Basically, the rule is never to put a cellulose **on top of** an enamel finish. If you are in any doubt about compatibility, try a test sample first. Remember that most paints take some time to harden completely, so painting is not a job you should rush.

There are two ways of applying paint; using a brush or spraying it. Both require dust-free, warm conditions to get the best results. A tack cloth is mildly sticky and if you wipe one over the surfaces just prior to painting it will help to remove any settled dust. Ian Peacock's *Painting and Finishing Models* (see page 243) gives comprehensive advice on the whole subject.

Brush work

It is almost impossible to get a reasonable paint finish without a quality brush of the right size. What you need is a big floppy brush for painting large areas and a smaller one for lines. In either case, avoid cheap brushes which will shed hairs on your work as you proceed.

Enamel is much easier to apply than coloured dope, and the matt varieties cover better than glossy ones, bearing in mind that both are likely to need a final coat of fuel proofer. Having

Figure 6..8 To get a top finish you need a paint spray or airbrush. This one is powered by an inflated tyre.

achieved a smooth surface ready to accept the paint, cellulose requires rapid application with no attempt to brush in the paint, while enamel should be carefully worked in using a back and forwards brush movement.

Do remember to read the manufacturer's instructions, particularly about how to clean brushes after use. Cellulose thinners or white spirit are what you should normally use for this task. Clean the brushes and leave the painted model in a dust-free environment to dry, letting the paint have plenty of time to harden. If using matt enamel, avoid touching the finished surface with your hands as the natural grease in them will mark the finished paint surface. A coat of fuel proofer will solve this problem but will also slightly darken the colour of any matt paint.

Spray painting

You may be lucky enough to own an airbrush or paint spraying equipment, but the majority of modellers make do with aerosol cans. While these are more expensive to use in the long term, unless you envisage undertaking a great deal of spray work, the investment in an airbrush or spray gun is hard to justify on economic grounds.

Figure 6.9 *Most model shops stock a selection of self-adhesive and water slide decoration. Car accessories shops are also a good source.*

The main problem with spray painting is that much of the paint ends up where you least want it. This means it must not matter if the place where you spray gets a light dusting of paint. Furthermore, you must wear a mask as otherwise it will also get into your lungs.

You will have to mask off any part of the model which you do not want to be painted. Masking tape and old newspaper are perfect for this task.

The basic rule of spraying is to use many thin coats to avoid paint runs, which you will find difficult to sand flat. Spray paint must be thin enough to pass through the nozzle of the gun, although this is not a problem with aerosols provided you thoroughly shake the can as indicated in the instructions. This is usually for a period of two minutes, and you will hear a small bead inside the can rattling about to help the mixing process.

Unless you are going to build very large models, a large airbrush or a small capacity spray gun will meet all your needs. Powered by a small air compressor, you should thin the paint with an equal amount of the appropriate thinners.

Try to choose a dry day with warm dust-free conditions. Hold the nozzle some 300mm (12") away from the surface you are going to spray and keep the gun moving horizontally back and forth until you have covered the whole area.

Let the paint dry and then add additional coats until you obtain an even covering. Remember, the more paint you spray on, the more weight you add to the model. The best finish involves rubbing down the model between coats and finishing off with a coat of fuel proofer or varnish, unless you are building a glider or electric model.

Decoration

Even the final decoration of a model requires some forethought. It may add a little weight and, with a bit of luck, attractiveness. For a gifted few it can convert a dull looking model into a truly memorable one. Transfers or decals, whether self-adhesive or water slide add interest. You can find letters and numbers in both these forms as well as on dry rub sheets.

You can purchase thin self-adhesive stripes from car accessory shops and use them to emphasise the lines and speed potential of your model, as well as providing a good divider between different coloured areas. You can obtain larger

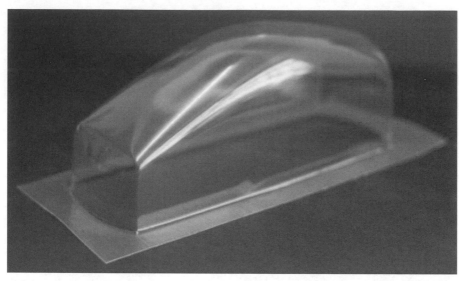

Figure 6.10 Any commercially available canopy can be modified and cut to size. (Photo courtesy Vortex Plastics.)

sheets of self-adhesive coloured film in model shops, a typical product being Solartrim.

Fuel proofing

For any model powered by an internal combustion engine, some sort of fuel proofing is essential. The weight of one or two coats of a suitable varnish must be considered when arriving at an estimate of the final all-up weight.

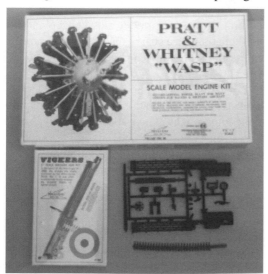

Figure 6.11 There are many plastic kits for items such as radial engines and World War I machine guns.

The engine and fuel tank bay may benefit from additional coats.

There are two types of fuel proofer that you can apply. The best is a two part epoxy which provides a truly fuel-proof surface. Polyurethane and acrylic varnishes are better classified as fuel resistant, as are many specialist fuel-resistant paints.

Their success depends on the contents of the fuel and the time you leave spilled fuel and exhaust goo on your model. Glow fuel with nitro content is the worst for attacking fuel-resistant paint, while diesel fuel is relatively benign.

Clearly, fuel proofing is quite unnecessary on any electric powered model, unless you use it to provide a more durable finish to your aircraft.

Adding realism

Even the most basic of trainers can be made to look more realistic by using the right colour scheme and adding a cockpit and pilot. Some of you will revel in adding details to your models, others will be happy with a purely functional machine. Just how far you go will depend on you own personal choice. Later, if you try scale modelling, you will find that most of your time will be spent adding realism.

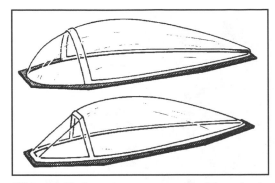

Figure 6.12 Sometimes you can find exactly the canopy you want. (Pictures courtesy Chart.)

Canopies

A canopy may be decorative rather than functional. Kits will include this item, but when building from a plan, you may find a suitable commercial one specified.

The alternative is to make one yourself. You can form clear plastic sheet in a variety of ways, all involving heat, some also involving vacuum forming, over a plug. You can also use household mouldings, such lemonade bottles or Easter egg coverings.

Commercial canopies are available in a wide range of shapes and sizes and you may use them as they are or crop them to provide an alternative

Figure 6.13 An Action Man is heavy but makes a very realistic pilot when suitably clothed. The flying teddy bear is inexpensive and can make a real fun pilot.

shape and size. Their use may increase the realism of any model for a negligible increase in weight and only a small increase in drag. Think about adding one to make your model a little different from the average.

Figure 6.14 The detail of the instrument panels in this Harvard makes the model come alive. (Photo courtesy Geoff Lamb.)

Figure 6.15 A moulded plastic 'head and shoulders' pilot before and after painting. (Photos courtesy Vortex Plastics.)

Instrument panels

An open cockpit is very desirable on certain types of models, such as biplanes, to improve their looks. Such a cockpit cries out for a simple instrument panel and a pilot. You can make a panel from a sheet of card, or thin ply, by painting or sticking pre-printed instruments in place. You can make a more elaborate panel for a better effect, from a sandwich of panel with holes, a sheet of transparent acetate and instrument dials on card. You can even photograph a full sized instrument panel, or cut a picture from a magazine to achieve the right effect.

Pilots

Many people feel a model aircraft without a pilot has something missing. If you are of this view, then the key factor to remember is that apart from adding visual appeal, a pilot also adds unproductive weight to the model.

Fortunately, pilots made from balsa wood, silicon rubber or vacuum formed all add very little weight to the finished model, while adding to the realism, even of the most basic design. You can select the one you want from the wide range available commercially. Head and shoulders usually suffice. An alternative is to find a doll,

Figure 6.16 A US Navy colour scheme, some decals, a pilot and ejection seat plus shark's teeth painted on the nose identify this model clearly as a Corsair 2.

such as Action Man, but the weight may make this solution unacceptable.

Stores

A range of items can add interest to almost any model and make it look more realistic. Machine guns, bombs, rockets or guided missiles can all add character to the simplest model without adding much weight or causing a loss of performance.

You can make any of these items from bits of balsa and plastic gleaned from your scrap box or buy from a wide range of kits which are quickly assembled. Figure 6.17 shows a 500lb bomb easily made from balsa and card. Its weight is

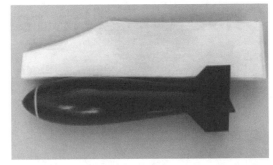

Figure 6.17 You can produce bombs from balsa and card. They will add considerable interest when hung beneath the wings of your model.

negligible, construction time minimal and you can attach it to the wing of the most basic of trainers.

Figure 6.18 The look of this large Sukhoi is much enhanced by its superb colour scheme. (Photo courtesy Airplanes Etc.)

Figure 6.19 You can have just as much fun finishing a model like this Baby Magic, a half size version of the Magician. (Photo courtesy Malcolm Corbin.)

Chapter 7 The radio equipment

System overview

A radio control system consists of a hand-held transmitter, on which all the user controls are mounted and a receiver which accepts the transmitted signals and distributes them to a number of servos. An internal battery powers the transmitter, while a separate pack with its own switch powers the receiver and the servos.

Servos can be regular sized, miniature, micro or high power. The size you use will depend on the type and size of your model as well as the speed at which it flies.

Most, but not all radios available today are compatible, which means that any servo can be plugged in to any receiver, provided the correct plugs are fitted.

Although it is possible to power R/C equipment with dry batteries, it is a far from satisfactory solution, both from a safety and a cost of ownership point of view. Wait until you have saved a little more money and buy a set powered by rechargeable nickel cadmium (nicad) batteries. These can be recharged overnight as many as 1,000 times before you need to replace them. A customised charger, included with the radio, allows you to charge the transmitter and airborne battery at the same time.

Virtually all model aircraft flying in the UK takes place in the 35MHz band, which is exclusively reserved for aircraft. Model boats and cars either operate in the 27MHz or 40MHz band.

Matched pairs of interchangeable crystals control both the transmitter and receiver frequencies. There are, in fact, three frequency bands in the UK on which it is legal to operate radio control equipment; 27MHz, 35MHz and 459MHz

The first, 27MHz is largely discredited as it is shared with R/C cars and boats as well as citizen's band radio. Any of these can easily cause sufficient interference to make your model crash. The 459MHz band has few users due to the lack of available commercial radios.

The almost universal choice today is for equipment operating in the 35MHz band. This frequency band is divided into 26 discrete frequencies, labelled 60 – 85 and based on 10kHz frequency separation. These frequencies, controlled by pairs of interchangeable crystals, theoretically allow up to 26 aircraft to fly at the same time.

The main limitations on their use come from modellers themselves. BMFA competitions

Figure 7.1 *At the dawn of radio control, before servos, rubber powered escapements could only move the control surfaces to full deflection and back to neutral!*

allocate odd frequencies for powered flying, even for gliders. Some clubs only allow the use of every other frequency to avoid interference between adjacent channels with older equipment. Of course any group of modellers will want as few users as possible on any particular frequency. To avoid disappointment and further expense, ask at your club which frequency they can allocate to you before you buy your radio.

If you are considering entering competitions at some time in the future, a second pair of crystals on a different frequency will prove invaluable. However, not all crystals work with any radio set, so make sure you get the correct brand.

The radio is the heart of any R/C model and you must take care to provide positive slop-free connections to the controls. You must protect all airborne parts from vibration and the possibility of an unplanned impact with the ground.

Most people buy their first radio as a complete set of units which will operate satisfactorily together. It is important to make the right purchase decision as this is the single most expensive item you are likely to buy.

Fashion is a consideration and shows in the rate at which new R/C systems appear on the market. They may look shiny and exciting or matt black and professional depending on the current fashion, but they do not necessarily work better. They may have more facilities, but you must decide if you need them. Rather like computers, new models are appearing all the time but few of you need to change to a new model, though you may well want to keep up to date.

Deciding what to buy

It is important to look at the features an R/C system contains and decide which ones you are likely to need. The following paragraphs should help you to arrive at a decision.

How much to spend?

As an expensive item which should last a considerable time, it seems sensible to allocate

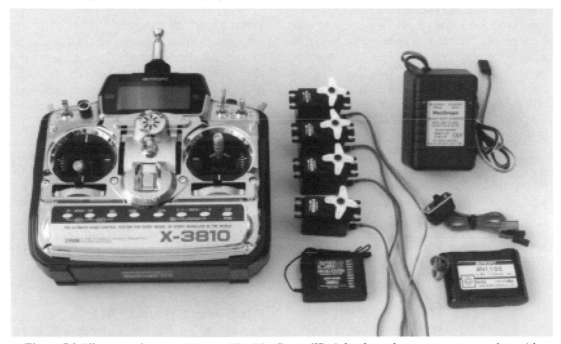

Figure 7.2 All you need to get airborne. This MacGregor/JR eight channel system comes complete with transmitter, receiver, battery pack, four servos and a charger.

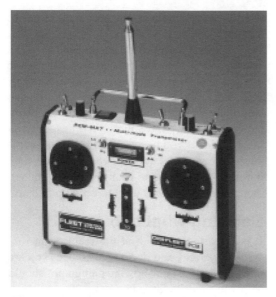

Figure 7.3 A typical basic transmitter. This is the seven channel British-made Fleet PCM-MX7. It has well laid out controls and is easy to use.

a reasonable sum of money for the purchase of your radio control system. Prices in 1997 vary from £150 for a four channel set up to £1,000 for a top of the range system. The low end includes systems designed to be cost effective for sports fliers. They will, with care, last for many years. At the top end are the precision sets built for daily use by pilots competing in aerobatic and other competitions. They are full of bells and whistles unlikely to be used by the average flier.

Which make of radio to buy?

While not recommending any particular manufacturer's radio, you need to think about a

Channel	Control
1	Elevator
2	Rudder
3	Throttle
4	Ailerons
5	Retracts
6	Flaps
7	Ancillaries

Table 7.1 Typical use of seven channels.

number of factors. Assuming you have joined a local club, what type of radios do the members use, which are the most popular and which manufacturers have a good reputation for servicing and repairs. If you wish to buy a British radio, then the only surviving and well established manufacturer is Fleet Controls based in Hampshire. There are a number of Far Eastern sets with a first class reputation including Futaba, Hitec, MacGregor/JR and Sanwa. In all probability, the factors which follow will dominate your choice.

Where to purchase the radio?

Radios do need servicing and crash repair from time to time. When choosing a supplier, think about how easy it will be to return the set when necessary and/or buy additional items.

A supplier local to your home or place of work is the obvious choice. If they hold a range of ancillary items and spares for the radio, so much the better.

What about the range?

All radios operate to a range where it impossible to see the model to control it. Typical ranges of a kilometre (half a mile) on the ground and at least twice that in the air are common. In a word, don't worry.

How many channels?

Four is really the minimum for powered flight, giving control of elevators, ailerons, rudder and throttle. If you have ambitions to fit retracts and flaps as you gain experience, a six (or more) channel system costs little extra if still supplied with only four servos. You can purchase the additional servos later. However, it is worth noting that the vast majority of club fliers never employ more than four channels.

What about FM and PCM?

Radios are no longer produced which use AM. The reason for this is that FM (sometimes called PPM) gives a far more interference-free performance. The difference is similar to listening to your favourite show on an AM and then on an FM radio. PCM is a technique to improve the quality of the radio link further, albeit at a small increase in complexity and expense.

What frequency?

Almost all aircraft modellers in the UK fly with radios operating in the 35MHz band. These are the most widely available. It is illegal, not to mention outright dangerous to use them in R/C boats or cars. Pairs of plug-in crystals for the transmitter and receiver allow you to select any one of 26 channels in the band. You must attach a matching flag to your transmitter aerial to indicate your frequency to other fliers.

When deciding which channel you are going to use, there are a few basic rules. First, there may be club rules which demand that you operate either on even frequencies only, or on odd ones only. Next, there may be a log of members' channels and it is sensible, or you may be asked, to operate on one of the less populated channels. Next, if you have any aspirations to compete, you will need an odd frequency for a powered model but an even one if you fly gliders.

Number and type of servos

Four is the ideal number to start and normal size, economically priced ones are fine. You will use them to operate the elevator, ailerons, rudder and throttle. You can fly some trainers on just three channels, eliminating ailerons, and a few without even a throttle, though this means that you have to fly until the engine runs out of fuel. This can be awkward if you get into any type of difficulty.

Remember, you can always buy more servos later if need be. You should only consider specialist servos if you have firm ambitions to fly electric, small models, very large ones or models equipped with retracts.

Buying second-hand

If you are forced by lack of funds to buy second-hand, find out why is the set being sold. There may be a genuine reason, such as a desire to move to a new set giving additional channels or facilities. Carefully check how the set has been looked after. Is it in its original box with a clean set of instructions? Carefully check the airborne items for any signs of crash damage and ask if the radio has been involved in any crashes. Find out where it was purchased and where it is serviced. Ask for a service history and check on spares availability. It's a bit like buying a second-hand car. If you can get an experienced R/C flier to accompany you, so much the better.

Which features do you need?

Let's assume you are buying a radio with four functions and trims for the two sticks. If you require a fifth and sixth channel, you should opt for a switch to operate retracts and a slider for flaps. The rotary knobs fitted to some transmitters are less than ideal as you cannot sense their position by feel alone.

Dual rate switches

These switches allow you to alter the maximum control throw of the elevators and ailerons in flight. This is a very desirable feature when it comes to test flying a new model.

Servo reversing switches

Reverse switches make fitting the servo connections much easier, but do bring about their own dangers. When you build a second model, you may need some servo reversing switches in a different position to your first model. If you take them both to the flying field at the same time, you have an accident, caused by control reversal, waiting to happen.

Voltage indicator

A meter or digital indicator, and preferably one which indicates transmitted power, provides an important way of knowing that your transmitter has sufficient power in its batteries. A low battery alarm, either audible or visual, gives an added safety factor.

Stick length adjustment

This feature allows you to customise the stick length to suit the size of your hands and, more

Figure 7.4 You can program the MacGregor/JR X3810 transmitter for powered models, gliders or helicopters. It has a 10 model memory and a programmable trainer function.

importantly, to adjust the length to suit hand holding, use of a neck strap or use of a tray.

Control stick spring tension adjustment

This enables you to choose between a strong reaction to stick movements or a soft one. The choice between these extremes is purely a personal one.

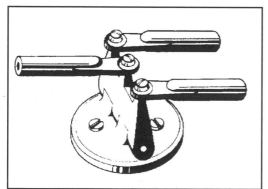

Figure 7.5 A mechanical mixer which attaches neatly to the top of a servo. (Picture courtesy Chart.)

Mode conversion

Almost all sets allow you to choose whether to have the throttle on the left- or right-hand stick. This is important if you decide to fly mode 1 (see Figure 7.7) or are left-handed. You should check if you can do this yourself (without invalidating the guarantee) or whether you have to return the set to the supplier.

Coupling

Many transmitters provide a switch to couple ailerons and rudder together, as some models only turn satisfactorily if the use of these two controls is co-ordinated in the turn. While this can be done manually, the coupling feature makes accurate flying much easier.

Mixers

The mixing of elevators and ailerons to provide an elevon output is useful if you fancy flying deltas or flying wings. Flap/aileron and flap/elevator trim mixing are both useful if you envisage fitting flaps. Note, however, that you can purchase both mechanical and electronic on-board mixers at a later stage, though they do add slightly to the weight of a model.

Snap roll switches

Providing instant full aileron, these switches are a useful adjunct to the serious aerobatic flier. They are of virtually no use during the early stages of learning to fly, but they cost little and you may be happy to find them included.

Computerised radios

The use of microprocessors in so-called computer radios provides a host of features not available in more conventional basic R/C systems. They are particularly useful if you plan to fly helicopters as well as, or instead of, fixed wing models. As you might expect, they are also more expensive. Thus, you need to be absolutely certain you will continue in the hobby before making such an investment.

The various facilities are programmed using a liquid crystal display and series of push buttons. You should check how easy it is to feed your model details into the transmitter and to alter them.

Number of models – memory

A computer radio will store all the various features and control settings you have chosen for your model. Most allow you to retain several models' settings for future use. It is well worth checking the number of models the memory can retain as re-programming a radio is not the most interesting of tasks. Clearly, however, more memory equals more money.

Exponential

This feature enables the servo to move a small amount for a given stick movement near neutral, yet give large deflections when the stick is moved to its maximum deflection. This gives smooth control at high speed yet plenty of control at low speed.

Sub trim

You can alter the neutral position of each servo arm to provide correct in-flight trim without the use of the transmitter trim controls.

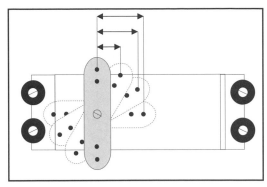

Figure 7.6 The linear movement of a servo output arm is not proportional to the angle of movement. Exponential can correct this and provide more movement at extreme angles.

Throws (end point adjustment)

You can vary the amount of movement of the servo arm each side of neutral to alter the amount of control deflection in either direction. This is particularly useful when adjusting the throttle at the flying field as it is luck whether you have mechanically set the tick-over accurately.

Equally, you can introduce a little bit more or less control deflection if the model's flight performance dictates this. The alternative of altering the distance of the clevis from the servo centre (out for more deflection) or at the control horn (in for greater control throw) is not as easy to do in a hurry.

Mixers

All computer radios provide facilities for mixing channels together. Most allow you to mix all of the commonly required channels, such as elevator, aileron, rudder and flaps, in the normal combinations. They also allow such helicopter combinations as tail rotor/throttle and collective/throttle mixing.

Fail safe

The ability of the radio to set the controls to neutral positions and close the throttle automatically should you lose radio contact can avoid a 'flyaway' and also minimise damage in the ensuing crash. The fail safe positions are set up with the other features for each chosen model. Some systems also provide an internal flight

IT'LL BE ALRIGHT! ... IT'S GOT A FAIL SAFE!

battery pack monitor which senses when the battery is all but flat and switches in the fail safe while there is still sufficient power remaining to move the servos.

Programmable controls and switches

Some transmitters have programmable controls and switches which allow you to set them to give a particular amount of servo movement in a particular direction for use with ancillary functions such as bomb release. You may need some thought to set the control to give a natural direction of movement when operated and to ensure that it comes readily to hand when you need to operate a particular function.

Decision time

By now you are probably feeling fairly confused, so it is a good idea to talk to someone who has some experience. This could be a model shop proprietor, though such people do have a vested interest in parting you from your money. Club members can be very helpful, but you may get conflicting advice.

The questionnaire opposite may help you arrive at a final decision. Having made your purchase, do spend time reading and understanding the manual which comes with your radio.

Transmitters (trannies)

There are basically, as you have seen, two main types of transmitter used today, those with a built-in computer and those without. The number of channels can vary from 2 – 9 or more, depending on the current and future needs of the owner. There are two basic systems of controls, known as mode 1 and mode 2. These are shown in Figure 7.7.

Which you choose must very much depend on your choice of instructor, since you will have to choose the same mode. Left-handers often choose left-handed mode 1 or 2, but although I am left-handed and learned to fly left-handed

How much do you plan to spend?	No of channels				Computer	No of servos
	2	3	4	5+		
£100	✓					2
£150		✓				3
£200			✓			4
£250 or more				✓	✓	5 +
Do you expect to fly models controlled by:						
Rudder/aileron and elevator only	✓					2
Rudder/aileron, elevator and throttle		✓				3
Aileron, elevator, rudder and throttle			✓			4
Do you want to fit retracts or flaps at some stage?				✓		5 + retract
Do you want to fly electric?		✓				3 + speed cont
Do you want the latest 'bells & whistles' radio?					✓	
Are you happy to program a computerised radio?					✓	

Table 7.2 *Planning your expenditure on an R/C set against your likely future needs*

mode 2, I later converted to conventional mode 2 and find it much more satisfactory to be compatible with everyone else in the club where I fly.

The argument in favour of mode 1 is that elevators and ailerons are the most used controls and their separation onto different sticks makes accurate flying easier. The advantage of mode 2 is that it mimics the full size practice of having a single stick for elevator and aileron. In truth it really doesn't make much difference and you will soon adjust to either system. A few radios still exist that have a twisting rudder control on top of a single stick, operated by one hand while the other arm, which cuddles the transmitter, has a separate hand-operated throttle knob. This is ideal for some disabled modellers.

It is essential to establish the maximum ground range of your system with the transmitter aerial collapsed. You should carry out this check when no other transmitters are switched on. With the receiver aerial stretched out horizontally, walk away from your model, checking the controls from time to time until the servos start to twitch and move away from neutral. This is what happens at extreme range.

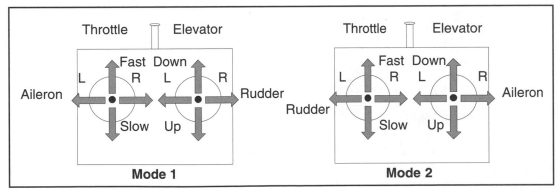

Figure 7.7 *The two main transmitter control modes. Left-handed mirror image operation is also possible.*

Check the number of paces back to your model; usually around thirty to fifty. This establishes the performance of your R/C system and you can regularly check it. Remember, this distance is far less than the range with the transmitter aerial extended.

Straps, trays and mitts

While many pilots are happy to grip their trannies in two hands with their thumbs on the sticks, others find it more convenient to grip the stick, while a neck strap or transmitter tray takes the weight. The main advantage is the potential to make more delicate stick movements. The snag is that it makes it harder to just pick up your tranny and get airborne once you've started your engine. It can also make solo hand launching a real problem unless you have a helper.

When flying in cold weather, frozen fingers are not conducive to good control of your model while gloves remove a fair degree of feel. The type of mittens which have no ends to the fingers are one solution, but a transmitter mitt which encloses both the transmitter and the hands gives the best possible protection.

Figure 7.8 *A modern PCM receiver is a masterpiece of miniaturisation. This is the MacGregor/JR NER-649S nine channel unit.*

Receivers

You can consider the receiver as a black box, which receives signals from the transmitter via a short length of insulated wire. Do not alter the length of this wire as it is 'tuned' to the radio's frequency band. Do not fold it back on itself, as this effectively reduces its electrical length.

The receiver has a socket containing a plug in crystal and sockets (or occasionally leads) for plugging in the airborne battery pack and required number of servos. Where the number of servos used is less than the maximum capability of the receiver, you can safely leave the spare sockets blank. What is important is to use sticky tape to ensure that the crystal, battery and servo leads cannot become disconnected in flight due to vibration.

Servos

The servo is the part of the radio system that moves the control surfaces (or throttle). It incorporates a small electric motor that moves an output arm to the required position, using a feedback potentiometer to achieve the correct positioning.

The output power of the servo depends on its size and design, but all consume a fair amount of electrical power when moving the controls. This power can increase dramatically should there be any stiction in the linkage or hinging of the control surface.

You need to cut many servo arms to avoid fouling the clevis and connection to the control surface. This is shown in Figure 7.10.

Despite the miracle of modern computerised radios, you still need to work out the geometry of the control connection. The reason for this is to ensure that the control follows the movement of the servo in a linear fashion, or gives differential movement if that is what you require. The next chapter, which deals with connecting the controls, examines this in more detail.

The use of ball races rather than plastic bearings on the output of a servo effectively reduces wear, and the resultant floppy output

Figure 7.9 Three different sizes of servo from MacGregor/JR. Left is the large and powerful NES 605, middle is the standard NES-517 and right the tiny NES-341 which only weighs 18g *(just over half an ounce).*

arm, to zero. You should always use ball-raced servos where loads are high – on large fast models – where you want long life or when precision is important. As usual, there is a small price penalty to pay.

Sizes and weights

The so-called standard servos from all manufacturers are similar in size and weight and are ideal for models from 3.5cc (0.20cu in) powered trainers to 10cc (0.61cu in) powered aerobatic models. Smaller models need mini- or micro-sized servos as do the most electric

powered models. Not surprisingly such servos are both more fragile and more expensive. A microservo is around twice as expensive as a standard one and one-third of the weight. Furthermore, microservos are less powerful and thus you should not use them on larger models.

At the other end of the range, larger servos are made for big models. Powerful but slower moving ones are produced especially to operate retractable undercarriages. It should thus be clear that when starting in the hobby, a radio with four – three if your budget is tight – standard servos is what you need.

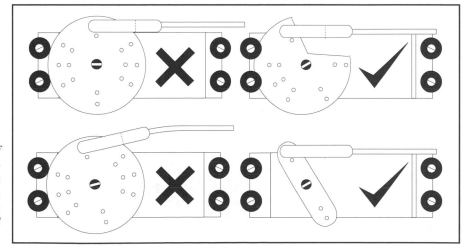

Figure 7.10 If you use a circular output arm on a servo, you must cut away a sector to avoid the clevis fouling.

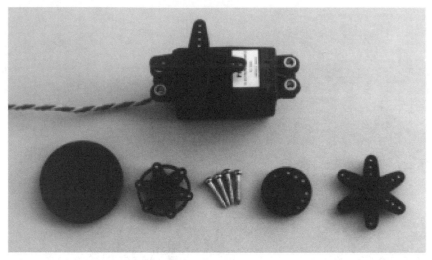

Figure 7.11 A typical low-cost servo comes with a selection of output arms and mounting screws.

Plugs, sockets and leads

Although the various manufacturers produce plugs and sockets which look very similar, they are not identical, and you must not mix them, even though most servos will work with most makes of receiver. Extension leads and Y leads can prove invaluable during installation, particularly if you want to use a pair of aileron servos.

Batteries

The nickel cadmium rechargeable secondary cell is the almost universal choice for powering radio control equipment. These batteries provide an excellent power to weight ratio and will recharge as many as 1,000 times. They provide a relatively constant output throughout their discharge cycle, are capable of providing high levels of power and only lose charge slowly over a period of weeks. They require custom-built constant current chargers, which are usually supplied as part of the radio system.

They do have a few shortcomings – basically memory and black lead. Once understood, both of these are easily avoided and should not cause you any significant problems.

Memory is a feature found in cells which are constantly partially discharged and then fully recharged. After a time, the battery capacity may reduce to that from fully charged to the previously discharged point.

This, unfortunately, is typical of the cycle of R/C operation. You can overcome it by fully discharging your batteries from time to time, followed by a full charge. Battery cyclers are available to undertake just this task.

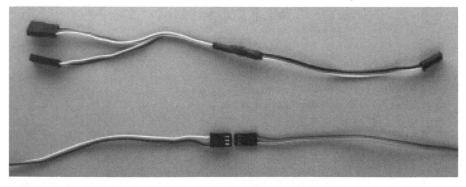

Figure 7.12 Top, a Y lead and, bottom, a typical plug and socket. When joined, it is sensible to tape the plug and socket together to avoid them coming apart in flight.

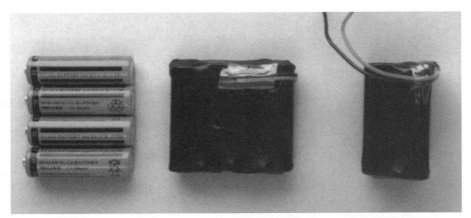

Figure 7.13 The four separate nicad pencells which make up into a flat or square airborne battery pack.

Black lead is a problem which occurs only on the negative battery lead and you can recognise it by pulling the insulation up from the battery connection and observing if the bare wire is clean copper or steel coloured, depending on the type of wire, or whether it is blackened.

The discoloration is thought to be caused by a chemical reaction and is exacerbated by damp conditions. In severe cases, the resistance of the wire will increase until it can pass insufficient current to operate the radio correctly. The only cure is to replace all the wire which exhibits this blackness underneath the insulation. The effect does not occur on the positive battery lead, but can in bad cases affect the switch connected to the battery.

Transmitters almost invariably include a display which indicates the remaining capacity in the battery. For airborne packs, a ground plug-in checker, or airborne go/no go indicator gives a good idea of whether you can safely undertake further flights.

Other ancillaries

Fail safes

A fail safe may sound the answer to the beginner's prayers, but it only fails safe in terms of freezing one or more of the controls at a pre-set position. Invariably, the throttle is closed. With the controls set to neutral, a stable trainer may glide safely down to earth, but for any less stable model, a

crash landing is the almost inevitable result. The philosophy is that it's better to lose the airframe in a controlled crash than the airframe, radio and engine in a flyaway.

Autopilots

Do not think that an autopilot does what it says. It will not fly the model for you. However, any device which makes learning to fly an R/C model easier is worth consideration. Autopilots are available which will level the wings of a model once the controls are released. This can be ideal

Figure 7.14 A plug-in tester indicates remaining airborne battery capacity on a row of coloured LEDs.

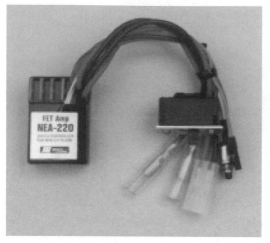

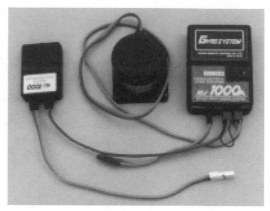

Figure 7.15 The diminutive MacGregor/JR NEA-220 electronic speed controller handles 50 amps and acts as the throttle 'servo' for an electric motor.

Figure 7.16 The latest gyros have no moving parts. The MacGregor/JR NEJ-1000 piezo-electric gyro comprises sensor, amplifier and remote gain controller.

for the inexperienced flier who panics in a spiral dive. On the other hand, autopilots are not cheap and add to the complexity of the radio system.

Speed controllers and switches

For those who fly electric powered models, a speed controller in place of the throttle servo gives proportional control of motor speed. A less expensive solution is to use an electronic on-off switch, or a microswitch operated by the throttle servo.

Figure 7.17 A field charger for fast recharging of transmitter and receiver batteries from a 12 volt battery. (Photo courtesy MainLink Systems.)

A speed controller may also include a BEC or battery elimination circuit. A BEC will provide power to the receiver as well as the main motor and will include a safety feature which cuts off power to the motor while the battery pack still has sufficient power to carry out a safe landing. As the typical consumption of an airborne pack is only some one-hundredth of that of a main drive motor, it seems a good idea to use a BEC and save the weight of the airborne radio battery.

Gyros

A gyro is a device mainly used in helicopters for keeping the tail pointing in the right direction. It also has applications on fixed wing models, for example in keeping the wings level.

The gyro consists of a rotating wheel or, in the latest designs, a solid state equivalent. There is a small unit containing the amplifier and other drive electronics, which fits between the receiver and the servo you wish to control.

Most gyros also allow you to change their gain or effectiveness in the air via an additional channel on your transmitter. The gyro stops the model changing attitude in the selected channel due to turbulence or other external influences, but allows you to over-ride it with control inputs. You should mount the gyro as close to the centre of gravity of your model as possible.

Figure 7.18 A unit like this Wide Range Analyser by MainLink gives you peace of mind by checking capacity. It will also help you maintain your batteries in tip top condition. (Photo courtesy MainLink Systems.)

Battery charging

The ubiquitous nickel cadmium battery needs a constant current charger. Do not try to hook it up to your car battery charger! Radio systems are supplied with a dual charger which will recharge the transmitter and airborne batteries at the same time.

LEDs indicate that charging is proceeding satisfactorily. A nicad should be charged at its C/10 rate. This means that, knowing the capacity of the battery, say 600 mAh, you charge the battery at one-tenth of this hourly output current i.e. $600 \div 10 = 60$ ma or milliamps.

Figure 17.19 Most people charge their radio batteries using the dual unit supplied by the radio manufacturer.

Battery cyclers

You can overcome some of the less desirable characteristics of nicad batteries by the use of a battery recycler. This unit fits between the charger and the airborne pack.

With the charger switched on, the cycler first discharges the battery completely and then fully charges it, at which stage it stops any further charging. It does stop capacity reducing memory and ensures the battery is given a completely full charge.

Chapter 8 Connecting the controls

Planning the installation

It is a mistake to build a model without giving early thought to the installation of the radio equipment. For a small model, this may, in any case, involve a fair amount of shoe horning in of the various radio components. Moreover, it is only too easy to get to a stage where, for example, you cannot get your hands into the rear fuselage to feed through the connections to the control surfaces.

Installation

You should use the radio and particularly the battery to balance the model, rather than adding lead ballast. A larger battery is a good idea if long flights are planned or if the model needs ballast to bring the centre of gravity to the correct position.

For all models, the positioning of the servos and the routes for the control linkages need plenty of forethought so that you can build in the necessary mounts and control runs before it is too late to get access.

One thing that often gets forgotten is where to put the receiver aerial. This is not normally a problem, except with small models and un-conventional ones. It should exit the top of the fuselage behind the wing and run to the top of the fin, where you can fix it in place with a pin and a small elastic band. You will have to plan carefully with a pusher layout as the propeller is ideally placed to cut through the aerial wire if it is left to trail. You can make a route out to a wing tip using a snake outer or drinking straws.

You should use foam rubber to protect the receiver, but take care to ensure that it is not the type which crushes to nothing when you squeeze it between your fingers. The type which is textured is much firmer and provides excellent protection for the delicate electronics in the event of an unscheduled arrival. Model shops sell custom-made foam tubes which fit most receivers.

Figure 8.1 This internal view of a Hi-boy shows the rudder, elevator and throttle servos plus a fly lead for the aileron servo. The receiver is protected by foam rubber.

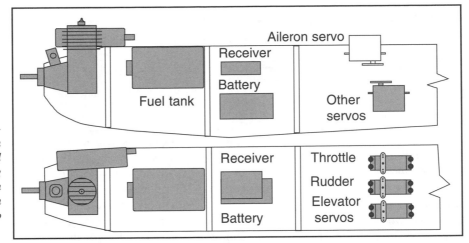

Figure 8.2 A typical installation of a four channel system showing the ideal location for the main items of radio equipment.

Number and positioning of servos

Thinking about a four channel model, it is common sense to mount the elevator, rudder and throttle servos in the fuselage, but what about the aileron servos? One in the wing centre section is usual, though care must be taken to ensure it does not foul any items in the fuselage when the wing is fixed in place.

The alternative is a pair of servos, each located behind an aileron itself, if the wing is thick enough to house them. This does ensure short slop-free connections. Figure 8.3 shows two different sized boxes which you can install in your wing to house the servos.

Servo arms come in a variety of shapes and sizes. When working on control linkages, think about the most suitable type of output arm. It must be long enough to give the desired movement. It must also have holes in the required positions if you are going to incorporate offset

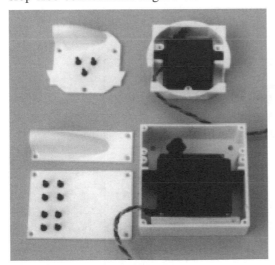

Figure 8.3 Two neat sizes of box by Pettipher Plastics for installing aileron servos in wings.

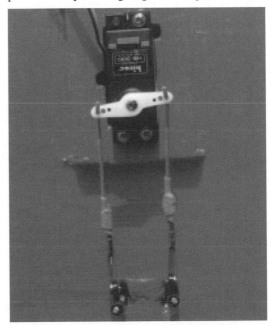

Figure 8.4 An aileron servo mounted under the wing of a Hi-boy, directly connected to strip ailerons.

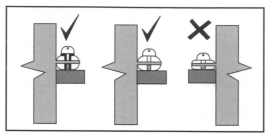

Figure 8.5 Pre-drill holes for the screws and never tighten them so much that they squash the grommets which will then be unable to absorb vibration.

movement without resorting to a computerised transmitter.

Servo mounting

The installation of servos requires attention to detail as it is important to isolate them from airframe vibration caused by the engine. There are several ways of mounting a servo in a model, and the use of special boxes for aileron servos has already been mentioned.

You can fit a pair of servo rails the right distance apart, which is the length of the servo casing plus 1.5mm (1/16") and screw each end of the servo to one of the rails. You can use a ply plate with a suitably sized cut-out for each servo, or you can use a ready-made servo plate, usually supplied by the manufacturer of your radio.

In all cases, securely fix the servos in place, so that they do not move when the control is deflected under load. At the same time, it is

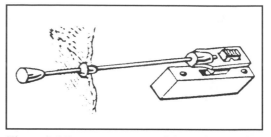

Figure 8.6 Remote operation of the radio switch is often easier than fitting it to the side of the fuselage. (Picture courtesy Chart.)

important to isolate the servos from engine vibrations and small grommets, usually four per servo, are provided for just this reason. It is essential that you do not over-tighten the screws passing through these grommets or you will lose their anti-vibration qualities. Some manufacturers also supply a small brass spacer which fits inside the grommet to prevent you squashing it when the screw is tightened.

You can also attach servos to the side of a model with double-sided servo tape, having first put a coat of clear dope on any bare balsa surface to prepare it for the tape.

Getting the controls to work

Whichever method you employ for connecting the servos to the controls, it must provide a lightweight, free movement without slop, parts touching or rubbing. Moreover it must give

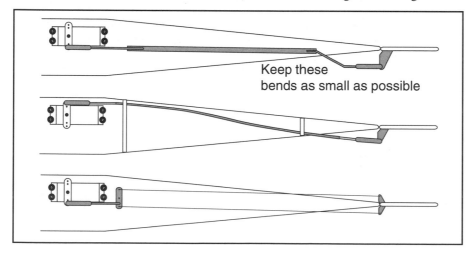

Keep these
bends as small as possible

Figure 8.7 The three basic ways of connecting a servo to a control surface. From top to bottom a push rod, a snake and finally closed loop.

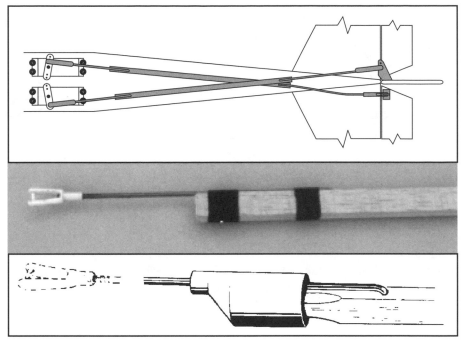

Figure 8.8 Crossing push rods gives a neat connection for elevator and rudder to a pair of servos mounted side by side in the fuselage.

Figure 8.9 You can bind and glue the clevis rod in place. Alternatively a purpose-made nylon pushrod end firmly fixes the clevis rod to the push rod. (Picture courtesy Chart.)

the correct amount of control movement of the control surface for any particular transmitter stick deflection.

The three basic ways of connecting any servo to a control surface are shown in Figure 8.7. You can use a stiff push rod, you can fit a snake, which is a form of Bowden cable or you can use a pair of thin wires in a push-pull configuration. This last is known as closed loop control.

There are many specialist fittings for each of these three connecting solutions and they offer a quick and reliable way of connecting the servos to the control surfaces.

Push rods

The use of push rods to connect rudder and elevator is common. The rod must be rigid and unable to flex. It should also be as light as possible. This is why the preferred material is hard 6mm (¼") to 12mm (½") square balsa, depending on the size of model, with wire fittings at each end. You can attach the wire to a balsa push rod using a special end fitting like the one shown in Figure 8.9.

Alternatively you can bind the wire to the push rod with thread, then smear the binding with glue. Push rods made from alternative materials such as birch dowels or GRP arrow shafts are equally acceptable providing they do not increase the rear end weight of the model. Try to make sure that the push rod and its end fittings run in as straight a line as possible, though you will normally have to make a double bend where the wire end exits the fuselage.

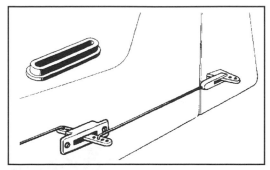

Figure 8.10 A linkage transfer assembly neatly brings the pushrod outside the fuselage, reversing the throw at the same time. Top left is a tidy exit guide. (Pictures courtesy Chart.)

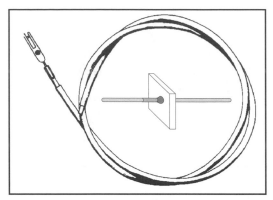

Figure 8.11 A snake with clevis attached to one end. (Picture courtesy Chart.) Centre, use a former, bulkhead or fuselage exit point to secure snake ends.

Snakes

Snakes are available as multi-strand metal cable running in a plastic outer, or as a plastic inner running in a plastic outer. The best plastic snakes have a gear wheel shaped cross section on the inner to minimise flexing and friction.

Snakes are widely used for connecting up the throttle and steerable noseleg if fitted. They are the only direct connections which do not have to run in a straight line. As a result they are also popular for awkward linkages, such as those to inset ailerons.

However, any substantial curve may involve slop in the linkage, resulting in a variable neutral and the possibility of flutter. You should balance this source of slop against the same phenomenon found if you employ a pair of push rods and a bell crank to turn a control run through ninety degrees.

Securely attach snakes to the airframe at each end and support them along their length to avoid

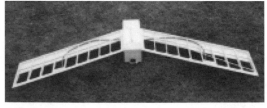

Figure 8.13 Glue snakes where they pass through ribs/formers to reduce slop and the risk of control flutter.

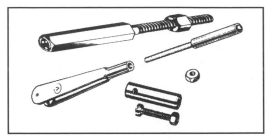

Figure 8.12 The top adaptor screws on the nylon inner of a plastic snake so you can fit a clevis on the end. The middle one solders onto the metal inner of a snake, while the bottom item enables you to attach the snake directly to the servo arm. (Pictures courtesy Chart.)

the outer tube moving or flexing. Roughen the outside of the snake or wrap masking tape around it and glue it in place, preferably with epoxy

Closed loop

The use of specialist multi-strand wire or fishing trace to provide closed loop controls gives a light, positive method of operating controls without any slop. It can, however, cause wear to the servo main bearing if not ball raced.

You can use an intermediate arm to overcome this difficulty and also make trim adjustments simple. In addition, you can purchase commercial closed loop systems with a built-in tension adjuster. Figure 8.16 shows just such a solution.

Some thought is necessary to ensure that the wires can run straight to the control surfaces without fouling any part of the airframe, particularly at the point where they emerge from the fuselage.

Closed loop controls do minimise the weight of the control connections at the rear of the model and this alone can justify their use. They are also widely used on scale models of vintage and veteran aircraft.

Clevises

All linkages require a screwed-on fitting at one end to allow fine adjustment of the control surface position with the servo at neutral. This is

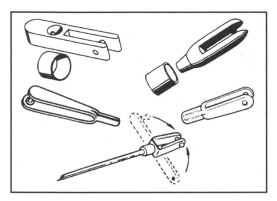

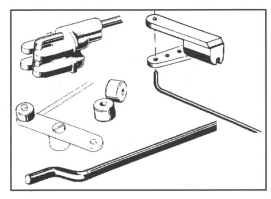

Figure 8.14 From top left clockwise, a nylon clevis with plastic safety keeper, the same with a metal pin, a snap link, a fold snap link and a spring steel clevis. (Pictures courtesy Chart.)

Figure 8.15 Three ways of retaining wire with a right-angle bend to a servo arm or horn. Bottom, a jiggle can be used at one end of a control link. (Pictures courtesy Chart.)

true even if you use a computerised transmitter with neutral adjustment, since it is important to maintain the correct control geometry at the neutral position to avoid undesired differential movement. You do not need an adjustment at the other end of the control linkage.

Attaching clevises to control rods and snakes can provide some difficulties, especially as there seems to be several variations. Most people tend to find their favourites and stick to them. No doubt you will find the ones that suit you.

While clevises are supplied by themselves, it is more common to find them attached to a short length of threaded wire, similar to a bicycle spoke. If you use a snake with a metal inner, you can soft solder an adaptor to the snake and screw a quick link in place, using the fitting shown in Figure 8.12. You can use a short length of studding of the right size for hollow plastic inners.

Because only one end of a control linkage needs to be adjustable, Z bends or jiggles provide a simple and economic solution at the other end. You can make the Z bend with just a pair of pliers but the investment in a purpose-made bending tool will soon pay for itself and make the job a simple one.

Alternatively, you purchase ready-made Z links and then solder them to snakes or attach

them to push rods. Whichever solution you choose, make sure your joints are securely fixed.

Horns

The connection from the clevis to the control surface requires the use of some sort of horn. There are several important factors to remember when selecting the correct control horn for any particular application.

The first is the length of the horn; the longer it is, the less control surface movement for a given servo movement and vice versa. Figure 8.17 overleaf shows some of the wide range of horns.

The second issue is the position of the horn in relation to the control surface hinge line.

Figure 8.16 Both the elevator and rudder are connected by the Flair closed loop system on this model.

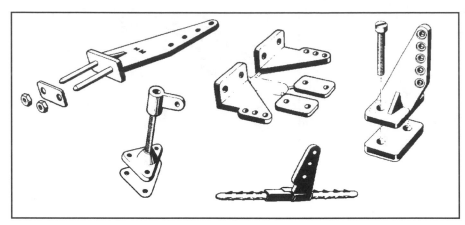

Figure 8.17 *Top are three conventional horns. You can adjust the height of the horn, bottom left, by screwing the connector up or down, The horn, bottom right, is an integral part of a barb hinge. (Pictures courtesy Chart.)*

The more offset it is from the hinge line, the more control differential you will get. Figure 8.18 shows two typical differential horns.

Horns come in a variety of sizes, with different amounts of offset and a number of different attachment methods. Alternatively, you can make horns from good quality plywood or plastic sheet and glue them into the material of the control surface.

When screwing a horn in place, do not tighten it so much that you crush the wood but make sure that you fix it securely in place.

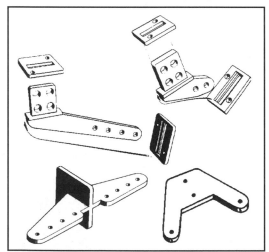

Figure 8.18 *Two offset horns specially designed for use with aileron (top) and below two for use with closed link systems providing connections each side of the control surface. (Pictures courtesy Chart.)*

Ball joints

As an alternative to the conventional horn and clevis, the ball joint is an attractive solution and is particularly popular on helicopters. The two main types involve a socket which clips onto a ball with a built-in thread and bolt for attachment. The other type has the socket permanently connected to the ball, which is held in place by a nut and bolt passing through it. Both require thread-locking adhesive on the nuts and bolts, and are illustrated in Figure 8.19.

Bell cranks

When installing control linkages, particularly to ailerons, you may sometimes need a bell crank.

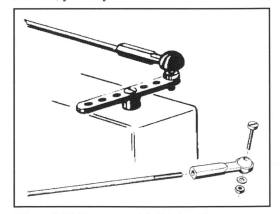

Figure 8.19 *Two types of ball joint. The upper one clips onto a ball attached to the servo arm or horn, the lower one has an integral ball and the whole assembly bolts in place. (Pictures courtesy Chart.)*

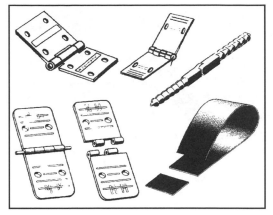

Figure 8.21 *Five types of hinge including barb and bottom right mylar strip. (Pictures courtesy Chart.)*

Hinging

It is common, when building a kit or from a plan to find that you are left to select the type of hinges you will fit to the control surfaces of the model. While a personal choice soon develops, initially the hinges selected should be:

- Simple to fit and align.
- Strong and secure when fitted.
- Slop-free and easy to move.

There are many different types of hinge on the market and each type has its advantages and snags, shown in Table 8.1. They divide conveniently into three categories; those which rely on the flexibility of their material, those that use a rotating hinge, and finally those employing a row of sewn stitches.

In addition, when building high performance models, you may want to use a hinge which prevents air leaking though the joint between the control surface and the rest of the airframe.

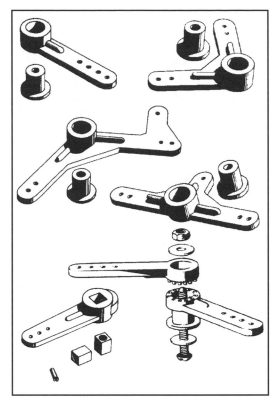

Figure 8.20 *A selection of bell cranks of which the 90° one is widely used to connect inset ailerons. A variable angle crank can be set in 30° increments up to 180°. Bottom left is a tiller arm for operating a steerable noseleg. (Pictures courtesy Chart.)*

Where you want to turn a corner or where you need differential control movement, they are invaluable. They are normally available with an angle of 90° or adjustable in 30° increments. They are usually mounted on a small piece of ply and glued in position.

Table 8.1 The characteristics of the various types of hinge help you to choose the right one for any particular requirement.

Type		Ease of fitting	Flexibility	Strength
Flexible material	Mylar strip	Difficult	Good	Medium
	Moulded flexible	Moderate	Good	Medium
	Film covering	Difficult	Good	Medium
Rotating hinges	Leaf and pin	Moderate	Excellent	High
	Point barb	Easy	Excellent	High
	Tube and wire	Difficult	Excellent	High
Stitching	Stitched material	Easy	Good	High

Figure 8.22 This hinging tool has four main parts, a cutting tool (the V blade) in two sizes, a wood removing tool (the hook-shaped blade) and two alternative jigs for finding the centre of the wood.

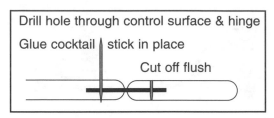

Drill hole through control surface & hinge

Glue cocktail stick in place

Cut off flush

Figure 8.23 How to secure hinges in place using cocktail sticks.

By far the best hinging method for this is to use film covering or stitched material.

Fitting leaf and pin or flat moulded hinges requires you to cut matching pairs of slots in the control surface and the part of the airframe to which it attaches. Cutting the slot for hinges can seem at times impossible. A simple tool eases the task considerably by ensuring the slot for the hinge is placed centrally in the control surface and trailing edge of the primary surface.

First, you locate the centre of the wood where you want the slot, then you insert the double-pronged blade to just over the depth of the hinge. Finally, you use the hooked blade to remove any wood left in the slot. You will need to make a dry check of the hinges for position and freedom of movement before gluing them in place with epoxy.

Using an old knife blade, smear glue inside each slot, and then a touch on each side of one half of the hinge, sliding it into the slot but stopping just before it is completely in to

remove any excess glue with a cocktail stick or similar. Then push it right in. Repeat for each hinge on a single control surface and then repeat for the other half of the hinges, though these will have to be slid into their slots all at the same time. Make a final check that there is no glue in the hinge joints and leave to dry.

If the hinges have holes in them, the glue will effectively form locking pins through the hinges to hold them secure. In the case of mylar or other hinges without holes in the flat surface, drill small holes right through the control surface and hinge and then glue a length of cocktail stick though the hole for added security. Repeat for both halves of every hinge.

Pointed barb hinges present much less difficulty, requiring you to drill a simple hole, rather than a cut slot. Furthermore, when glued with epoxy, the barbs will prevent the hinge from pulling out. The only important consideration is that the axis of rotation must lie along the hinge line after you have inserted the barb.

Making hinges from iron-on covering material is straightforward. Using an elevator

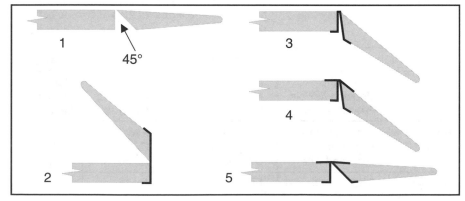

Figure 8.24 The five stages in making a hinge from iron-on covering material.

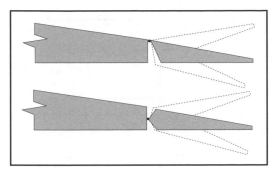

Figure 8.25 *You may find ailerons hinged at the top or in the middle.*

hinge as an example, you should sand a 45° gap between the control surface and the tailplane. Two strips of the material are needed, about 25mm (1") wide. Figure 8.24 shows the process as first the underside strip and then the top strip of material are ironed in place. You can similarly fix material with a stitched hinge in place with a hot iron. It is normal to do this type of hinging before covering the elevator and tailplane in matching material.

To reduce the effort required by the servo, the hinge line is sometimes moved back from the leading edge on more advanced designs to reduce the loads on the servo. However, a hinge line on the leading edge is much more common and always used on trainers.

Aileron hinges

Aileron hinges are rather different from the hinges used on other control surfaces. For a start, they can be hinged at the top or in the middle. The hinges are sometimes inset.

Inset ailerons are harder to make and hinge properly than elevators or rudders. Tube and wire hinges are sometimes preferred since they give freedom without slop.

The generous up and down movement required normally calls for a short control horn. The push rod is often located within the main wing section, although this is obviously not essential.

Strip ailerons are hinged directly to the wing trailing edge in the same manner as rudders or elevators. However, the necessary linkage can be simplified to a degree, as shown in Figure 8.4.

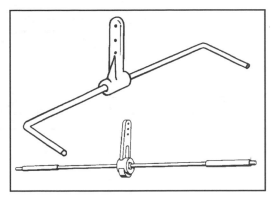

Figure 8.26 *Elevator joiners with a built-in horn neatly solve the problem of moving two elevator halves from a single servo. (Pictures courtesy Chart.)*

Customised connections

Having looked at how to connect servos to controls, you should note the special factors which affect each of the individual control surfaces.

Elevator

Elevator joiners with built-in horn are useful for joining separate elevator halves and are epoxied into suitable holes drilled in the elevators. Some designs specify a strip of hardwood to join the two halves of the elevators.

All-moving tails

The connections to all-moving surfaces differ from those required for conventional control surfaces. First, it is even more important that they are slop-free as the angular movement is often quite small. Second, they commonly use a special type of horn, shown in Figure 8.27, which is custom designed for the task; the long arms reducing the angular movement from the servo.

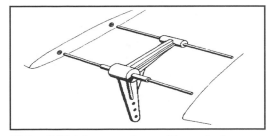

Figure 8.27 *A long-arm horn with two bushes, purpose designed for all-moving tails. It is available with angles of 80° or 105°. (Picture courtesy Chart.)*

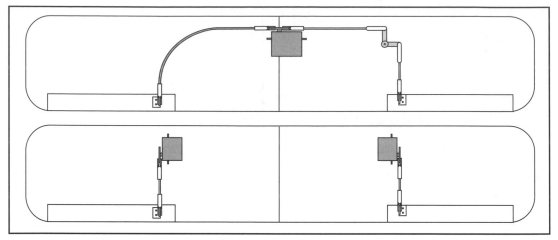

Figure 8.28 *You can connect ailerons by snakes or push rods and bell cranks. Alternatively a pair of mini servos provides a positive linkage.*

Ailerons

There are several ways of connecting up ailerons. With a single servo, you can use push rods and bell cranks, snakes or torque rods. The other option is to employ a pair of mini servos. Figure 8.28 shows three alternatives. For strip ailerons, it is normal to make the connection via a torque rod and Figure 8.29 shows three different types.

Steerable nose and tailwheels

Usually connected to the rudder servo, the linkage needs some form of flexibility to avoid transmitting bumps back to the servo. Figure 8.30 shows two alternatives.

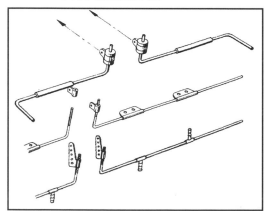

Figure 8.29 *A number of different aileron torque rods are suitable for use both with strip and inset ailerons.*

Setting up the control throws

All kits and plans specify the recommended control throws of each control, usually as a distance each side of neutral. You must set up the throws and the neutral position of each control surface with care. By altering the length of each control rod or snake in turn, you should be able to position the control surface in line with its main surface at neutral. By moving the clevises in or out on the horns and/or servo arms you should be able to get the throws just right as well.

Differential ailerons

To avoid adverse yaw, and the consequent reduction of effectiveness when ailerons are

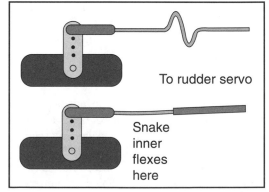

Figure 8.30 *Two ways of building in flex in a steerable nose or tailwheel.*

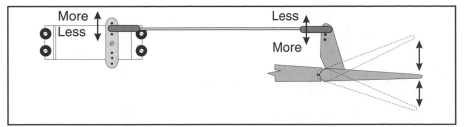

Figure 8.31 You can obtain more or less control surface movement at either end of the link.

used, differential ailerons are the solution. The ways in which you can do this are as follows:

- Offset aileron horns.
- Offset servo arms.
- Offset interconnecting bell cranks.
- A pair of servos and the facilities of a computerised transmitter.

Differential is simple to build into the linkage and Figure 8.32 shows a number of alternatives. Whichever solution you choose, it is important to make a decision before construction starts, rather than when you are finally installing the radio.

Control flutter

Flutter caused many fatal accidents to full size aircraft in the 1920s and 1930s and is an increasing problem for R/C model aircraft as engine powers increase and models fly faster. Flutter usually has disastrous results. It is almost always due to sloppy linkages from the servos to the control surfaces or poor hinging. It can occasionally result from making minor changes when building a proven design or fitting a more powerful motor so that the model exceeds its tested maximum speed.

Flutter is a violent vibration of the airframe and/or control surfaces caused by the interaction of their mass and aerodynamic loads. Models normally experience failure of an elevator or aileron control linkage or hinge, accompanied by a loud buzzing noise. This is followed by loss of control and impact with the ground. Of the three main types of flutter which affect the wing,

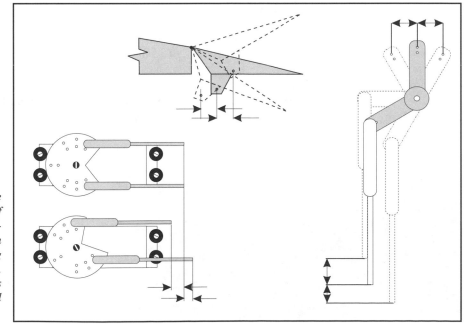

Figure 8.32 Three possible ways of obtaining differential aileron movement, using an offset horn, offset servo arms or a 120° bell crank.

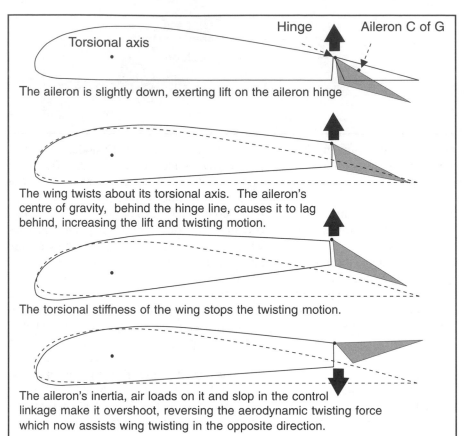

Hinge   Aileron C of G

Torsional axis

The aileron is slightly down, exerting lift on the aileron hinge

The wing twists about its torsional axis. The aileron's centre of gravity, behind the hinge line, causes it to lag behind, increasing the lift and twisting motion.

The torsional stiffness of the wing stops the twisting motion.

The aileron's inertia, air loads on it and slop in the control linkage make it overshoot, reversing the aerodynamic twisting force which now assists wing twisting in the opposite direction.

Figure 8.33 Control surfaces are vulnerable to flutter, especially if there is slop in the linkages.

only torsional flutter is likely to be a real problem. This effect is illustrated in Figure 8.33. The second half of the cycle is similar to the first, but in the opposite direction.

A good stiff linkage from the servo to the aileron will prevent this, while sloppy linkages will encourage it. Exactly the same problems can affect elevators or rudders, although the stiffness of tailplanes and fins, compared to wings, makes flutter of these control surfaces less likely.

All forms of flutter only occur above a critical speed, so the problem is more likely on a high speed model. You can avoid flutter by ensuring that none of your control linkages are sloppy.

Figure 8.34 The result of flutter with an all-moving tail was an expensive disaster for this model.

Chapter 9 Providing the power

Basic choices

There are several ways you can power any R/C model. By far the most popular is to use a two stroke, glow plug engine. Rather less common, but still widely used are four stroke glow motors, diesel and petrol engines as well as electric motors. At the advanced end of the hobby are multi-cylinder piston engines, ducted fans and turbojets.

Your choice of first power plant is likely be affected by your choice of trainer, and vice versa, as well as your future ambitions in the hobby. A summary of the basic features of the various engine choices may help you to make up your mind. You should bear in mind that you will have to add the cost of batteries to that of any electric motor.

It is increasingly clear that the noise created by many model aircraft internal combustion engines is unacceptable to the vast majority of the general public. Noise reduction has thus become an important, if not the key factor in ensuring the retention of flying fields. Most engines are supplied with a silencer but, with a few notable exceptions, these rarely meet the

Figure 9.1 The Enya SS40 is representaive of the most popular size of two stroke R/C power plants. (Photo courtesy Enya UK.)

Department of Trade and Industry guidelines of 82 dB at 7 metres. Many clubs are demanding noise limits below 80 dB and make regular tests of individual models. Methods of noise reduction are examined on page 115.

Noise reduction has been one of the main reasons for the dramatic growth in the popularity of electric flight. There is a good selection of electric power systems that will allow you to obtain an excellent flight performance and this subject is covered in the next chapter.

Table 9.1 Some of the important factors when choosing a power plant for a model.

	Cost of engine	Power to weight ratio	Noise level	Ease of operation/ maintenance	Suitable for first trainer
Glow 2 stroke	Medium	Very high	V. high	Easy	Yes
Glow 4 stroke	High	High	High	Less easy	Possible
Diesel	Medium	High	High	Less easy	Possible
Petrol 2 stroke	Med/high	High	V. high	Less easy	No
Petrol 4 stroke	High	Medium	High	Least easy	No
Electric	V.low	Low	V. low	V. easy	Not ideal
Geared electric	Low	Low	V. low	V. easy	Not ideal

	Ability to swing large propeller	Vibration level
Glow 2 stroke	Poor	Medium
Glow 4 stroke	Average	High
Diesel	Good	High
Petrol 2 stroke	Average	Medium
Petrol 4 stroke	Good	High
Electric	Poor	Trivial
Geared electric	Excellent	Trivial

Table 9.2 The different types of engine vary considerably in their ability to turn a large prop and the amount of vibration they create.

As you advance in the hobby and gain more experience, you may see two other factors as increasingly important; the ability of a given engine to swing a large propeller and the amount of vibration created when the engine is running. Table 9.2 compares these two factors for the various types of engine.

Internal combustion engines

The origin of the internal combustion engine used to power R/C models, as well as cars, motor bikes and full size aircraft dates back to the last century when a German called Herr Otto formulated the Otto four stroke cycle. Another German, Rudolf Diesel invented the type of engine named after him. Developed over the last 100 years, the power output of small model aero engines is fantastic, their ability to throttle excellent and their life, given reasonable care, years if not tens of years.

How they work

Any model engine works by sucking a mixture of fuel and air into its combustion chamber, compressing and igniting this explosive mixture and using the power of the explosion to drive the output shaft of the engine. The way this is done depends on whether the engine is a two stroke or four stroke design. In addition, the method of ignition of the fuel air mixture may vary. Figures 9.2 and 9.3 illustrate the difference between a two stroke and a four stroke.

In a diesel (compression ignition) engine, the heat of compression causes combustion of the mixture. These engines have much higher compression ratios than other designs and, as a result, tend to be heavier. In model diesels, there is a contra piston at the top of the cylinder which you can screw up and down to alter the timing of the ignition to suit the operating conditions.

A glow motor uses a small glow plug which is heated by the passage of an electric current for starting. The element heats, igniting the mixture and once running, the glow is maintained by the heat of combustion.

A petrol engine uses a spark plug for ignition, and a spark must be provided at exactly the right time in each cycle. The spark is normally produced by a coil which transforms the low voltage from a battery to a high enough voltage to cause a spark in the combustion chamber. The timing of the spark is set by a sensor attached to the crank case behind the propeller. A few larger engines are fitted with a magneto for spark generation.

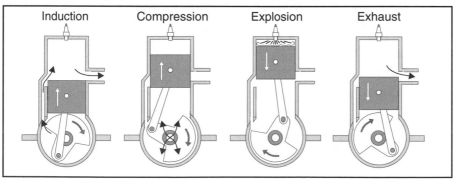

Induction Compression Explosion Exhaust

Figure 9.2 The cycle of a two stroke motor takes only a single revolution.

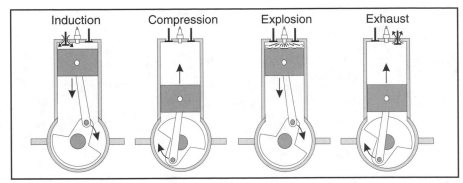

Figure 9.3 The cycle of a four stroke motor occurs over two complete engine revolutions.

Two stroke glow engines

For powered models, two stroke glow motors are still by far the most popular and with good reason. Their construction is basic and light-weight, there are few moving parts and the only adjustment necessary is the fuel mixture. They are not difficult to operate and provide an excellent power to weight ratio.

Mention must be made of the Wankel engine, of which the OS version of 5cc (0.30 cu in) is the only one in production in 1997. Wankels are compact cylindrical-shaped motors which turn small propellers at high rpm, even compared to conventional two strokes. That apart there are few practical differences.

Current motors provide power outputs between 75 watts (one-tenth of a horsepower) per cubic centimetre (0.06 cu in) for sports motors and four times that amount for racing or ducted fan engines. Fuel consumption can vary by a factor of two to one between sports motors and high powered variants of the same capacity.

All two strokes require a good silencer and most come complete with a manufacturer's unit. The efficiency of these silencers varies and you will often need a second one if you are to meet the noise limit of 82 dB at seven metres.

The disadvantage of all glow motors is the need to fuel proof the complete airframe to protect its paint finish from attack by methanol and nitro-methane. A few two stroke engines come with a remote needle valve behind the cylinder head. This increased distance from the rotating prop does improve safety when adjusting the mixture.

The most popular sizes of engine for initial trainers are in the 4 – 7.5cc (0.25 – 0.40 cu in) range, the smaller size minimising costs and the size of the finished model. The larger size, on the other hand, offers more flexibility in future models as your skills develop. Your choice will probably result from cost and model size factors.

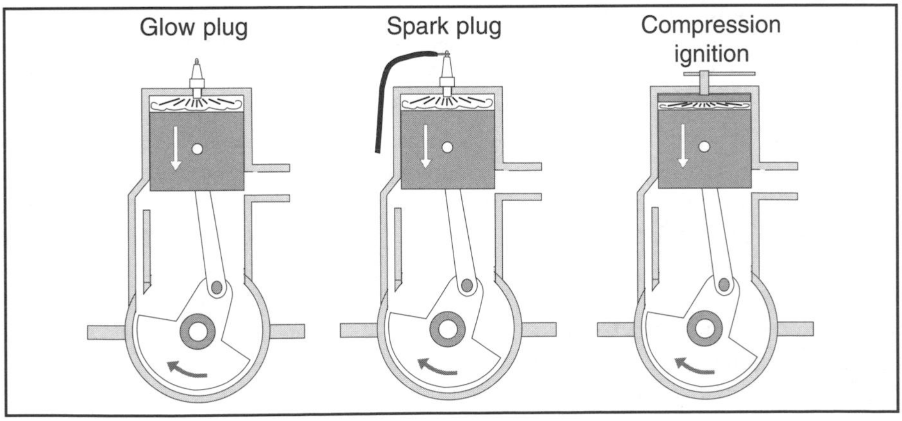

Figure 9.4 The three types of ignition systems each have their own advantages and shortcom-ings.

Figure 9.5 This selection of Lazer four stroke engines – from the 70 to the 150 – are powerful, efficient and beautifully made. (Photo courtesy AGC Sales Ltd.)

Four stroke glow engines

Four stroke engines are more complex in design and construction, heavier and less powerful for a given capacity than two strokes. They have the added complexity of a pair of valves and springs, rocker arms and push rods, not to mention a cam shaft and reduction gearing to drive it.

They are also more expensive and require more complex maintenance. On the other hand, they are very economical, having only around half the fuel consumption of a two stroke, and are inherently less noisy.

These two factors help reduce the total installed weight to a similar figure to a two stroke engine, and the lower fuel consumption helps to offset the increased initial purchase price.

Four stroke motors are not recommended for the beginner for two reasons. You have to check the tappets from time to time and, when required, adjust them. If you have a serious crash and damage your engine, repairs or replacement will cost you significantly more than for an equivalent powered two stroke.

Glow plugs

The humble glow plug lives in a very high stress environment at the top of the cylinder. It consists of a small coil of wire which is heated electrically to a bright orange colour during starting and continues to glow from the heat of combustion and a catalytic effect once the engine starts and you remove the electric power.

Depending on the design of the plug, it can be hotter or cold, the 'heat' affecting the ignition timing. Thus it is important to following the engine maker's recommendation on the right type of plug. Some glow plugs are fitted with an idle bar to protect the element from being over-cooled by droplets of neat fuel at low speeds. These claim to give more reliable slow running.

Diesels

Diesel engines rely on the compression of the fuel/air mixture to cause ignition. They were very popular in the Europe after the Second World War, but their popularity reduced after the introduction of the easy starting glow engine, first from the USA and later from Japan.

There are both pros and cons with diesels. First, they do not require any battery to power a glow plug for starting, reducing the amount of equipment carried in the flight box. Second, they are able to swing larger propellers than an equivalent capacity glow motor, a great plus for models with large radial cowls. Their fuel consumption is around half that of a glow two

Figure 9.6 A diesel engine has a compression adjusting control, in this case with a locking lever as well as a normal needle valve for fuel control.

stroke and the fuel is less likely to attack the finish of the airframe.

On the down side, diesels tend to be slightly heavier and vibrate more than their glow equivalents. There is an additional compression control to set and they do produce a black oily goo from their exhausts. They can be harder to start and operate as there are two controls, mixture and compression, for you to set correctly.

These skills are not difficult to learn. Diesels have historically been harder to throttle reliably and have been manufactured only in smaller sizes, up to 5cc (0.30 cu in). However, recent developments have resulted in successful diesels up to at least 10cc (0.61 cu in) capacity.

Petrol engines

Petrol engines are the most economic of all to operate, as petrol is cheap and consumption miserly. However, there is the added complication of a magneto or coil to produce the spark and the need to ensure that the spark does not interfere with the radio. Do not use silicon fuel tube, as it reacts negatively with petrol, but clear ordinary plastic pipe is ideal.

The equipment to generate a spark adds both to the weight and expense of this form of power. Petrol engines are much more common in larger sizes of 15cc (0.90 cu in) upwards and particu-

Figure 9.7 A large petrol engine is by far the most reliable running internal combustion engine.

larly prevalent are converted chain saw motors. As with diesel engines, kits are available to convert glow motors to petrol usage.

Silencers

There are few places in the UK where you can fly an unsilenced engine and many clubs make you submit each model for a noise check at full power. It is thus essential to fit an effective silencer. Almost all engines are supplied with a silencer to fit, almost invariably of the side-mounted type. This is satisfactory providing it meets your local noise limits. Should it fail, and especially if the noise limitations where you fly are particularly tough, a second silencer in series will normally solve the problem. There are two other types of commercially available silencer.

- Dumpy/dustbin.
- Tuned pipe.

The former are very useful on some cowled models allowing you to conceal the silencer. Tuned pipes are normally only fitted where you require the highest power outputs, in pylon racing and competitive aerobatics for example. Some people make home-made silencers but this requires basic silver soldering skills as soft solder will not withstand the high temperatures.

115

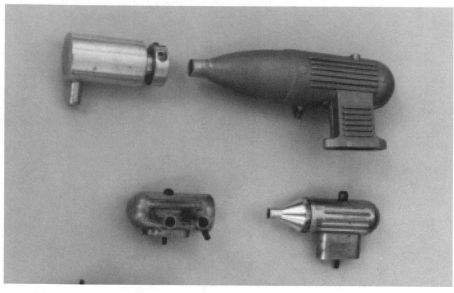

Figure 9.8 Top, a conventional silencer with an add-on unit, bottom, a heli-copter-type dumpy silencer and a small conventional silencer.

Which type of silencer you select will depend on your choice of model, type of engine and, to some extent, your personal choice. It will also depend on the extent to which you wish to reduce the noise from the exhaust.

The title of this section might better be silence than silencers as the exhaust is not the only source of noise from a model I/C engine. Certainly, it is important to consider how the silencer will fit the airframe; the more so if a second silencer is to be fitted.

Will the silencer be mounted inside the model or externally? If the former, how will it be cooled? Modern silencers are bulky and get very hot. They must be securely installed, preferably so that any exhaust oil is thrown clear of the model.

The noise from propellers can be significant, so you should consider the size and pitch of the propeller, particularly if the model has a large cross section fuselage. Generally, the larger the prop, both in diameter and pitch, the less noise the engine will emit. The prop itself will create some noise and, the less flexible the prop, the less noise it is likely to generate. Also, some brands of prop claim to be quieter than others by design.

A cowling around an engine helps suppress noise as can an anti-vibration mount. Open structure airframes with taut covering can act as excellent loudspeakers amplifying any noise produced by the engine. You may find this quite marked on a nylon covered open structure wing, resulting in a noisier model than the same design with a foam wing.

Propellers (props)

There is a bewildering choice of propellers for internal combustion engines made from a variety of materials in a number of different

Figure 9.9 The use of a tuned pipe will improve the power output of an engine. (Photo courtesy Parc-Amber.)

Figure 9.10 A prop balancer is straightforward to use and quickly indicates the heavier blade. (Photo courtesy Balsacraft International.)

colours and of varying diameters and pitches. The main materials used for making props are:

- Wood.
- Plastic.
- Composite materials.

Wooden props give the best performance but are quite unsuitable for learning to fly as they are so easily broken if the model noses over on take off or landing. Nylon props tend to flex under load, reducing thrust. Glass-filled plastics are the most popular, combining performance with reasonable strength.

Under no circumstances ever try to repair a prop by gluing it back together. This practice is potentially lethal. You should also never use a prop which has been damaged or nicked.

Spinners

A spinner will help to streamline the nose of a model as can be seen in Figure 9.12 overleaf. It is important to select the right size of spinner to suit the dimensions of the engine bay. You may also have to cut away some of the plastic to fit your propeller without distortion.

Prop balancing

Do not for one moment think that any new propeller is perfectly balanced. This is an extremely unlikely occurrence. More to the point, any imbalance will cause vibration which will:

- Try to destroy your airframe and radio.
- Reduce the power output of your engine.

- Cause increased wear in your engine.
- Try to undo any nuts and bolts.

Vibration is a great enemy and you only need to talk to any ducted fan flier to hear about the dangerous effects of vibration. Fortunately, the cure is simple.

Drill or ream the hole in the prop to fit your motor. Then use a prop balancer such as the one is shown in Figure 9.10. Once you have identified the heavier blade, a little work on the trailing edge with some sandpaper will quickly bring the prop to a perfectly balanced condition. It is then ready for you to fit to your engine.

Figure 9.11 Propellers come in a wide range of diameters, pitches and shapes, with two or three blades.

Figure 9.12 An upright installation provides easy access to the engine and straightforward starting.

Installing engines

Any good trainer will include detailed instructions on how to install the engine, though the one chosen may be different from your own. A basic upright installation simplifies starting and adjustment of the engine once it is running. It may not look particularly attractive, but you should reserve good looks for later models you may build. It is essential that you incorporate the recommended amount of up/down and side thrust when building the airframe.

There are many factors which affect the way you install an engine in a model. The first factor is your choice of a particular motor. The following list indicates the main factors you should take into consideration.

- Engine size.
- Glow, diesel or petrol.
- Two stroke or four stroke.
- Power output.
- Location of engine.
- Location of the exhaust.
- Location of throttle arm.
- Type and position of mounting lugs.
- Up/down and side thrust.
- Vibration level.
- Fuel consumption.
- Upright, inverted or sidewinder.

It is important to remember the increased length of a four stroke engine when fitting it in a model designed around a two stroke one, the increase resulting from the space required for the valve gear.

Conventional wisdom states that an upright engine installation is the best for ease of starting and running. You may well ask why any other configuration should even be considered. Generally, the answer is that it's simply a question of aesthetics. Figures 9.13 and 9.14 show that a typical sidewinder or inverted engine can provide a much more pleasing nose shape.

In the case of a sidewinder, viewed from the favourable side, only part of the silencer hangs beneath the fuselage. For an inverted installation, just the top of the cylinder head shows, but the whole of the silencer is visible from one side.

Figure 9.13 A sidewinder layout gives a clean profile to the top of the fuselage and locates the silencer underneath it.

Figure 9.14 An inverted engine also gives a well streamlined nose shape but a two stroke silencer still comes out of one side of the fuselage.

45° mounting

A compromise that has found favour is to angle the motor over at 45° to the vertical. This can produce a neat installation, but you will normally have to use a commercial engine mount or some other form of bulkhead mounting.

Pushers

The main differences between a tractor and a pusher lie in the silencer mounting and the fuel system. The exhaust exit of a normal silencer mounted on a pusher faces into the air stream and causes some back pressure. It will not fit the other way round. A dumpy silencer is an ideal solution. The fuel tank must still point forward, resulting in longer fuel pipes. A nose-up attitude after take off will make the engine run richer, rather than leaner as on tractor layouts.

Pylon mounting

For powered gliders and seaplanes you can mount the engine and tank in a pylon above the wing. This layout keeps the prop clear of the ground but requires a fair amount of up thrust (down for a pusher) to compensate for the high thrust line. Figure 17.8 (page 222) illustrates this layout.

Figure 9.15 This fun scale MiG 25 is fitted with an inverted pusher engine and prop combination.

Figure 9.16 This model has a built-in ply plate giving side thrust. To the left is a removable plate, which may be replaced if a change of side thrust is needed.

Engine bearers and plates

The use of a pair of beech engine bearers is one of the oldest methods of attaching an internal combustion engine to a model. The main snag is the need for accurate cut-outs in the relevant formers, the need to adjust the spacing of the bearers to suit the chosen engine and the difficulty of making adjustments to the engine thrust line.

Bearers can still be used as mountings for an engine plate made from ply, paxolin or aluminium

Figure 9.17 Anti-vibration mounts are becoming increasingly popular. This Super Tigre 3000 is mounted on one and fitted with a transverse silencer. (Photo courtesy Parc-Amber.)

and this type of installation has much to recommend it for any new model. You can replace the plate if the side thrust is incorrect or if you wish to fit a different, more or less powerful engine. Finally, you can place wedges beneath the plate to adjust the up/down thrust.

Plastic and metal engine mounts

Commercial engine mounts have most of the advantages of engine plates. They come in a wide range of sizes to suit most engines and some are adjustable for spacing of the engine mounting lugs. More recently, ones with absorbent mountings help reduce engine vibration and noise. You can still adjust side and up/down thrust, and many make provision for attaching a noseleg to the engine firewall. The plastic ones are generally only suitable for smaller sized engines.

You must learn to drill holes in the right place and vertically. You can easily achieve the first by the use of a punch to mark the place where the drill is to enter the hole. You can use a sharp nail if you have nothing better available.

Getting the hole vertical is much harder, unless you have access to a vertical pillar drill. Some power drills are now sold with a spirit level built into the end, which allows verticality in one plane to be set. You can achieve verticality in the other plane by viewing the drill from the side. The size of the holes should suit the bolts which will pass through the engine mounting lugs.

Figure 9.18 Four different engine mounts, left with and without noseleg mounting and right, adjustable for width. (Pictures courtesy Chart.)

Fuel systems

It is essential, and should be self-evident, that you should locate the fuel supply as close to the engine as possible and at the correct vertical position in relation to the engine, **unless a pumping system is used**. While a pump gives freedom to position the fuel tank at the centre of gravity, it does tend to increase the weight, complexity and cost of the total fuel system. It is therefore not a particularly common solution.

Tanks

Invariably, R/C trainers use what is known as a clunk tank. This is a type of fuel tank where the fuel feed from the inside of the tank consists of a weight (clunk), connected by flexible pipework to the fuel intake of the engine. You can purchase fuel tanks in a variety of shapes and a range of sizes. You should follow the manufacturer's recommendation on size. The most popular are round, square or rectangular in cross section. Trainer kits usually come complete with tank, but for other models, the choice is up to you. The key factors are the capacity of the tank and its ability to fit in the tank bay. If you use a round tank, you must prevent it rotating under the influence of engine vibration as this will twist the connecting pipes and stop the fuel flow.

Figure 9.19 Fuel tanks come in all shapes and sizes. The cross section may be round, rectangular, oval or square.

121

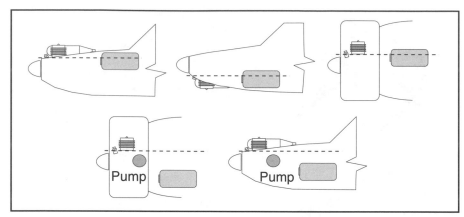

Figure 9.20 Locate the fuel tank so that when two-thirds full, the fuel is in line with the needle valve. A fuel pump (lower two drawings) allows greater flexibility in positioning the tank.

You can also make a tank by hand from tinplate or brass sheet if you have an awkward space to fill and if you have the skill to cut and soft solder one to shape.

Locate the tank so that the engine spray bar is level with the fuel when the tank is two-thirds full. Securely mount it, horizontally as close to the engine as possible. Particularly on two strokes, use fuel tank pressurisation from the silencer to ensure positive fuel transfer. Figure 9.21 shows how to connect the pipework.

Fuel pumps

R/C engine fuel pumps generally rely either on vibration or crank case pressure variations to provide a pumping action. The one shown in Figure 9.22 operates from exhaust pressure. Pumps give the freedom to position the fuel tank some distance from the engine. This solution is ideal for aerobatic and scale models.

Filters

Any internal combustion engine will only continue to run if it is provided with an adequate flow of fuel. There are two common reasons why this flow fails. The first is when you run out of fuel and is easily overcome by fitting an adequate size of tank and using a flight timer. The second is to use a filter to remove any small particles of dirt which may find their way into the fuel system. The most common cause of this dirt is grass seed, commonly found on flying fields during the summer months.

Fuel tube

Silicon rubber tube is ideal for making the various fuel and breather connections for a glow motor. You should take care when handling silicon rubber to ensure you do not cause small tears or pin holes in the tube when fitting it in place. As the tube comes in several diameters,

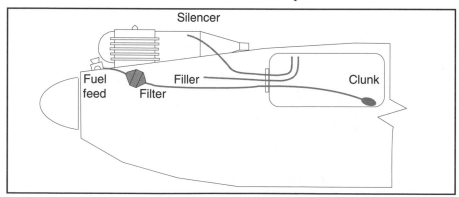

Figure 9.21 Fuel pipes run from the carburettor to the clunk pipe and from the silencer and filler to the two pipes terminating at the top of the tank.

Figure 9.22 Fuel pumps are ideal for advanced aerobatic and some scale models. This is the Fuelmaster by Airplanes Etc.

check it fits onto the engine and tank before making a purchase. Unfortunately, diesel fuel will attack silicon rubber and you will have to choose a suitable plastic pipe which has a more shiny finish. The same applies for petrol fuelled engines.

When connecting up the fuel pipework, cut the pipe lengths slightly too long rather than too short. Then, if you damage the end of a length of tube, you can trim it off and still have sufficient length.

Fuels

Most of you will recognise that the average garage sells several different types of fuel and that diesel in a petrol-driven car and vice versa is catastrophic. The same is true of model aero engines. While the vast majority use glow fuel, both diesels and petrol engines are increasing in popularity. Both of the latter are more economical in fuel consumption terms, and the fuel for petrol engines is far cheaper than for either of the other types. What fuel to use depends very much on the type of engine, the model you fit it in and, most important, the recommendations of the manufacturer.

Glow motors

A basic 20% castor oil 80 % methanol is recommended for running in most glow engines. It is economically priced and provides more than adequate lubrication during the early life of the engine. Later, you can safely reduce the percentage of lubricant, change from castor oil to a mineral oil and include a small percentage of

Figure 9.23 You should use a filter on the outlet from your fuel storage container as well as at the output of your fuel tank. Open it from time to time to clean the gauze.

nitromethane. This additive can increase power and improve throttling. You will rarely need more than 10% nitro and this is a good thing in view of the rapid price increase as you need more nitro.

It is also worth noting that nitro has an adverse effect on the bearings of four stroke motors, which are not flushed clean by the flow of fuel through the crank case, as is the case for two stroke engines. A breather nipple on the crank case of a four stroke will dribble a little oil when running and provide access for post-flight oiling. A flush through of a water-repelling oil via this breather at the end of each flying session will keep a four stroke's bearings in tip-top condition. Glow fuel and the exhaust residue from glow motors will attack most paint finishes, calling for the use of fuel proofer or fuel resistant paints.

Diesels

A mixture of one-third each of castor oil, paraffin and ether is the basis of fuel for diesels. The ratios of these three ingredients may vary and again, there are additives which can boost performance. Diesel motors tend to throw out a more oily black exhaust, but it does not attack paint

Figure 9.24 Once you have removed the rocker cover, the tappets are straightforward to check and reset.

finishes to the same extent as glow fuel. Model diesel engines, as in the full size case, are very economical in terms of fuel consumption.

Petrol

Petrol engines can safely be run in on standard two stroke mix which is 95% petrol, 5% oil. There is little exhaust mess and, as with diesel engines, less tendency to attack paintwork.

Maintenance

It goes without saying that you should never strip down a model engine unnecessarily. Furthermore, unless you know what you are doing, DIY repairs can easily prove more expensive than paying a professional to do the job for you.

Basic two strokes require virtually no routine maintenance apart from oiling them well before laying them up, say over winter. If you use a castor-based fuel, the fins of the cylinder head will tend to get caked with baked-on fuel residue, which you can remove with a proprietary cleaner. Very occasionally, the carburettor may get blocked, which requires removal of the needle valve and a good blow through the spray bar.

Four stroke tappets need a regular check. To do this, you will find the engine is usually supplied with a pair of feeler gauges and a set of spanners and Allen keys. You will also need a small screwdriver.

First, remove the tappet covers and, with the engine rotated one full turn beyond the point where the inlet and exhaust tappets have moved down, insert the thinner of the two feeler gauges, which should be a tight fit. If it is loose, see if the thicker gauge will fit. If not, all is well and no adjustment is required. Carry out a similar check on the second tappet. If you have to make an adjustment, loosen the nut holding the tappet in place, slightly tighten or loosen the tappet screw and retighten the nut. Check the clearance as before and further adjust until the thinner tappet just fits. Put a few drops of oil on each tappet and replace the covers, ensuring the bolts are tight, but not so tight as to strip the threads in the aluminium cylinder head.

Petrol engines use an ignition coil to provide the spark to the plug. While most modern engines use a contactless system for generating the spark at the right time, some are still fitted with contact breakers. These must be kept clean and smooth, and adjusted to the right gap, again using a feeler gauge and screwdriver adjustment. Even with contactless breakers, it is essential to adjust them to give the correct timing to get the best performance from the engine.

In addition, the plug itself may well need regular cleaning to clear carbon from the electrodes and insulator; the more so if there is any oil contamination. Sand blasting is the easiest solution for cleaning a plug, but use of a cocktail stick, though more time consuming, is just as successful.

Chapter 10 Electric flight

Advantages and disadvantages

Electric power, while far from ideal as the motive power for a first trainer, is sometimes the only choice in a noise conscious society. Rapidly growing in popularity, the advantages of this power source are noteworthy. It is virtually silent in operation and does not cover the airframe with an oily residue. Furthermore, it is vibration free and avoids the need for fuel proofing.

While power to weight ratios cannot yet match those of internal combustion engines, progress has been rapid in recent years. For anyone wishing to explore the subject in more detail, the book *Fly Electric* by Dave Chinery (see page 243) provides a great deal more information on this specialist subject.

The easiest type of electric model to fly is the powered glider, but anything from a pylon racer to a vintage model, from a scale Spitfire to a multi-engined giant is practical with electric power.

The rapidly rechargeable nicad is used to store the electrical power. Its weight, and its restraint in the event of a heavy landing, are the two major challenges facing electric flight. A final advantage is the ability to fly a multi-engined model without fear of an engine cut and the trials and tribulations of an asymmetric landing.

As already mentioned, one area where electric flight lags well behind is in the power to weight ratio of the total system. For a given power output for a period, say, of five minutes, the weight of an internal combustion engine, fuel and tank is still dramatically less than that for an electric motor and battery. Thus, in building a model for electric flight, the weight of the airframe must be as low as it is humanly possible to avoid ending up with an excessively high wing loading. It is in this area that the main challenge lies and is one of the reasons for not starting with an electric model.

Figure 10.1 Climbing away from a safe launch, an electric powered glider is an ideal introduction to electric flight.

Figure 10.2 The Flair Tara pylon racer is fast and highly manoeuvrable.

Motors

As with internal combustion engines, electric motors come in a wide variety of sizes and shapes, with an equally wide range of power ratings. You can also use them with or without a gearbox. Unfortunately, unlike internal combustion engines, it is much harder to understand their sizes. Mabuchi use 280, 380, 540, 550 and 750 to define the sizes of their range of motors, while Astro motors are labelled .035, .05, .15,

.25, .40 and .90 in an attempt to match their performance to that of glow motors. Graupner terminology for their range of motors is 400, 600 and 700. As with glow engines, there are hot motors and 'cooking' ones. When you come to choose a motor, you may be able just to buy the one recommended by the kit manufacturer, but this is often not possible. If making a selection from scratch, the following factors need your consideration:

Figure 10.3 The Graupner Junkers JU 52 tri-motor looks just the part with three electric motors fully concealed in their cowls.

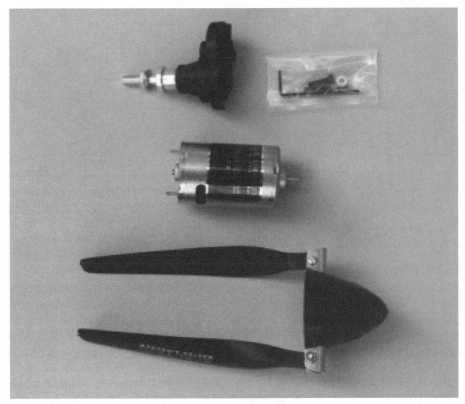

Figure 10.4 You can purchase an electric motor complete with gearbox and folding propeller. This is Flair's electric flight pack for their Volture.

- Size.
- Weight.
- Power output.
- Revs at maximum power.
- Voltage.
- Current consumption.
- Cost.

The first two define the size of the motor mount, the third affects the size and weight of the model, the fourth impacts on the choice of propeller size and the use of a gearbox, while the next two are major considerations in arriving at the size of battery.

As with most things in life, you get what you pay for. There are several types of magnet from low cost ferrite to rare earth materials, flux rings to give higher torque at lower revs, different numbers of winds on the armature affecting the voltage and current the motor can handle, as well as the option of adjustable brush timing.

A basic 540 motor will set you back a few pounds, while a ball-raced wet magnet motor may approach £100, but give several times the power output.

Gearboxes

The choice of whether to use a gearbox will depend primarily on the maximum speed of the model. Gearboxes give more thrust at slower speed, but are unsuitable for faster models. Geared systems are thus best suited to slower flying aircraft and are an advantage for designs with large cowls. You will be able to fit a larger propeller to a geared motor, the actual size depending mainly on the reduction ratio.

The price of gearboxes varies considerably with their method of construction. The least expensive use a belt drive or simple spur gear. At the top end, an epicyclic gearbox will provide an output shaft roughly in line with the input shaft.

127

Figure 10.5 A standard 540 motor is low cost. One with a belt reduction drive will handle a large prop.

Motor controllers

There are basically three ways that you can control an electric motor from your radio. You can fit a microswitch to the top of your throttle servo, arranged to turn on the power at full throttle and off again as you close the throttle. You can do the same thing with an electronic flight switch, which is less expensive than a speed controller, which allows you to vary the speed of your motor at any time using your throttle stick. It is essential that you choose a flight switch or speed controller capable of handling

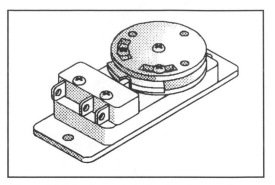

Figure 10.6 A microswitch fitted to the top of a normal servo allows an electric motor to be turned on and off in flight. (Picture courtesy Flair.)

the current which flows through your motor at maximum power.

BECs (Battery elimination circuits)

A BEC is an electronic part of a speed controller which enables you to power your radio receiver and servos from the main electric power battery. This eliminates the need to carry the weight of a second battery for the radio. Within the BEC is circuitry to shut down power to the main motor when the battery capacity has fallen to a pre-set low level, leaving plenty of electric power for the radio to continue the flight and land safely.

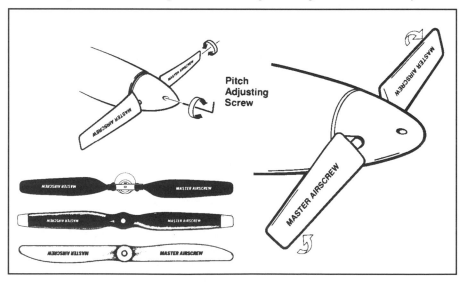

Figure 10.7 An electric variable pitch feathering prop compared with, bottom left-hand corner, an electric folding prop, a conventional prop and an antique style prop. (Picture courtesy Chart.)

Propellers

Fitting a propeller to an electric motor shaft requires an adaptor and one is illustrated in Figure 10.8. Securely fixed to the motor shaft with grub screws, it allows you to fit any standard prop.

With so many electric powered models being flown without undercarriages to reduce weight to a minimum, folding propellers have become a popular choice. A wide choice of sizes is available and a typical example is illustrated in Figure 10.4.

It is essential that you select a prop to match your model and its motor. The kit manufacturer or plan designer will hopefully make some recommendations. Failing this, experience and an understanding that at the end of a flight, an over-hot motor means you have too large a prop and should reduce diameter and possibly pitch. On the other hand, a poor performance by the model in the air and a cold motor after landing suggests too small a prop.

Batteries

At the time of writing, the nickel cadmium rechargeable battery rules supreme, both for

Figure 10.8 An adaptor allows you to fit a normal prop to a thin electric motor shaft. (Picture courtesy Chart.)

electric flight and for powering airborne receivers and servos. This may change in the future as battery technology continues to improve rapidly, fuelled by the needs of portable power tools and telephones. In any case the weight and size of nicads is reducing year by year. Table 10.1 overleaf shows the state of the technology in mid-1997.

By way of a comparison a nickel metal hydride cell will produce 1.2 volts and is claimed to have a 30 – 50% performance advantage over the best nicads, no memory effects and is free

Figure 10.9 The Stratus 2000 is an almost ready to fly electric powered thermal glider. It has a 1.9 metre (76") wing span and comes complete with motor and prop.

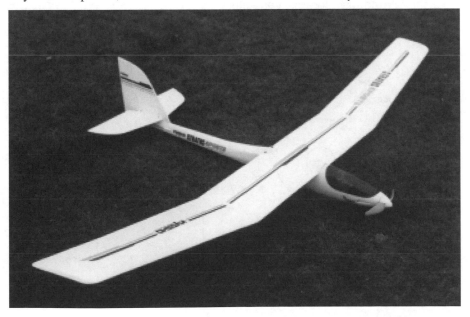

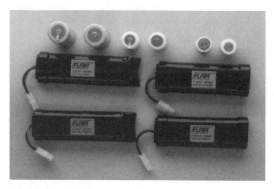

Figure 10.10 Battery packs vary in size depending on the number of cells and their capacity. It is possible to assemble your own pack from individual cells.

Capacity mAh	Wt g	Wt oz
500	19	2/3
700	22	0.8
850	25	0.9
1200	28	1
1400	52	1.8
1700	54	1.9

Table 10.1 The weight of a nicad battery varies according to its capacity, as does the time it will produce power to your motor..

from toxic or hazardous effects when the time comes for disposal.

The power available from a flight pack and how long it can provide power varies in two ways. Each nicad cell has a nominal voltage of 1.2 volts and a number of cells make up a battery or flight pack.

The more cells you use the greater the total voltage, though this must match the voltage rating of your chosen motor. The larger each cell, the more current it can happily produce. It can also produce the same current as a smaller cell, but for a longer time.

The power passed to the motor in watts is a multiple of the voltage and the current. More of either will increase the power output. The duration of the powered part of the flight depends on the current drawn and the size of the cells in the battery. The size is measured in milliamp hours (mAh) and is the current the battery will produce multiplied by the time it will deliver this current. The actual output time reduces disproportionately as higher current levels are drawn. It is important to remember that increasing the number of cells has two effects. For a given motor, it will increase the power output, but because more current flows, the duration will reduce.

For most applications, a seven cell pack is normal, with six cells a good choice for lighter weight and longer endurance, albeit with reduced

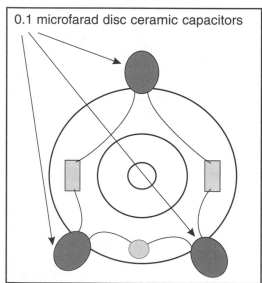

0.1 microfarad disc ceramic capacitors

Figure 10.11 Small disc ceramic capacitors are simple to solder to the brush gear and motor casing.

Figure 10.12 Installing an electric motor is much easier than an internal combustion engine.

Figure 10.13 The Volture is specifically designed for beginners and features a foam wing and comprehensive recommendations for motor battery and prop.

power output. Larger numbers of cells are generally used with high performance motors in larger models.

Using popular C sized cells with capacities in the range 1200 to 1700 mAh, you can easily relate the number of cells to the required power. Increasing the number increases the power available with an increasing weight penalty. Of course, you will need fewer cells in a slow flying old timer than in a fast aerobatic model.

Installation

Since electric motors produce virtually no vibration, installation is quite straightforward. You can use a tube of card, balsa or thin ply, that fits around the motor. Alternatively, you can attach a commercial electric mount or the fixing lugs found on many gearboxes to suitable hard points.

The brush gear of an electric motor can generate considerable radio interference, but fortunately this is simple to suppress. The

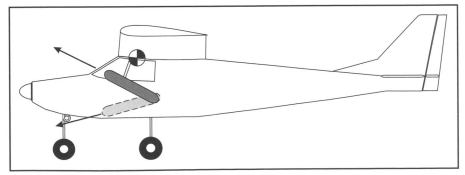

Figure 10.14 You should locate the battery so that it can slide forward with minimum damage in the event of a heavy landing.

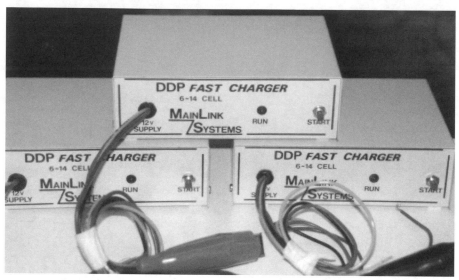

Figure 10.15 A fast charger for your flight battery is really an essential item for electric flight. (Photo courtesy MainLink.)

recommended solution may be given by the motor manufacturer in the instructions, but failing this, connect three small capacitors across the brushes as shown in Figure 10.12.

It is best to mount the battery near the centre of gravity as it is by far the heaviest component. Wiring to the battery needs careful planning. The cable must be thick enough to carry the high current and will normally run via a switch, fuse and speed controller. You must select the fuse to match the maximum current your motor is likely to draw, plus fifty percent to stop the fuse blowing during normal operation. With all that electrical power, it will prevent damage should the motor stall due, for example, to an unplanned landing.

You can save weight by replacing the receiver battery with a BEC, but you must fit the BEC on the battery side of the fuse to prevent radio failure

if the fuse blows. This is shown in Figure 10.16.

Motors and batteries get hot during flight so you should never neglect their cooling requirements. You may wish to change batteries at the end of each flight so that you can continue to fly while recharging the battery you have just flown. For both these reasons, you should ensure easy access to the battery pack.

Chargers

The nicad batteries used to power electric models require a different charger from that supplied for your radio equipment. You will need a high rate of charge to cope with the higher capacity of these batteries and for large packs, the ability to deal with a high voltage. You will probably want facilities to charge your batteries from a mains charger at home, but fast charge them from a 12 volt battery at your flying field.

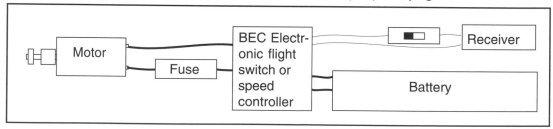

Figure 10.16 The right way to install a BEC system, with the fuse between the BEC and the motor.

Chapter 11 What to build

Kits or plans?

There are a number of differences between kits and plans as a starting point for a new model; some obvious, some less so. For many people the obvious starting point is a kit.

Kits

All the materials are selected by the manufacturer and there should be few additional items to purchase. Engine and radio, of course, glue and covering materials, possibly a fuel tank and wheels. Most, if not all, of the parts should be already cut out and wire components like the undercarriage bent to shape. This approach means you must select a kit from the range available and hand over your hard-earned cash.

The quality of materials varies quite a lot. Sometimes the wood is not of the ideal quality, sometimes the parts don't fit together very well. This latter problem is rapidly being overcome by the use of computer-cut parts from a CAD drawing of the model. Do take the time to read reviews of the various trainers available in the modelling press and listen to the advice of members of your club.

When you have made your purchase and returned home gleefully with the brimming box under your arm, PRTM – **Please read the manual**. The manufacturer has written some comprehensive instructions to help you build the model with the minimum of difficulty. Do not ignore this advice. It can save the heartbreak of having to undo work to gain access to a part that was not fitted at the right stage. It can save cutting a long piece of wood when the correct shorter piece is in the box and you will need the longer piece for another part of the model. It is also advisable to dry fit pieces together before applying any glue.

ARTF

Almost ready to fly models are increasingly available for those who lack time for building rather than money. These models come in two basic types. There are those of built-up construction where the building has been done by the manufacturer, usually in the Far East where labour costs are low. The other type feature a lot of prefabrication during the manufacturing process, usually by the extensive use of foam

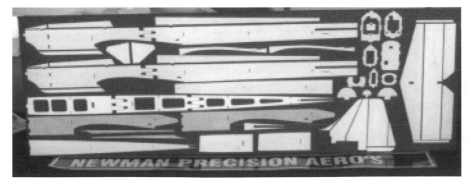

Figure 11.1 These are the wooden parts of Terry Westrop's Loaded Dice 40S. There are over 60 CNC machined items.

Figure 11.2 An ARTF model like this 1500mm (60") wingspan VMAR Cessna 40 takes only a few hours to complete. (Photo courtesy MacGregor Industries.)

and plastics. A coloured finish is printed on the exterior so you do not even have to paint it.

All that is left for you is to install the engine and radio. Providing that suitably sized equipment is available, this task only takes a few hours. The down side is that you get no experience of construction, nor are these models easy for a beginner to repair except by replacement of complete items.

Some model shops offer ready-built models for sale, anything from a basic trainer to an accurate scale model. These models may have been built from a kit or a plan and are so far unflown. They can be a good buy provided they are well built and are suitable for your engine and radio. Equally they may have flown extensively and are effectively offered second-hand. In this case, you should carefully examine them for damage caused either by old age or crashes.

Plans

Building from a plan requires more skill than assembling a kit but does offer a far wider choice of models for your next project. Furthermore, the cost of the aircraft can be spread over the time taken to build it, only buying materials when they are needed. It may not, however, be a significantly less expensive way of building a model. Kit manufacturers can buy raw materials far more cheaply than you can, and their profit often comes just from the mark up on the contents of the kit.

Remember that all you will get is the plan of your chosen model. There will be no box of pre-cut parts to glue together. For some more advanced plans, you can also purchase a cockpit canopy and engine cowl. Plans are usually published together with the designer's write up, and some, like Nexus Special Interests can usually supply a photocopy of the original article.

As with kits, PRTM! The instructions and pictures from the original article will certainly help you to understand the plan and realise how the model goes together. You may worry about working everything out yourself, deciding what materials to buy and acquiring them, marking and cutting out all the parts before starting construction. Once you've tried it, you may be surprised to find it an enjoyable task. However, it takes more time than building from a kit, but once you have cut out the parts, you have what is, effectively, your own kit.

In buying the materials, a little extra time in careful selection will pay dividends. Strip wood should be straight both in terms of its grain and physically. Looking along the length will produce some surprises in terms of curves in what appears at first glance to be a straight piece of wood. You must be equally careful in selecting balsa sheet for its required role.

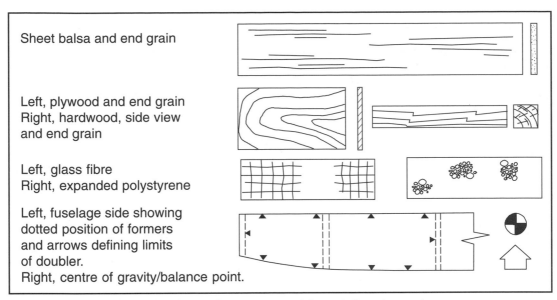

Sheet balsa and end grain

Left, plywood and end grain
Right, hardwood, side view
and end grain

Left, glass fibre
Right, expanded polystyrene

Left, fuselage side showing
dotted position of formers
and arrows defining limits
of doubler.
Right, centre of gravity/balance point.

Figure 11.3 How the various materials are indicated on a plan.

Different wheels of the same size can vary in weight considerably. You should think in terms of selecting lightweight ones.

How plans indicate different materials

There are conventions used on plans to show the different types of materials and structural arrangements. The main ways of indicating various materials and construction points are shown in Figure 11.3. Line thickness variations make drawings more readable and emphasise complete components.

Thick lines – major items such as wing and fuselage.

Medium lines – structural items like fuselage longerons and wing spars.

Thin lines – wood grain; the type of lines showing the grain indicate the various different woods.

Primary dotted lines – indicate that the line is hidden behind a component or inside an assembly. Also used for similar parts where one has minor changes e.g. one whole rib shown in full and others with cut-outs dotted.

Secondary dotted lines (often chain lines; a long dash, one or two short dots, followed by a long dash and so on) – used where one

wing is drawn reversed on top of the other because space is short.

An examination of Figure 11.4 overleaf will show how these appear on a published plan.

Where there are several layers of materials, for example in a fuselage side view, part of the fuselage may be cut away with a pair of solid wavy lines. This gives a better idea of the internal structure between these lines.

To show full internal details, the side view of a fuselage may have all the near side omitted. This makes the large number of dotted lines easier to interpret. Sometimes the plan shows only one wing half, with its outer sheeting. The other half has the sheeting omitted to show internal detail. An alternative is a cut-away showing the external sheet covering most of the area, but removed over a complex part, to show you the interior detail. Often the cut-away area is bounded by curved or S shaped lines.

To minimise confusion in complicated parts, you may find a scrap view or a cross section. Cross sections show the structure as if it is cut right through. Right-angle arrows each side of the structure, marked 'Section A-A' or just 'A-A', show the location of the cross section. A

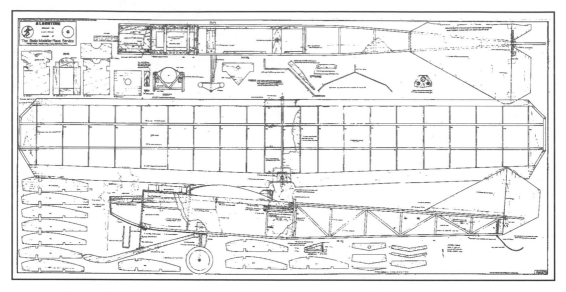

Figure 11.4 This Nexus plan of the Albertine shows the sort of information you can expect.

fuselage cross section will show the outline of the former, the fuselage top, bottom, sides and any doublers at that point. It can also show rounding of the square corners of a fuselage, reinforced with triangular stock, which you must sand to shape. Scrap views show additional detail, while constructional sketches in perspective demonstrate how parts fit together.

It is worth noting that side views of items such as cabane struts and undercarriage legs do not show true lengths, due to the angles of these items. A separate drawing will indicate the actual lengths with any bends marked by dotted lines.

When building over a plan, either cover it with transparent film, such as clingfilm or the backing from iron-on covering materials, or rub over the areas likely to be affected by glue with candle wax.

Choosing a trainer

There are many trainer kits, plans and ARTF models available. Most are practical designs that are easy to build and to fly. The one which is most suitable to you will depend on many factors.

What attracts you about R/C aircraft? Do you live life in the fast lane, or are you the quiet withdrawn type? Are you a perfectionist who will find building an end in itself, or do you prefer the idea of quick-build models which you can fly after a minimum delay? How much can you afford and what pleasure do you get from making every part, though it may take you longer.

You must find the balance which suits you and the model which appeals to your eye. Beauty is in the eye of the beholder and that's you. Any reputable design you select will provide plenty of enjoyment if you build it properly and look after it.

There is a bewildering number of trainer kits available today, and the main ones in production at the time of publication are listed, together with their recommended engine size, wing span and the number of radio channels required.

Probably the most important factors when choosing a first model are that you should find its looks attractive and that it should be suitable for its purpose, which is helping you to learn to fly. Those who, for one reason or another, feel confident enough to start from a plan, will again find a good choice in the Nexus Special Interests range. Table 11.2 shows some suitable plans.

Manufacturer	Name	ARTF	Engine	Wing	span	Radio	U/C
DB Sport & Scale	Rookie	✓	09	1727mm	68"	2	None
Kyosho	Auto Kite II	✓	10 incl	1090mm	43"	3	Tail
Thunder Tiger	Little Tiger 10	✓	10 incl	1118mm	44"	3	Tail
Global	Skylane		10 - 15	1229mm	48"	3	Nose
JP	Butterfly	✓	15 incl	1270mm	50"	3	Tail
MFA	Skyhawk		15 - 25	1168mm	46"	4	Nose
Precedent	Fly-Boy		15 - 25	1194mm	47"	2/3	Tail
Thunder Tiger	Tiger Trainer 25T	✓	19 - 25	1270mm	50"	4	Nose
Chart	Tyro Major		19 - 30	1371mm	54"	3	Tail
Micromold	Mascot		19 - 30	1473mm	58"	3/4	Nose
Pica	Flyer		20 - 25	1524mm	60"	4	Nose
DB Sport & Scale	Mentor		20 - 30	1321mm	52"	3/4	Nose
Cambrian	Flyer		21 - 25	1524mm	60"	4	Nose
Chris Foss	Uno Wot		25	1575mm	62"	3/4	Tail
Flair	Cub		25 - 40	1855mm	73"	3/4	Tail
MFA	Yamamoto		29 - 40	1420mm	56"	3/4	Nose
Precedent	Hi-Boy		29 - 40	1575mm	62"	3/4	Nose
Precedent	T180		32 - 40	1803mm	71"	4	Tail
Thunder Tiger	Eagle 30H	✓	36	1250mm	49"	4	Nose
Global	SST 40		40	1448mm	57"	4	Nose
Great Planes	PT 40		40	1473mm	58"	3/4	Nose
MFA	New Yamamoto		40	1420mm	56"	4	Nose
JP	Tipo 40	✓	40	1397mm	55"	4	Nose
Hobbico	SuperStar 40	✓	40 - 46	1524mm	60"	3	Nose
Thunder Tiger	World Trainer 40T	✓	40 - 46	1626mm	64"	4	Nose
MacGregor	Aero 40 Trainer	✓	40 - 47	1725mm	69"	4	Nose
US AirCore	Classic 40		40 - 46	1626mm	64"	4	Tail
US AirCore	Aircore 40		40 - 50	1626mm	64"	4	Nose
Thunder Tiger	Tiger Trainer 60T	✓	60	1829mm	72"	4	Nose
Precedent	T240		60 - 90	2400mm	94½"	4	Tail

Table 11.1 *A selection of kits suitable for use as initial trainers in order of recommended engine size.*

Take off

Remember that new kits for trainers are launched on the market from time to time and new plans published in the modelling press.

Conventional trainers

Most basic trainers use a high-wing, tricycle undercarriage configuration, and with good reason. Such a design is relatively easy to fly and has a number of forgiving characteristics. Low-wing models are harder to fly, but ideal for a second model, once you have gained some experience.

Avoid unconventional layouts at all costs during the initial learning period as they are difficult to orientate and often have flight characteristics ill-suited to learners. The delta layout is renowned for its high speed and fantastic roll rate; hardly what you want when learning!

High wing or low wing

A high-wing model will be more stable, all other things being equal, than its low-wing counterpart. None of the trainers listed in Tables 11.1 and 11.2 is low wing, though many manufacturers offer low-wing models as intermediate trainers, once experience has been gained on a high-wing model.

Plan No	Name	Engine	Wing	span	Radio	U/C
MW 2163	Step One	09 - 15	1229mm	48"	2	Tail
RM 40	Trotter	09 - 19	1168mm	46"	3	Tail
RC 1480	Steerone	10	1000mm	39"	3	Tail
RM 432	Jeepster	10 - 20	1216mm	47½"	3	Nose
RM 42	Roulette	19 - 40	1370mm	54"	3	Tail
RC 1642	Storm Petrel	20	1370mm	54"	3	Tail
RC 1176	Tyro Major	20 - 30	1370mm	54"	3	Tail
RC 1349	Bat	20	1245mm	49"	3/4	Tail
RC 1600	Pronto 9	30 - 40	1524mm	60"	3	Nose
MW 2008	Bright Spark	29 - 40	1473mm	58"	3	Tail
MW 2014	Ensign	35 - 40	1397mm	55"	4	Tail
RC 1556	Instructor	35 - 40	1448mm	57"	3/4	Nose
MW 2434	Grand Master	35 - 45	1829mm	72"	3/4	Tail
MW 2416	Pho-Tow	40	2000mm	78"	4	Tail
MW 2250	Solo	45 (4 Stroke)	1829mm	72"	3	Nose
RM 139	Unicorn	49 - 61	1816mm	71½"	4	Nose
RM 50	Big Wig	60	1880mm	74"	4	Nose

Table 11.2 Some plans of models suitable for use as basic trainers, in order of recommended engine size.

Manufacturer	Name	ARTF	Engine	Wing	span	Radio	U/C
US AirCore	Skymaster	✓	Incl	867mm	34"	3 incl	Tail
Kyosho	Cessna Cardinal EP	✓	Incl	1190mm	47"	4	Nose
Great Planes	PT E		Incl	1473mm	58"	2/3	Nose
Hobbico	Dymond	✓	Incl	1700mm	67"	3	Nose
Flair	Volture		Incl	1800mm	71"	2/4	None

Table 11.3 A selection of trainers designed for electric power in order of increasing wing span.

Noseleg or tail leg

Most trainers feature a noseleg, because they are so much easier to keep straight on take off and there is little difficulty from the propeller digging into the ground as the model noses over. However 40% of the trainers listed use a tailwheel configuration and the advantages include a lower weight and less stress on the model on take off and landing.

Powered gliders

Quite a few R/C pilots start their careers in flying by learning on a powered glider. The single major advantage of this approach is that gliders fly slowly and there is more time to correct mistakes made when airborne. There are some problems to offset this major advantage, the main ones being the construction of an accurate wing and the tendency of such a model to tip stall. Chapter 17 gives more information about gliders.

Large or small

By and large, bigger models are easier to fly because things seem to happen more slowly and they get to a distance where they are difficult to see less quickly. On the other hand, they are more expensive to build and power, and also more expensive to repair.

Probably the optimum size of trainer is in the range 1250mm to 1900mm (49" to 74"). You can normally power this size range with a 20 – 60 size engine, of which a 40 is by far the most useful and practical, although you may prefer a 25 size for cost, space or transportation reasons.

Electric flight

While it is possible to learn to fly on an electric model, its higher wing loading and more fragile construction makes it far less suitable as a training aircraft. In addition, it takes some experience to build down to a weight where the best flight performance is achieved. Table 11.3 shows a number of electric powered trainers, and it is noticeable that the majority of them are ARTF models.

Building the model

You will have seen in Chapter 5 that there are many different ways of building models. For a first model, a simple box fuselage with a parallel chord foam or built-up wing has many attractions. Such a trainer is straightforward to build and relatively easy to repair. It is also quick to build. You do want to get airborne don't you!

It really does not matter what model you choose to build, but unless you have built the finished aeroplane square and unwarped, it will not perform as the designer originally envisaged.

There are several stages in construction where you can produce warps and out of true structures. The use of a really flat building board is essential, while the use of a building jig can help as well. You should develop a good eye by viewing what you are building from the right angle.

To give an idea of what is involved in building your first model, two particular trainers are selected for detailed examination in the next chapter.

Figure 11.5 The Mentor is a classic four channel high-wing trainer, with a tricycle undercarriage. (Photo courtesy DB Sport & Scale.)

Always study the plan until you understand the complete building sequence. Cross referring between the elevation, plan view and sections will help, as will written suggestions on the plan or in the instructions.

Planning the installation of the R/C equipment and control runs will save time and effort later. Most plans indicate the location of R/C equipment, but you may need to adjust these to suit your own R/C. The same is true for your engine and fuel tank.

Some older plans show obsolete R/C equipment which is usually larger than its modern replacement and occasionally very different. You should ignore it when planning your installation.

Areas to consider are the engine and fuel tank bays, the battery area, the location of the on/off switch, receiver, servos and control linkages. There are two important points to remember.

> **Tips**
> Avoid building over-weight.
> Don't build warped wings or a banana shaped fuselage.
> Make sure the wing and tail are rigged correctly and the C of G is in the right place.
> Ensure you fit a reliable fuel system.
> Take care with the radio installation.

- Never install any of the radio equipment or the engine and its fuel system so that you cannot remove it later for servicing.
- Avoid finishing any part of the airframe until you are sure that you do not need further access. It is easy to finish the fuselage and then find you cannot get your hands inside to fit snakes/push rods in place.

Building from a plan
The materials
The main difference between building from a kit and building from a plan is that in the latter case you will have to obtain and cut all the materials to shape yourself. You should start with a materials list. Some helpful designers provide this but if not, you will have to work it out for yourself.

The plan should specify the type and quality of balsa needed for the various parts. Hard straight grained balsa is normal for the fuselage, softer for the fin and tailplane. Medium cross grain balsa is ideal for ribs and formers. You can cut out a tracing or photocopy of the ribs and fit it over a standard sheet of balsa to see how much wood you will need to make them.

The smallest size of plywood you can buy measures 300mm (12") square. This is more than you are likely to need but the remainder can be

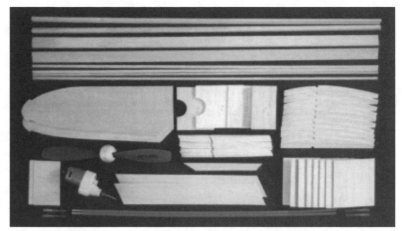

Figure 11.6 Once you have cut out a kit for yourself, building from a plan is no different from building a kit model.

used on your next model. In the same way that some kit manufacturers offer accessories packs with wheels, tanks and items like hinges, horns and clevises, so you will need to make a similar list of hardware. Make sure you know the crank case spacing on your engine when buying an engine mount and the length of noseleg from the firewall to the axle.

Marking out the parts

You will have to copy the parts from the plan onto the correct thickness and type of wood. There are three commonly used methods:

- Carbon paper.
- Pinning through.
- Ironing photocopies.

In all three cases, if the part you are marking out has one straight edge, use a fresh, straight edged sheet of wood.

To use the carbon paper method, put the wood under the plan with the carbon paper face down between the two. Then gently manoeuvre the wood into place so its straight edge matches the line of the part.

A couple of pins pushed through the plan on the desired line helps the location process. Further pins through the plan and the wood will stop any relative movement. Using a ball point pen, mark over the part and the lines will be transferred to the balsa. Be careful with very soft wood as heavy pressure will squash and damage it.

Instead of using carbon paper, a pin can be stuck through the plan into the wood at 50mm (2") intervals, closer where there is a tight curve, and then removed. The pin pricks on the wood outline the component and you can join them up with a ball point.

Finally, you can cut up a darkish photocopy of the plan into the various parts and transfer the outline of each to the wood. This is done by using a hot iron over the desired part of the plan, placed face down onto the wood.

In all three cases, where there is more than one identical part, use the first as a template, taking care not to modify the original outline when cutting out the second part. It is also essential to ensure that the wood grain runs in the required direction.

Cutting out the parts.

The grain of balsa can cause problems when cutting as it will try to make the knife follow the grain. Always cut balsa so the grain pulls the knife away from the part you are cutting. Use your ruler whenever cutting straight lines. Thin balsa up to 1.5 mm (1/16") will cut with a single stroke of the knife, but thicker wood will need several cuts to go right through. A cutting mat will prevent damage to the work surface. You should lightly sand any rough edges of the finished components.

Strip wood is better cut from sheet than bought as individual lengths. Due to the widely

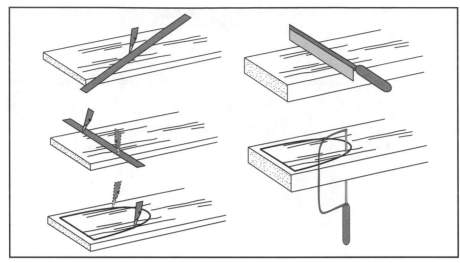

Figure 11.7 Correctly cutting balsa wood requires some skill, whether using a balsa knife or, on thicker wood, a razor or coping saw.

varying nature of balsa this is by far the easiest way of matching strength, weight and hardness; important if you are to build an un-warped airframe.

Even so, you should cut the wood from a homogeneous sheet of balsa and it is easiest using a purpose-made balsa stripper or even a small circular saw. Otherwise, the importance of using a steel rule and keeping the balsa knife blade vertical are key factors. Remember to mark one end of the sheet so that all strips can be used with the marked ends together. If you do decide to buy ready cut strip, holding seemingly similar pairs by one end and noting if they droop a similar amount will give a good indication of matched strength.

It is easier to cut strip wood to length with a razor saw as knife blades tend to crush the wood and it is hard to achieve a square end. When cutting hard sheet over 6mm (¼") thick, use a fret saw on curved lines but a knife for the straight ones.

To make identical wing ribs, use a plywood template. A pair of pins pushed through the template will allow you to cut the rib out directly from balsa sheet. Make sure the grain runs along the length of the rib. For these and other curved lines, try to cut outside the line and then sand to

size. You can pin identical ribs into a stack and sand them as a block to ensure that they all end up an identical size.

Accuracy in marking out and cutting components is important since incorrectly sized parts make construction awkward and may result in a misshapen structure. If a part is wider than a single sheet of wood or if the grain direction varies, mark out each part and join them later. Cutting the parts oversize and gluing them together before final marking can avoid problems of misalignment when you come to join them.

You should always cut plywood with a fret saw, apart from thin 0.4 and 0.8mm where you can employ a razor knife. However the blade will quickly lose its edge.

Cut piano wire parts to length with a junior hacksaw, but the use of a vice or a specially designed wire bender will make shaping parts far easier than struggling with a pair of pliers.

In effect, the only difference between building from a plan and a kit is that you have three extra tasks:

• Deciding what materials you need.
• Buying the materials.
• Cutting out the parts.

From this point, building from a plan is exactly like building a kit.

Chapter 12 Building the Hi-boy and the Cub

The Hi-boy

Certainly by far the most popular trainer in the UK, approaching 100,000 kits have been purchased over the last two decades and that must be an indication of the suitability of Balsacraft International's Hi-boy for its role as a trainer. It has been adopted by a number of leading model flying clubs as their standard club trainer, and many thousands of trainee pilots have learnt to fly using it. The building instructions which follow are based on those included in the kit for the Hi-boy.

The model is easy to build, its strong all plywood fuselage and obechi veneered foam wings enable it to survive hard knocks. The wing section is semi-symmetrical, so that although the model flies slightly faster than one with a flat bottom wing, it has smoother flight characteristics. This type of wing section is also able to handle gusty wind conditions better and helps make Hi-boy an all weather trainer. Landings are slow, but with positive control. The four channel version is fully aerobatic, which you will appreciate as your flying abilities improve.

As you can see from the following illustrations, the Hi-boy Series 2 features a high degree of interlocking die cut litely parts. All parts are individually numbered and these numbers are also included in the list of parts and on the comprehensive assembly drawings. Letters are used on parts of the wing, numbers for all other components. Some trial assembly of the parts, without the use of glue, will help. You will need two types of adhesive; epoxy, both rapid and slow setting variants as well as PVA white glue.

You should have your engine and radio to hand to check their fit as construction proceeds. The first Hi-boy three channel model was powered by an Enya 0.29 (5cc) motor using a 23mm x 15mm (9" x 6") propeller. Under full power

Figure 12.1 The Hi-boy is the UK's most popular trainer and is available as a three or four channel model. (Photo courtesy Balsacraft International.)

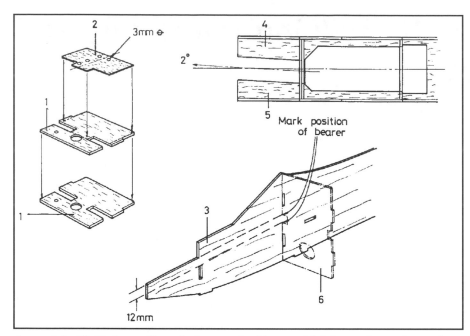

Figure 12.2 How the formers interlock to give the correct amounts of side and down thrust.

the model will climb steadily and when a safe altitude is reached you can ease back on the throttle to half power to maintain height.

Hi-boy can handle the power of a 0.40 (6.5cc) size motor. The extra power makes this the choice if you plan to fit the aileron wing at a later stage or you are flying in a restricted area. The take off run, even on grass can be quite short and the climb away steep. Propeller size could be 28mm x 10mm (11" x 4") to start and 25mm x 15mm (10" x 6") for maximum power, though you will need more down thrust on the motor in this case.

Dry assembly of the fuselage
Carefully remove the die cut parts from the sheets using a sharp knife to relieve if necessary. Clean out the punched slots in the fuselage sides and formers. Before starting to glue the fuselage together identify where all the bits go, looking carefully at Figures 12.2 and 12.3.

Dry assemble the fuselage parts in your hands, retaining the top and bottom fuselage pieces in position using clamps or rubber bands. Note that the main bulkhead shown in Figure

12.2 is made up from three pieces of wood laminated together, and that one slot is cut deeper. This is to accommodate the engine bearers which are shaped to build in engine side thrust to offset effects of torque. Make sure the hardwood engine bearers fit into former 1, having noted that there is a left and right bearer. When correctly fitted these point the motor to the right, viewed from above and in the direction of flight. This is shown in Figure 12.2. Notice also that the line of the bearers points slightly downwards to give some down thrust. The gap between the engine bearers may need adjustment to provide a perfect fit for your chosen motor. You should do this before gluing the bearers in position.

Fit the motor between the bearers so the propeller boss just overhangs the front of the fuselage, not forgetting that there is still a 3mm (1/8") ply plate to go on the front. Don't drill the mounting holes at this stage, just sand or carve one of the bearers so that the motor will fit snugly between them when the fuselage and bearers are glued up. When doing this maintain the 2° of offset (side thrust) already built into them. Make sure all the slots and tabs fit nicely, and that the

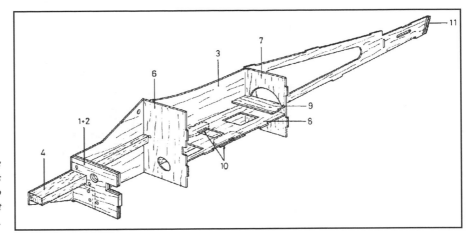

Figure 12.3 The way the formers and the servo mounting tray fit into the fuselage.

formers butt closely to the fuselage sides, before taking apart for gluing up.

Pre-assembly

Insert former 6 into its slots in one fuselage side and mark the position of the engine bearer as shown in Figure 12.2 and draw a line on the fuselage side, so you can glue the bearer exactly in the correct position. Repeat for the other fuselage side remembering you need a right and left; not two the same! Glue both parts 1 and 2 together with epoxy and put under a weight to keep flat until set. Make sure that the slots line up and that the punch marks are uppermost.

The noseleg is mounted on the front of the bulkhead with the bend at the top pointing to the right (the wider engine bearer slot) and is shown in Figure 12.4 overleaf. Drill the four holes 3mm ($^1/_8$") for the clamp retaining screws and the 4mm ($^5/_{32}$") hole for the throttle control snake. There are two punch marks in former 12 for the elevator and rudder control snakes. Drill these 6mm ($^1/_4$") and check that the snake outer tubes fit. Open out slightly if necessary to keep the cable run as straight as possible to exit through the fuselage side.

BUT THE INSTRUCTIONS SAID TRY A DRY ASSEMBLY FIRST!

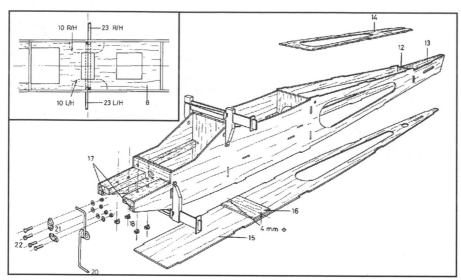

Figure 12.4 The second side of the fuselage, top and bottom pieces and noseleg are fitted in place.

The punch marks above the vertical slots in the fuselage should be drilled out to take the two wing 7.5mm (5/16") retaining dowels. The dowels are glued into the fuselage after the model is finished and covered. The wings are retained on the fuselage by the use of strong fuel proof rubber bands. These are stretched over the dowels which span the fuselage. This is a sensible method as trainers take a fair amount of punishment while you are learning to fly. When you arrive at the happy state of affairs that the wheels are the first thing to make contact with the ground on landing, you can use a cleaner and more permanent method like plastic wing bolts. These certainly look neater but have no give. Bands, on the other hand, will allow the wing to twist off the fuselage. If the wing hits something hard it's better that it parts company with the fuselage, absorbing the energy of the impact, rather than break. Don't cross the bands from side to side, although many modellers do, as the wing then cannot twist off and something will break!

Drill out the two marks in lower fuselage parts 15 and 16 using a 4mm (5/32") drill.

Hi-boy has a built-in servo tray which holds the rudder, elevator and throttle servos, with a place for the on/off switch. The openings in the tray are designed to take standard servos but you may need to enlarge them to fit your particular servos. Some R/C sets come complete with a plastic servo mounting tray. In this case you will need to fit it into the ply servo carrier. This should be done now before assembling the fuselage. Fit the servos, drill holes for the servo mounting screws and fit the on/off switch across the fuselage. When satisfied, remove the servos and switch.

Fuselage assembly

Using epoxy, fit the engine bearers 4 and 5 to the previously marked right- and left-hand fuselage sides. Check Figure 12.2 again to ensure your engine points offset to the right when viewed from behind before you finally glue these. Lay the right-hand fuselage side down flat on the bench, engine bearer upwards. Using plenty of PVA glue, attach formers 6 and 7, the servo bearer and control snake support in place. Before it dries, glue the other fuselage side directly over the first, holding down with weights or clamps until set. Spring the front bulkhead (engine firewall) assembly into position and glue well.

Figure 12.4 top left is a top view of the fuselage between formers 6 and 7 which shows that one main undercarriage leg fits immediately

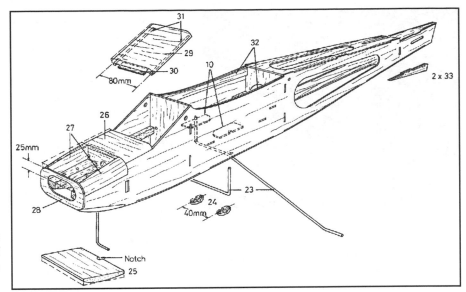

Figure 12.5 The mainwheels and the hatches are now completed.

ahead of the other. They are retained with double width saddle clamps on the bottom of the fuselage. This means that the tops of the legs are staggered through the notches in the servo bearer. One leg rests against the front of the slot and the other against the back of the opposite slot. Ply doublers locate both underneath and on top of the servo bearer, locking each leg in its position. Using epoxy, glue one of the four doublers in position as shown underneath each side of the servo bearer. Make sure that the holes which will carry the legs are clear of glue. Leave the upper doublers for the moment. Figures 12.3 and 12.5 also show details.

Glue the balsa tail post in place along the back edge of one fuselage side. Checking the holes for the undercarriage correspond with the stagger you have allowed for in the servo carrier, and using PVA, glue the fuselage underside and reinforcing plate together. Clear any glues from the holes. Bring the rear ends of the fuselage together and fit and glue the top and under sheeting in place at the same time. Use plenty of glue squeezed into the joints and hold the assembly together with clamps or masking tape while it dries. Before it does so, look down the assembly from the rear to make sure there are

no twists in it. Glue the lower cowl doublers under the bearers flush with the fuselage sides.

Position the motor between the bearers and mark the holes for the screws. Remove the motor and drill these 3.5mm ($^9/_{64}$"), or to suit the holes in your motor lugs if different. Counter bore from underneath to allow the neck of the captive nuts to seat. Push a mounting screw through, and attaching a captive nut underneath, tighten up until the captive nut is drawn into the bearer. Secure each nut with a smear of epoxy but do not get glue into the thread. At this stage apply a couple of coats of fuel proofer to the parts inside the tank bay and underneath the engine bearers ahead of the front bulkhead.

Fit the noseleg to the bulkhead using the short screws provided with washers and nuts inside the tank bay. The shorter arm of the noseleg fits against the bulkhead and the coil faces rearward as shown in Figure 12.4

Referring to Figure 12.5 epoxy the remaining two doublers to the top of the servo bearer, aligning the holes for the main undercarriage legs with those already made. When set, clean out the undercarriage holes from underneath the fuselage with a 4mm ($^5/_{32}$") drill. Push the legs into position and position the double clamps.

Figure 12.6. The engine pipework to allow filling, pressurisation and flow to the carburettor.

Mark the holes for the screws and drill 3mm (1/8"). The clamps are retained with nuts and washers after the fuselage is finished and covered. Glue the engine bay floor in place cutting a notch to fit around the noseleg. Don't make this a tight fit as it will also serve as a drain for spent fuel in the bay. Glue the tank cover and upper cowl blocks in place. When set, sand the front end of the engine bay flush with the front of the engine bearers. Then glue the front plate in place. The top of this should be exactly 25mm (1") above the top of the engine bearers.

Noting Figure 12.5, chamfer the front edge of the windscreen to fit snugly against the tank cover and glue the locating tab in place. Glue the balsa locating strips as shown so that they fit against the inside of the fuselage. The windscreen serves as an access hatch to the tank bay and is retained with a small rubber band across the front wing retaining dowels.

When completely set, carve and sand the windscreen, tank cover, cowl sides and engine bay floor to match the curve of the front end plate. Use 180 grade abrasive paper wrapped around a flat block and sand the whole fuselage smooth, rounding off the corners between the sides, top, and bottom.

Use model filler in any gaps. Depending which motor you are using, you may need to cut a slot in the upper cowl to allow the fuel needle to seat. If so, make it large enough to allow you to adjust the needle.

Glue the wing supports in place; these give the wing a wider platform to sit on. A sponge wing tape can be added after covering if desired. The tail skid is best covered and fitted after the fuselage is completed.

Fixing the motor and fuel tank

Refit the motor. If fitting a 0.40 (6.5cc) motor, extra down thrust will be required. The exact degree will depend on engine power output and choice of propeller. Start by putting two washers between the bearer and the motor on the rear engine bolts. This will tip the motor forward a couple of degrees. You may need more and this is covered in Chapter 9.

Correctly connecting the three tank pipes can be a mystery to a beginner, but this is exactly how to do it on the Hi-boy.

Assemble the tank fittings, clunk, thin-walled feed tube, sealing washer and connector as shown in Figure 12.7. This is the main fuel feed to the motor. The two outlets on the top of the tank are for a filler and a breather. Both of these are connected to a tidy tank filler which is let in to the fuselage side near the top of the tank bay, on the opposite side to the silencer. To fill up, you simply attach your fuel pump or bottle to one of the inlets and when fuel comes out of the other, which is a breather, the tank is full. However, when the door shuts on the tidy tank it also blocks the air supply. Used in this way you must cut off one of the little tubes moulded into the door of the fitting thus allowing it to act as a breather. Cut off the one nearest the door hinge and the door will snap shut on the remaining one.

The ideal position for all fuel tanks is with the middle of the fuel tank level with the spray bar in the carburettor. This is because model engines generally do not have fuel pumps and rely on suction. Obviously when the tank is full, and the fuel level higher than the carburettor, this is easier than when the tank is less than half full and the level lower. It can mean that

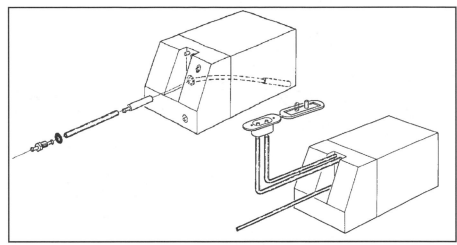

Figure 12.7 The correct way to install and connect up the fuel tank.

several adjustments are necessary to the needle jet in order to run a whole tank of fuel through the motor. These can be a bit difficult to do when the model is airborne! One answer is to start off with the needle open more than really needed (rich) so that as the fuel level drops, things improve. A better answer is to pressurise the system. It's easy to do, has many advantages and is described in detail in the instructions.

When plumbing in the tank, don't cut the tubes too short. Nothing is more irritating than trying to lift the tank, perhaps to get at the nicad, and finding you have to disconnect the pipes to do it.

You will notice that the tank sits on top of the nicad. Cut a piece of foam and sit the tank on it so the tank is in the highest position in the tank bay. Cut a slot in the foam so that the nicad fits into it. Pack foam at the tank sides to hold it in position, but not too tightly otherwise it will transmit any motor vibration.

While on the subject of vibration do balance your propeller, even a new one, as an out-of-balance one can cause havoc. Never use a damaged propeller and never try to repair one. Vibration can cause hinges, linkages and even your radio to fail. It can literally shake the motor out of the airframe in serious cases. It can also be extremely unpleasant when holding your model during final checks on the ground.

The tail surface and wing construction of the Hi-boy follows a similar pattern to the fuselage. If you start with a three channel Hi-boy and want

Figure 12.8 The completed Hi-boy ready for action.

WHEN LANDING, BEGINNERS ALWAYS SAY THAT OBSTACLES JUST SEEM TO MOVE IN FRONT OF THEIR MODELS!

to convert to four with aileron control, a complete wing set is available as an extra, as is the fuselage and the tailplane. The Hi-boy looks attractive, flies well and has introduced many thousands of beginners to the joys of flying radio controlled aircraft. Happy landings.

The Cub

Supposing, however, that you are not enamoured with the idea of a conventional looking trainer like the Hi-boy. There are alternatives, such as the Flair Piper Cub, of which well over 10,000 have been produced. Actually, it was designed as a high-wing, tail dragger trainer which was made to resemble the Piper Cub. It is not a true scale model, though many people think it is.

With a suitable colour scheme, there is no doubt that it will convince many people of its pedigree. So, as with the Hi-boy, we will look at what is involved in building a Cub.

The five sheets of instruction include a kit contents schedule, hardware schedule, and die stamped litely part numbering schedule. The manufacturer can supply a full range of spare items.

The kit is available for three or four channels, the latter with an aileron wing. The wings can be built-up or foam, though only the latter is considered here. All parts are numbered on the

Figure 12.9 The Flair Piper Cub may look like a scale model, but is, in fact, an excellent high-wing trainer.

Figure 12.10 *You can purchase the Cub mail order directly from the manufacturer.*

actual piece of timber, and on the comprehensive plan/instruction sheets.

The following instructions refer to the figures taken from the instruction sheets. We assume here that you have completed the fuselage.

Tailplane assembly

Figure 12.12 Make the tailplane by butt gluing 39 to 40. Add 6 x 12mm stiffeners to the inboard ends of the elevators 41 as shown. The fin is made by butt gluing 43 to 42 and a 6 x 12mm stiffener is added to the bottom of the rudder 44.

Figure 12.12 top centre. Sand the tailplane overall and radius the leaning edge. Note that the trailing edge is kept square. Take the stock

Figure 12.11 *The kit includes a plan with comprehensive instructions and a pair of foam wings.*

length of 12swg wire and bend as drawn to make an elevator joiner. Drill and groove both elevators for the joiner so that the overall span of the assembly matches that of the tailplane. Sand the

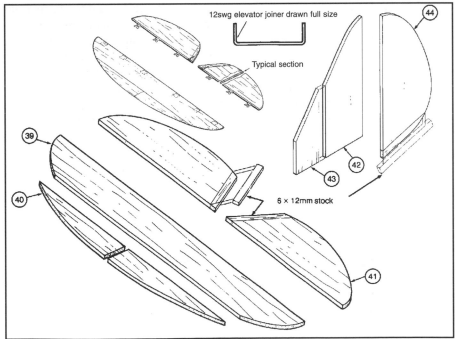

Figure 12.12 *How the tailplane and fin go together.*

151

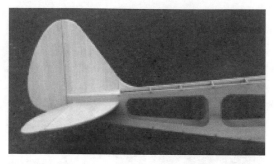

Figure 12.13 The tail surfaces have been fitted to the fuselage and the tail surface hinges are in place.

elevator overall, radius the trailing edge, the inboard edge of the stiffeners remain square, and form a blunt (obtuse) angle point, along the leading edge to allow for movement (see section). Mark out three hinge positions on each elevator and with a sharp modelling knife make a slit at each position. If the slit is too tight initially run the square back edge of the blade to each end of the slit. Dry fit the hinges and with the elevator joiner also dry fitted offer up the assembly to the tailplane and repeat the process.

Figure 12.14 left Place the elevator joiner through the tailplane slots in the fuselage sides. Mark the centreline on the tailplane and slide into position. Do not apply any adhesive yet. Check that the tailplane is central. Check that it is square looking down on it by measuring from each tip to former 9 and ensuring both measurements are at least similar! Finally check that it

is level by placing a straight edge square across the wing seat and eyeing the tailplane against it from the rear. When satisfied accurately mark its position, withdraw slightly both ways applying adhesive as you go. When the tailplane is back in its position adhesive fillets can be applied to the two inside top corners between the fuselage sides and the tailplane. Glue the fin assembly to the stern post 19, the top of the tailplane and to the rear of former 21. Chamfer the inboard edges of the two parts 45 and glue into position.

Figure 12.14 right. Sand and shape the fin and rudder in similar manner to the tailplane and elevators. Hinge the rudder in the same way as the elevator.

Foam wings

Figure 12.15 Accurately butt glue the two wing cores together, weighting one wing panel flat down and packing the other one up as shown to give the correct dihedral. Because the section is semi-symmetrical place small packings under the weighted panel to stop it rolling. When joining note the wing panels have the dihedral angle already formed for the root end. When the central joint has thoroughly dried, mask off the middle 120mm and apply one layer of 100mm wide glass tape all round the root joint with the epoxy resin mixture, applied with a spreader made from card or plywood. Remove the masking when the epoxy is still wet.

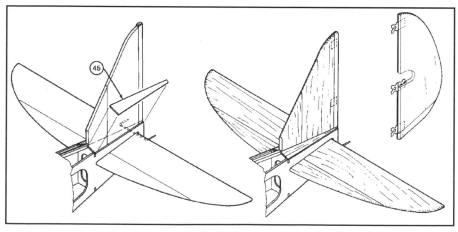

Figure 12.14 Installing the tail surfaces on the fuselage.

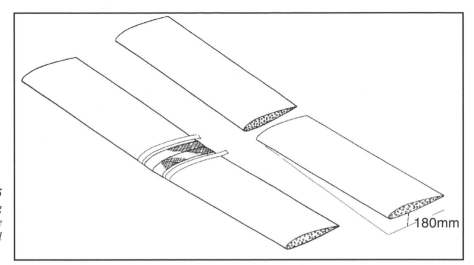

Figure 12.15 Joining the wing panels at the correct dihedral angle.

180mm

Figure 12.16 On a flat board make up two wing tip bows using parts 46, 47 and 48, before the glue sets make sure that measurements Y = X. Fit these assemblies to the tip ribs 49 using riblets 50, 51 and 52. Dry assemble initially to ensure all is well. Do not forget to make a pair! Glue the tip assemblies to the wing panels. Check alignment before the glue sets.

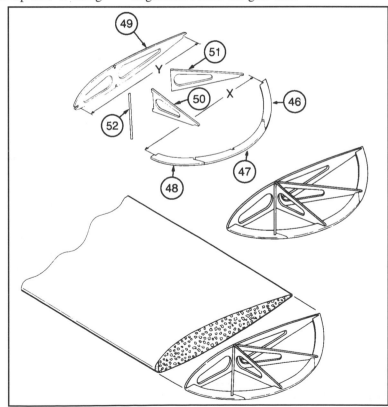

Figure 12.16 The construction of the wing tips.

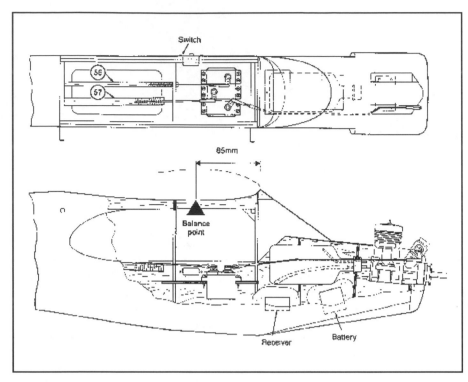

Figure 12.17 The location of the balance point and how to install the radio gear

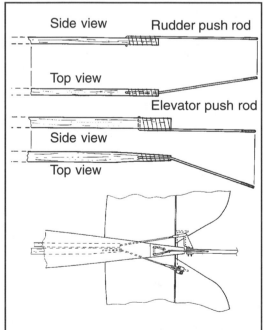

Figure 12.18 The control rod installation.

Covering, hinging the control surfaces and finishing the model

If you have followed the previous instructions correctly the wing fixing elastic bands will contact the wing only on the epoxied area. It is most important that this is the case to avoid deformation (and possible wing failure) of the wing veneer. Two extra 40 x 12 x 1.5mm ply pieces have been supplied to stiffen the trailing edge at the band positions. Glue them to the top surface with one long edge flush with the wing trailing edge.

Very important For normal flying use a minimum of six bands to secure the wing. For aerobatics and high 'G' manoeuvres use eight. (If the wing leading edge is allowed to lift from the fuselage in flight wing failure may rapidly follow.) Replace the bands with new ones of the same size when they start to become 'tired'.

Cover the model following closely the covering manufacturer's instructions. The prototype models were covered in Solarfilm, a British-made economical, heat-shrink iron-on material

Figure 12.19 Ready for take off at last. Inset, you can also finish the Cub in a military colour scheme.

that we strongly recommend. Do not use heavier materials, do not forget the object of the exercise is to defeat gravity and the heavier the model the harder this becomes! Add the fin strake 54 after covering the fuselage and before covering the fin.

Lightly sand the hinges on both faces, slit through the covering to reveal the hinge slots formed previously and using Flair Red Flash Cyanoacrylate fix the elevators and rudder.

Fix the wheels using the two star washers provided. You should by now have something that resembles an aeroplane.

Installing the radio control equipment

Figure 12.17 The radio installation shown here is only a suggestion but it is possibly the best from a centre of gravity point of view (loosely the 'balance point'). It is most important for the control surfaces to have a smooth and unimpeded movement. The movements for initial flights should be rudder 20mm each way, elevator 20mm each way.

Drill two 5mm holes in formers 11 and 12 to pass through throttle push rod. Cut rod to length and solder the adapter in place to facilitate

fitting a clevis to both ends. No side thrust is required but it will be necessary to cut the front formers and cowl to fit around the carburettor of a front induction motor.

Figure 12.18 This shows the rear end of fuselage viewed from underside showing control horn positions. The rudder horn is fitted on a level with the exit slot in side of fuselage.

The rear ends of the two push rods are drawn full size here. Make up as shown and fit in the fuselage. Make any necessary adjustments before cutting the front end to length and fitting the front metal rods, which should be kept as straight and short as possible.

Balance

Figure 12.17 The single most important facet of any fixed wing aircraft is the balance point. With the nose hanging down in the gliding attitude, it must be within 5mm of the dimension shown. Too far back and the aircraft would be uncontrollable, too far forward and the controls are deadened.

The instructions which deal with how to get the Flair Cub safely into the air, and back down on the ground, are covered in Chapter 14.

Chapter 13 Preparing to get airborne

Checking the model

At last you've finished your first model. You just can't wait to see it in the air. Hold on! There are some vital checks you must make before going to the flying field. You can also avoid disappointment if you get your potential flying instructor, or an experienced friend, to give your model a thorough ground check. First, check you have built a true and safe airframe:

- Are there any warps?
- Are the wings/tail set at the right angles?
- Are the controls neutral with the transmitter trims central?
- Are the control throws as specified and in the correct sense?
- Is the centre of gravity in the correct place?
- Does the model balance laterally?
- Is the radio installed securely?
- Are the control connections properly fastened?
- Have you run up the engine?
- Are the engine bolts still tight?
- Are there any fuel system leaks?

Is the centre of gravity in the right place?

It is easy to mark on your model's fuselage or wing where the centre of gravity should be. How do you check it is actually at that point, and what do you do if it is not?

First, suspend the model at its centre of gravity. This can be done with finger tips under the wing, but it is better to use a length of string attached to the model at the required centre of gravity. The model should sit, when suspended, very slightly nose down. Figure 13.1 shows the necessary corrections, for fore and aft positioning of the centre of gravity. You should also check and correct for lateral balance with a weight, such as a screw or bolt, in the high wing tip.

Flight box

Some form of flight box is absolutely essential for radio controlled flying and can vary from a simple plastic box to a custom-built wooden affair. Think about the likely contents, the distance you may have to carry the box and the available space, both in your transport and for storage at home.

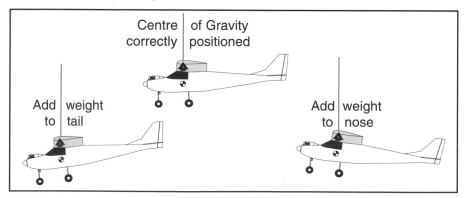

Centre | of Gravity
correctly | positioned

Add | weight
to | tail

Add | weight
to | nose

Figure 13.1 Add lead weight until you achieve the correct balance and then install the weights permanently.

Figure 13.2 This flight box carries two electrical distribution panels, one for operating a starter, fuel pump and glow plug, the other for recharging transmitter and receiver nicads. (Photo courtesy MainLink.)

You can go and fly a diesel engined model with just a container of fuel and your transmitter. An electric model requires only a recharging battery, which can be your car if parked conveniently, and your tranny. In both cases a few basic tools are advisable for on the field adjustments and minor repairs.

The much more common glow engine requires, as a minimum, a source of electrical power for the glow plug, which can either be a dedicated 2

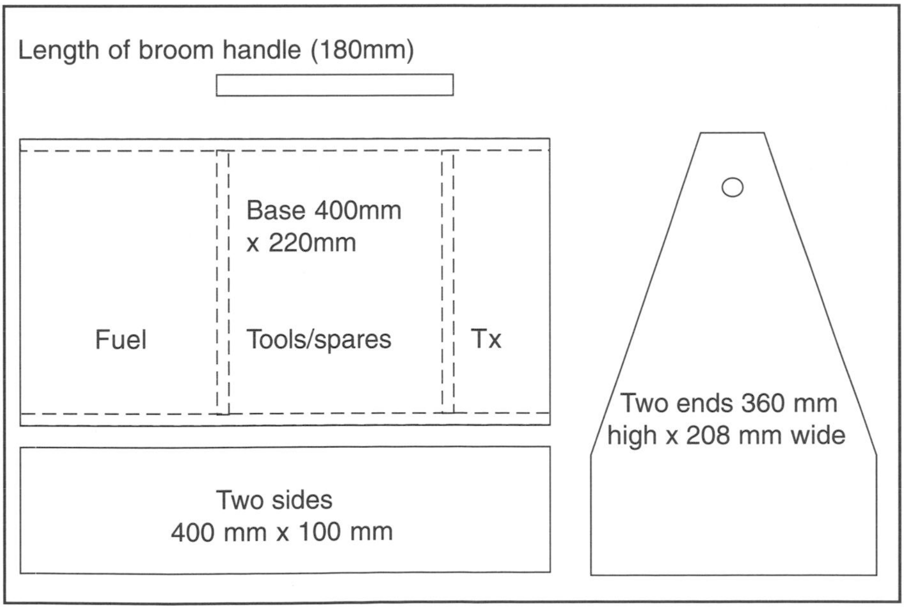

Figure 13.3 Plans for a simple flight box you can build from 6mm plywood. The fuel and transmitter are held in place with elastic straps.

Length of broom handle (180mm)

Base 400mm x 220mm

Fuel

Tools/spares

Tx

Two sides 400 mm x 100 mm

Two ends 360 mm high x 208 mm wide

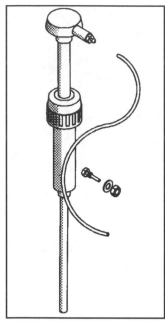

Figure 13.4 This fuel pump screws directly into the top of a plastic fuel container. (Picture courtesy Flair.)

volt battery or a 12 volt one with a power reducer. A starter is advisable, powered by the same 12 volt battery, as well as a container of fuel, fuel pumping system, spare glow plugs and props plus a selection of tools. To carry this large amount of equipment a custom flight box was first developed. Some proprietary plastic containers can be used or, if you have some basic carpentry skill, you can quickly assemble a box from scratch. A simple design is shown in Figure 13.3.

Carrying handle/wheels

Depending on how far you have to carry your flight box from your transport to the flight strip, it may be worth attaching wheels to your box. This can be in the form of a detachable trolley or the wheels can be a permanent feature. However, trailing a wheeled box over bumpy ground can give the contents a rough ride, so make sure everything is secure, particularly your transmitter.

Fuel

The size of your fuel container, normally five litres (one gallon) will depend on the number of flights you intend to make on each outing and the fuel consumption of your motor. It will also depend on whether you are using a glow motor, diesel or petrol engine. You will need to think about what fuel you will use. There is a bewildering array of possible fuels with varying amounts of nitro and different types of oil.

Glow fuel

Basically an 80% methanol 20% castor oil mix is a good starting point, particularly for running in a new engine. A small amount of nitro, say 5%, may improve the performance at tick-over, but will be more expensive than 'straight' fuel. More nitro really only benefits racing engines trying to extract the ultimate amount of power. Exceptions are the small Cox engines, which need some 20% nitro to run well.

You can do no better than to follow the recommendations of your engine manufacturer. The use of mineral oil in place of castor oil has caused the occasional problem in the past but does avoid the difficulty of an engine 'gumming up' when not in use for a long period. Some glow fuels offer a mix of mineral and castor oils to try to get the best of both worlds.

Diesel fuel

Basic diesel fuel consists of equal proportions of ether, castor oil and paraffin. As with glow fuel, these proportions can be altered to increase the paraffin content as this is the 'fuel'. The use of additives increases power output.

Petrol fuel

The petrol used in model aero engines is normal two stroke mix i.e. a mixture of petrol and two stroke oil. The mixture must be stored in the right type of container, and these are available in five litre (gallon) size from garages and car accessory suppliers.

Pump

You will need a pump to transfer fuel into your model's tank. At the simplest this is a straightforward mechanical device with a push/pull action like a bicycle pump or a rotary winding movement. More popular is an electric pump supplied from a 12 volt starter battery. You

Figure 13.5 A 12 volt starter simplifies engine starting and reduces the risk of damaged fingers.

should always fit a filter to the output of your pump.

Starter/chicken finger

To start an internal combustion engine you can either learn how to flick the prop until the engine bursts into life, or use an electric starter. On some smaller engines, a spring starter is built in.

For beginners, the biggest advantages of using a starter are that the skill is readily learned and it keeps vulnerable fingers away from the prop. A double-ended rubber insert in the starter allows you to use it on engines with and without spinners. For hand starting a rubber chicken finger which slips over the index finger will prevent a nasty knock from a back-firing motor.

Ground tether

It is essential that when the motor starts, you restrain the model from moving forward under its own power into the starter or, even worse, your hand. Most people use their left hand to hold the model but a restraint similar to the one shown in Figure 13.7 gives added security.

Glow connector

Glow models require a connection from a 2 volt battery, or a 2 volt supply derived from the main 12 volt starter battery, to the glow plug fitted in the cylinder head of the engine. At its simplest, the clip look and works like a clothes peg. The other main type is tubular and by pushing one

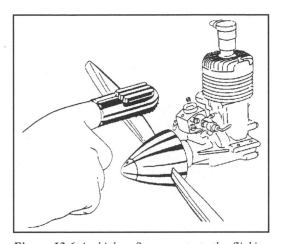

Figure 13.6 A chicken finger protects the flicking finger during hand starting. (Picture courtesy Chart.)

end and inserting the other over the glow clip, a permanent connection is made as soon as finger pressure is removed from the end. Similarly, a pushing action removes the clip. You can permanently wire the glow connector to its battery, or connect it by jack plugs and sockets.

Perhaps a better, and certainly a safer solution is to use a remote glow connection. In this case the glow plug is permanently connected to a pair of wires that lead to a socket mounted on the airframe, usually just behind the engine. This is

Figure 13.7 Some form of ground restraint stops the risk of a model moving forward on starting. (Photo courtesy Hoot Model Making & Tooling.)

Figure 13.8 A glow plug connector and spanner for changing both the plug and the propeller.

shown in Figure 13.10. Then, by plugging in a 2 volt lead, you can safely power the glow plug.

Batteries and chargers

Battery power is required for the glow plug and, if you decide to use them, a starter and electric fuel pump. You can obtain power for all three from a 12 volt battery, although in this case you will need a voltage reducer to the glow plug.

Sealed gel cells are preferable to 'car' batteries as there is no acid to spill and no hydrogen vented during charging. Gel cells do, however, require a custom-designed charger and a normal car battery charger will destroy them.

You cannot charge a 2 or 12 volt battery from your R/C charger. You need a different type of charger due to the difference in voltage and the

Figure 13.9 A 12 volt gel cell battery together with its special type of charger.

fact that you will be charging sealed gel type lead acid batteries rather than nicads.

Starter panel

A starter panel distributes electric power at the correct voltages to the glow plug, electric starter and fuel pump. As well as sockets and switches, there is normally a meter to indicate current flowing through the glow plug. It should read around 3 amps depending on the type and state of the glow plug. It will fail to register if the plug has blown and needs changing. A typical panel is fitted to the flight box in Figure 13.2.

Tools

A selection of hand tools is essential if you are to undertake even the simplest adjustments or minor repairs out on the flying field. Figure 13.11 shows pliers, spanners, a selection of screw drivers, Allen keys, a modelling knife,

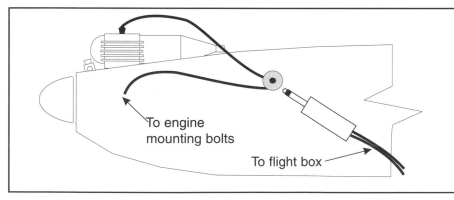

To engine
mounting bolts

To flight box

Figure 13.10 A remote glow connection utilising a 3.5mm jack plug and socket. The connection to the glow plug can be a commercially available item or the female half of a press stud.

Figure 13.11 It is amazing how many tools and spare items accumulate in a flight box over the years.

pins, epoxy and cyano glue, and a plug/prop spanner.

Spare parts

Initially, you will need only a few spares in your box, but as the years pass, such useful items as nuts and bolts, screws and lead weights will accumulate. However, there are a few essential items which are a must from the start.

Glow plugs

From time to time you will need to replace any glow plug, either because the element has broken, or because the plug has become so old that the engine will no longer run correctly.

Props

Any poor landing has the potential to break the propeller and terminate flying for the day unless you have a spare in your flight box.

Wing attachment

The problem with the elastic bands used to hold wings on is that they deteriorate and perish from the actions of sunlight and fuel. A few spares,

in a polythene bag hidden from direct light and with a little talcum powder to keep them fresh is an essential precaution.

If your wing is attached with wing bolts, it is possible that these will shear, as they are designed to do, during a cartwheel, without any other damage to your model. A spare pair of bolts will quickly get you airborne again.

Other items

You should also carry a length of fuel tube, spare wheel collets if you use them, alternative crystals for your radio, a rag for cleaning up and your club membership card and insurance certificate.

Starting an engine

You can just learn to flick the propeller, using a chicken finger. Adjust the prop so that it is in the 'ten to/twenty past' position, viewed from the front, as you feel the compression of the piston reaching the top of the cylinder.

In practice, electric starters are widely used and provide more reliable starting. Engines

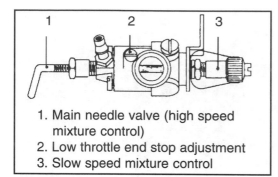

1. Main needle valve (high speed mixture control)
2. Low throttle end stop adjustment
3. Slow speed mixture control

Figure 13.12 A two needle carburettor as fitted to Super Tigre engines among others. (Picture courtesy Chart.)

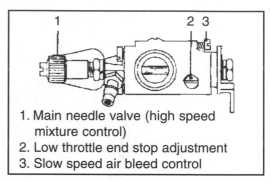

1. Main needle valve (high speed mixture control)
2. Low throttle end stop adjustment
3. Slow speed air bleed control

Figure 13.13 A single needle is used for the main mixture and an air bleed for slow speed mixture control.

under 0.061 cu in (1cc) capacity, sometimes use a coiled spring wound around the crank case as a recoil starter. Always check that the engine has not flooded and hydraulically locked the piston as you can easily damage the engine by applying your starter in this condition.

Glow

Glow motors are easy to start providing you observe a few sensible precautions.

While a carburettor is set up correctly when the engine leaves the factory, the type of fuel you use and the weather may require changes to these settings. There are normally four adjustments that will require attention.

First is the idle stop. This is simply a mechanical stop at the slow end of the carburettor and you must set it so that the servo does not stall when the throttle stick and its associated trim are fully back. This adjustment screw usually also retains the throttle barrel in place, so do not undo it so far that it may fall out.

Second, you must match the movement of the throttle arm to that of the servo arm. You can do this in several ways. Looking at Figure 13.14, you can set the connection on the throttle arm closer or further away from the pivot point and likewise with the servo arm. Finally, many trannies allow you to alter the amount of throw of the servo for full movement of the transmitter stick.

Kneeling in front of the model, check the needle valve is opened the number of turns recommended by the manufacturer, or if you do not have these, try two and a half turns. Rotate the prop by hand anti-clockwise for a couple of revs with a finger over the air intake to act as a choke. This will suck fuel through the carburettor and into the engine. Switch on the radio and open the throttle stick a couple of clicks from the closed position. Place the clip onto the glow plug and power it up. The meter should read around 3 amps, depending on the make and state of the plug.

Place the prop at the twenty to/ten past position and, holding the model with your left hand, sharply flick the prop upwards and to the left with your right index finger, making sure that your follow through brings your finger and hand well clear of the arc of the prop. Repeat this until the engine fires and bursts into life. Alternatively, push your starter cone onto the prop or spinner and close the starter switch, rotating the prop until the engine fires. Quickly remove the starter. (You should always use a starter on a four strokes.)

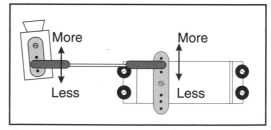

Figure 13.14 How to adjust the movement of your carburettor.

Carefully move behind the engine, open the throttle stick to full power and lean the main needle so that the engine just starts to two stroke (run smoothly if a four stroke motor). Carefully remove the glow connector. Raising the nose of the aircraft to the vertical should result in no drop in revs.

Remember that a slightly rich mixture will just mean the engine produces slightly less power. A lean mixture will damage the engine and may cause it to stop, usually at the worse possible moment.

There are two types of slow running adjustment which you set with the throttle closed after you have adjusted the main needle valve. The more common has a slow running needle valve allowing you to adjust the idling mixture. Less common is an air bleed adjustment which works in the opposite sense, richening the mixture as you screw it in.

If, when you start to open the throttle, the engine produces exhaust smoke and cuts, the mixture is too rich and needs weakening. Close the idle mixture needle or open the air bleed adjustment screw around ¼ of a turn and try again. If, on the other hand, the engine speeds up and cuts, you need to make the adjustments in the opposite direction to richen the mixture. Finally, mechanically adjust the throttle setting so the engine has a safe tick-over with the transmitter stick right back and the trim forward. Ensure the engine cuts when the trim is also back.

Diesel

Any diesel engine has two controls to adjust: the fuel mixture and the combustion chamber compression. With practice, this is not a difficult task.

Hopefully the compression lever is in about the right position. If not, suck in some fuel and adjust it until the engine gives a healthy plop when you flick the prop. Once the engine fires and starts to run, open the throttle and adjust the mixture, then alter the compression slightly until the engine runs smoothly.

Figure 13.15 Once you have started your engine, get someone to hold it vertically at full throttle to ensure the engine does not run lean or cut.

If you screw in the compression adjustment at full power, with the mixture right, until you hear the engine start to labour, turning it back about ¹/₈ turn is the correct position. Then readjust the carburettor as you would with a glow engine.

Petrol

Petrol engines are certainly easy to start providing the ignition battery is well charged. These engines are also less sensitive to fuel mixture and the need for adjustments is rare.

Electric

Surely, there are no starting problems with an electric motor. Wrong! The damage that an electric powered prop can do is no different from any other prop. The danger is that as soon as you turn on your radio, if the throttle stick is forward, an electric motor will go to full power

Wind force	Speed in mph	Definition	Observation
0	< 1	Calm	Smoke rises vertically.
1	1 - 3.5	Light air	Wind direction indicated by smoke drift; insufficient for proper indication by weathercocks.
2	4 - 7	Light breeze	Wind strong enough to be felt on the face, leaves on trees start to rustle; flags partially extend.
3	8 - 11	Gentle breeze	Light flags fully extended; leaves and twigs on trees in constant motion.
4	12 - 18	Moderate breeze	Small branches waving on trees; dust and paper on ground lifted by wind.
5	20 - 24	Fresh breeze	Small trees begin to sway.
6	25 - 30	Strong breeze	Large branches continually move; phone wires hum.
7	32 - 38	Near gale	Whole trees in motion; considerable resistance felt walking into wind.
8	39 - 45	Gale	Twigs/small branches broken off trees.
9	46 - 55	Strong gale	Some slates/tiles lifted off roofs; other minor structural damage likely.
10	55 - 65	Storm	Whole trees may be uprooted and houses damaged.
11	65 - 75	Violent storm	Damage to trees/buildings
12	> 75	Hurricane	Extensive damage to trees/buildings.

Table 13.1 The Beaufort scale helps you to relate wind speed to natural observations.

immediately, unless you have a safety feature on your speed controller requiring you to operate a start button with the throttle closed.

Watching the weather

The weather has a major effect on all model flying and may at times cause you great frustration. The key factors are the strength and

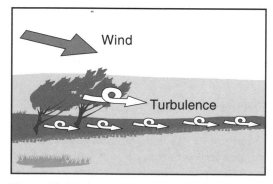

Figure 13.16 The worst turbulence is found in the lee of obstacles like trees and hedges.

direction of the wind, whether it is raining, drizzling, sleeting, snowing or hailing. Also important is the visibility, temperature and whether there is any thermal activity.

Wind

Wind strength is crucial in deciding if it is safe to fly a model. At the beginning of the 19th century, Admiral Beaufort invented a scale of winds ranging from 0 – calm to 12 – hurricane force and gave simple ways of observing the strength. He also provided methods of observation over the sea, but these are hardly what we want for normal R/C flying!

The Beaufort scale is very practical for use today. For all practical purposes, wind forces 1 – 4 allow normal R/C flying, although beginners should restrict themselves initially to force 3. Some slope soarers may fly well in stronger winds.

Remember that wind speed changes throughout any 24 hour period. All other things being equal, it is at its lowest value at night and increases from dawn to a maximum value during the middle of the day. This is why you so often wake up to a light breeze, only to find that by mid morning it is at or beyond the limits for flying. Furthermore, do not expect the wind direction to stay constant with time. Always check the wind direction before each take off and landing.

Turbulence

Turbulence is caused by wind blowing over an obstacle which breaks up the smooth airflow. Obstacles can be as small as hedgerows or as large as major wooded areas. The turbulence occurs in the lee or downwind side of the obstacle. The turbulence will affect a model by making it deviate from the required flight path without any control input. Turbulence is most dangerous when coming in to land as a model's speed is low and its controls least effective.

Temperature

Temperature changes affect the power output of an engine and will have an impact on take off performance. On a really hot day, the loss of performance of any model becomes noticeable. Changes in temperature and humidity will also mean you need to adjust your engine setting to ensure it gives the optimum power at full throttle.

Thermal activity

While thermals are used extensively by glider pilots, thermals also affect powered models. The lifting effect is caused by hot air rising and is normally found when there are cotton wool type clouds (cumulus) in the sky. Areas of tarmac, wheat crops in fields or even the roofs of barns can trigger the lifting action. The lifting air will cause a model to climb without input by the pilot, or descend more slowly. The effect on sports models is much less noticeable than on gliders.

Rain, snow and hail

It is possible to fly when it is raining, but apart from personal discomfort, there are other problems.

Figure 13.17 *The roofs of buildings or even piles of hay can trigger off thermal activity.*

First, water and electronics do not mix and water shorting out the transmitter aerial will result in total loss of control. Second, visibility is reduced, particularly if you wear glasses. Third, the structural strength of any model built with water soluble glue, such as most PVA glues, is significantly reduced. Finally, some rain is associated with a low cloud base and it is possible for a model to disappear into cloud with fatal consequences.

Visibility

Mist and fog can appreciably reduce the distance you can see your model, and life's already difficult enough. Mist is defined as a visibility not below 1000 metres (1100 yards) and should be OK for flying. However, beware! As the sun gets up in the sky, its heat effect will stir up the mist and often cause a significant visibility reduction before an improvement is apparent

---

Tip
Bad weather causes crashes:
- Watch a weather forecast on TV or the Internet, or listen to one on the radio or telephone before going out flying
- Learn to read the weather signs when you are out flying
- Always check the wind before take off and landing
- Stop flying if the wind gets too strong or the weather too adverse

---

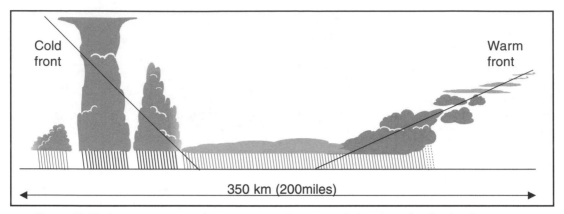

Figure 13.18 This cross section of a warm sector depression shows where the cloud and rain occur.

and the mist finally clears. Do not try to fly in fog!

Interpreting weather forecasts

The national and regional weather forecasts are a useful guide to tomorrow's weather, but with a little knowledge you can get a better insight from an R/C flying view point.

Probably the most common weather system to cross the UK is the warm sector depression. Its direction and speed of movement is easily forecast with accuracy and its intensity in terms of wind and rain is usually greater in winter than in summer. The cross section shows flying weather ahead of the warm front. Once the rain

has started flying conditions are unlikely again until the cold front has passed through, when blustery showers are likely for several hours. A low pressure system produces showers and longer periods of rain, while a high or ridge of high pressure usually gives a period of fine weather.

Short term weather problems

There are several hazards you should avoid once you are ready to get airborne. The wind will affect the direction of take off and landing and can change even during a short flight. Check it before take off and prior to landing. The danger of standing in the open during a thunderstorm is well known. The risks increase if you are holding your tranny with its aerial extended.

Flight safety

Transmitter control

Before thinking of turning on your tranny, you must check that someone else is not using your frequency. Put your peg on the board (or comply with whatever frequency control system is in use) and ensure your crystal matches the frequency you are going to use. A useful additional safety feature is to check who else at the field uses the same frequency as you. This knowledge will protect you as well as the others.

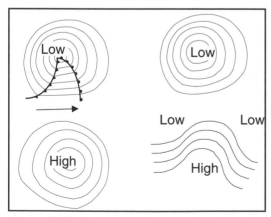

Figure 13.19 Top left clockwise: surface charts for a warm sector depression, a depression, a ridge of high pressure and an anti-cyclone.

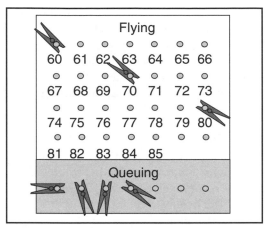

Figure 13.20 Many clubs use a peg board similar to this one for transmitter control.

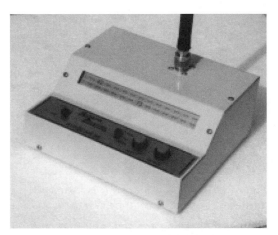

Figure 13.21 Some clubs own and use their own frequency monitor. (Photo courtesy MainLink.)

Frequency monitors

The cost of purchasing a personal frequency monitor is high but many clubs and almost all competition venues use them. They indicate which frequencies are occupied by an active transmitter and those which are not. They do increase peace of mind when flying at crowded locations, but unfortunately do not stop someone else turning on their transmitter when you are airborne.

Short circuits in flight boxes

Unless hand starting a diesel engine, there will always be a battery in your flight box. A fully charged 12 volt battery contains a great deal of energy, and a short circuit can quickly cause excessive heat followed by fire, particularly amongst the wood, rags and fuel found in virtually every flight box. Take care to protect the battery terminals and make sure that loose metal tools cannot bridge them.

Fire extinguishers and first aid kits

Common sense suggests that every flight box should include a small dry powder fire extinguisher of the type sold in auto accessories shops, together with a small first aid kit containing plaster, a sterile dressing, as well as some antiseptic and cotton wool to clean any wound.

Starting

One of the most common injuries to modellers is caused by accidentally putting a finger or hand into a rotating propeller. Even at tick-over, the injuries are particularly painful, not to mention crippling. One of the main difficulties is that a rotating prop is relatively invisible especially if it is black. Reaching over the prop to disconnect the glow clip or adjust the fuel mixture are times of maximum risk. Once the engine starts, move behind it before making any adjustments.

Electric fliers are also at risk, for the power behind an electric prop can equally easily cause a nasty injury. Safe practice means hands well clear of the prop and the throttle on the transmitter closed before you turn on the radio.

Checks

In the next chapter, there is a list of checks you should do before every flight, each day, and at longer time intervals. They are included to make your flying safer and an accident less likely. They are not rules for you to challenge but common sense precautions. Do develop the habit of always doing your checks.

Lookout

Being alert and keeping your eyes open can be a real life saver. Any model may go out of control

Figure 13.22 Military aircraft fly low enough to be threatened by possible collision with our models.

and, if it's heading for you, you may need to take rapid evasive action. The same is true in terms of avoiding a mid-air collision with another model, though this is difficult as you must never take your eyes off your own model.

Tunnel vision is common, particularly for beginners or for those doing complex manoeuvres or flying really fast models.

Full size aircraft

You may be irritated by full size aircraft flying low over your flying field, but if you collide with one, all you lose is your model: the other person may well be killed. If a full size aircraft approaches your strip while you are flying, preferably land or, depending on the height and track of the aircraft, descend to a low height and fly in the quadrant furthest from the aircraft. Do not forget to call out 'full size' to warn any other modellers who are airborne.

If the over flying is a persistent problem, contact the nearest RAF station in the case of military aircraft, civil aerodrome for civil aircraft or club for gliders and microlights.

Flight testing your first trainer

As if learning to fly is not difficult enough, to attempt the maiden flight of a new trainer model when you have never flown before, is asking for a disaster. It is no task for a true beginner and your flying instructor should undertake it. Watch all the checks he or she carries out, since, once

you have learned to fly safely, you will have to do the same on another model you have built. Your instructor should fly your model, trim it out and, if all is well, start your first lesson before making a safe landing. Then, after any necessary adjustments, you can start your flying training in earnest.

Learning to fly

While it is possible to learn to fly all alone, and this is what I had to do back in the 1960s, it is not the recommended way of learning to fly today. The five main choices are:

1. Learn alone.
2. Learn on a flight simulator.
3. Get yourself a flying instructor.
4. Get a flying instructor with a buddy box facility.
5. Pay for lessons at a flying school.

Of these, either 3 or 4 alone, or a combination of 2 and 3 or 4 will save a lot of grief. Number 5 depends on how far you are prepared to travel and how much you can afford to pay.

Flying fields

For most people, the local flying club will provide a ready-made flying site, but you should consider the conditions found at the field.

- Size of take off and landing area.
- Slope of the ground.
- Proximity of obstacles and their size (e.g. trees and hedges).
- Condition of the take off area (tarmac, mown grass, rough grass).
- Noise limitations.

All these factors should affect your choice of model. Hopefully now that you are ready to start to learn to fly, your model will suit the conditions you find.

If you have to fly alone, it is often difficult to find a suitable flying site. It needs to be at least 400 metres (¼ mile) from any inhabited building and further if there are several homes. It should be a flat grass field at least 200 metres (200 yards) square without any adjacent tall trees, power or telephone lines. It must be at least 5 miles (8 kilometres) from any active airfield. Approach the owner of the land for permission to use the field and mow a take off and landing area. Somewhere to park is important and give consideration to any animals that graze the land. In the interests of retaining the site, restrict flying to a reasonable number of hours each week.

Picking an instructor

Do you want a flying instructor? If so, how do you find and choose one? It is possible to learn to fly alone but it is not the recommended route, not the least because of the cost of repairing the inevitable damage.

The best approach is to spend a few weekends watching people at the flying club, seeing those who fly well and those who are less expert, those who help others and those who do not, those who find time to chat and make friends with you. Then is the time to choose a friendly face you know is a competent flier and ask if this individual will help you learn to fly. Some clubs have official instructors, which makes things a lot easier.

Remember that whoever helps you will give up a lot of prime flying time to tuition, so don't be surprised if you get a few rejections. Your chosen mentor may be an experienced teacher or new to this particular role. The purpose of this book is to give you sufficient grounding in the concepts and practice of flying to ensure that the time you spend under instruction at the field gives maximum benefit.

Continuity is vital to the learning process, so that both you and your instructor should try to fly whenever the weather is suitable; at least every week.

Many model fliers are good at their hobby, but cannot analyse how they fly and pass their skills on to you. A good teacher will watch, note a mistake and provide a brief explanation of how to overcome or avoid it. Many instructors see the mistake but cannot point out the cause. A comment like "You keep losing height" will not

Figure 13.23 Most modern personal computers will run an R/C flight simulator program. (Photo courtesy Tru-Flite Technology Ltd.)

help unless accompanied by either "Open your throttle a couple of notches" or "Feed in a couple of clicks of up trim".

It is essential that you relax and take time to make the correct control inputs as they are needed. Try to choose someone who is fairly laid back as an instructor, rather than an abrasive personality who may cause you to become tense. You will find it much harder to learn when stressed or under pressure.

Flight simulators

For many years pilots in full size aviation have learned to fly new aircraft using simulators. Emergencies are practised that cannot safely be done in flight. After making mistakes, pilots can practise avoiding them on the simulator. Models are also expensive to build and a lot of personal effort goes into their construction.

A flight simulator for model aircraft, not to be muddled with programs like Microsoft's Flight Simulator, helps to build flying experience without risking your model. However, investing in a flight simulator is not cheap. You will need a fairly modern PC and a compatible transmitter.

Furthermore, flight simulators do have limitations. They are not perfect either in terms of visual reality or in representing your particular model. However, if you already own a PC and

Take off

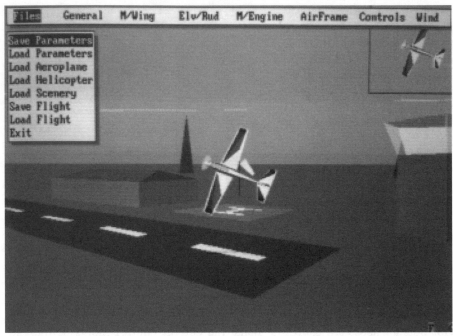

Figure 13.24 *The screen gives a realistic representation of what you see when you are actually flying an R/C model. (Photo courtesy Tru-Flite Technology Ltd.)*

decide to buy a flight simulator package, it can speed your learning process. It will allow you to practise flying at home when the weather outside keeps you in and ensures that you will not have to repair the models you 'crash'.

Over-controlling through excessive control movements is a major problem. Learning how to reverse lateral control movements when the model is coming towards you is also hard. There is little margin for error near the ground when landing or taking off. This skill must become instinctive.

You will need to handle variations in wind strength and turbulence. It is also important to practise unexpected out of trim conditions and recover from unusual flight attitudes. Very few models are in trim on their first flight. Excessive control movements to try to compensate after take off can result in disaster for those forced to learn to fly without an instructor.

Model simulators are slightly more difficult to fly than a model. By starting to learn this way, actual control of your model in the air becomes easier. This may explain why some experienced R/C fliers say that simulators are unrealistic.

A flight simulator will familiarise you with how to control a model from take off to landing and assist you in reacting instinctively to difficult situations in the air. However, you will still need a good flying instructor when the time comes to fly your own model.

Not many model aircraft simulators are available at the time of publication. The NHP/CSM 3 one in three simulator is typical and requires a moderately fast IBM-compatible PC (486 DX33), together with a suitable transmitter such as a 4-channel Futaba, JR, Graupner, Sanwa, or Airtronics, and a lead connecting the transmitter to the parallel port. The program provides good three dimensional graphics and a realistic response to control inputs. It is a simulator for fixed wing models, powered or glider, and helicopters.

You will probably crash a lot at first because of the control reversal required when the model is coming toward you. Practise this until it becomes instinctive. The quickest way to practise reversals is to fly away from yourself and then come back repeating it over and over again.

Then try to fly a rectangular circuit as you will have to get used to this at your flying field. Remember to make an equal number of take offs in each direction.

At first, flying a simulator seems impossible. You feel that you will never succeed in landing on the strip. This is because you remain positioned at one end. You can see only where the computer lets you look. The computer follows the model, but with only a limited field of view. After some practice, you will become familiar with the scenery and will know where you are all the time.

Use yourself as a reference point for landings. Fly your model directly toward you after a short base leg, bringing it toward the end of the runway. A slight turn lines the model up as the touchdown point comes into view. It also allows you to see your glide angle clearly. With practice, you should be able to land the model on the strip every time. It does, however, require concentration and skill similar to that needed to fly a real model.

You should aim for daily simulator sessions of half an hour. Even when you are proficient, you will find you still occasionally turn the wrong way. This usually occurs when things are happening rapidly or the model was almost out of sight.

Try to practise standing up, as you would at the flying field. If you start getting wound up, turning and looking over your shoulder may help. You may not be able to rid yourself totally of turning the wrong way. It takes a long time for this to become instinctive. Even then, after a period off flying, it may sometimes reoccur.

When you are ready, take your model to your field and get your flying instructor to check it, take it off and then let you have a go. You should be able to go solo far more quickly than if you had not used a simulator. During training, you can practise on your simulator any problems you have when flying. You can also help use it to rebuild your confidence if you crash your model.

Buddy boxes

A buddy box is a system which connects two transmitters by a cable, allowing the instructor

Figure 13.25 *Helicopter flight training is also possible. (Photo courtesy Tru-Flite Technology Ltd.)*

to give control to the student or take it back at the touch of a button. The system saves unsightly dives for the transmitter by your instructor if you get into difficulties. It is thus a near perfect dual system of learning to fly.

It does, however, require two compatible transmitters. It may be your reason for selecting a particular make of radio. The discipline of using a buddy box is quickly learned, and the words "you have control" and "I have control" indicate the transfer of control by the instructor. You must take care to ensure that you and your instructor turn together to follow the model in the air and avoid getting tangled in the connecting cable.

Relationship to full size flying

Any aeroplane which flies, whether full sized or a model, has to meet the same basic aerodynamic requirements. There is thus a great deal

---

Tip

Practise starting your engine before trying to learn to fly.

Get a flying instructor to teach you.

Get your model checked by someone experienced before its first flight.

Practise on a simulator if you have access to one.

Practise flying as regularly as you possibly can.

BUDDY BOXES HAVE OTHER ADVANTAGES!

to be learned from full sized aviation, although there is also much that is not relevant. It is certainly worth thinking about what does apply.

For those who have flown or still fly full size aircraft, the greatest difficulties arise from three areas. The first is the feeling that this cannot be anything like as hard as flying full size aircraft. The second comes from the fact that the ailerons are effectively reversed when the model is flying towards you. The last is that full sized pilots do not have to cope with a model orientation problem.

Many full size pilots, myself included, have come to grief through overconfidence. That said, a basic understanding of aerodynamics and aircraft control in a variety of roles from circuits and bumps to advanced aerobatics help immensely once you master the basics of radio flying.

Figure 13.26 Just because you can fly full size aircraft, like this Pitts Special, does not mean that you can instantly transfer this skill to R/C flying.

Chapter 14 Airborne at last

Airmanship

This is the skill of being aware of what is going on around you before, during and after each flight. Airmanship appears easy to learn when reading about it in the comfort of your armchair. It is more difficult to put into practice during the hurly burly of preparing a model for flight. It is even harder when concentrating on flying a model. For those who drive, remember how difficult it was to think about anything but the pure mechanics of driving during those early lessons, and how little you observed of the road ahead. It is the same when learning to fly.

Flying a model is very exhausting mentally, due to the high level of concentration you need in the learning phase. Restrict your time on the controls to five minutes if possible and ten minutes as an absolute maximum. You will be surprised how quickly time passes when you are in control, so let your instructor monitor the time.

There is another important lesson here. Running out of fuel in the air guarantees a forced landing and puts the model at risk. A ground run of the engine can establish fuel consumption at full power and, from the size of the fuel tank, you can decide on a safe flight endurance. A timer set to bleep after this duration from start up is a useful safety feature.

When learning to fly, everything seems to happen incredibly fast and you may wonder how you will ever cope. It helps to think slowly through each part of the flight in turn on the ground. This chapter describes each manoeuvre in detail. Learn exactly what to do. Then sit, relax, close your eyes and try to visualise each part of the flight as if it is happening. After some

practice you will find that the manoeuvres are ingrained and you will not have to think about them while flying as well.

Disorientation is probably the biggest single problem that any tyro pilot has to face, and part of the problem is well illustrated by looking at Figure 14.1 which you can see in two different ways. The other difficulty is freezing on the sticks and doing nothing to control the model and fly it where you want it to be.

If it is a sunny day, think about where the sun is and avoid flying near or into it. If you do, close one eye to avoid being blinded by the sun, only opening it when the model has passed through the sun. If it is windy, try to do the majority of your flying upwind of you, since, with a model downwind, a turn in the wrong direction can quickly result in the model becoming too far away to see which way it is flying.

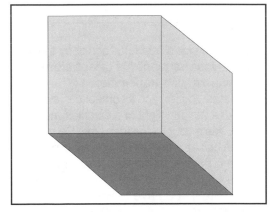

Figure 14.1 Does this look like a box seen from below, or looking inside an area with a floor and two walls? You should be able to change easily from one view to the other.

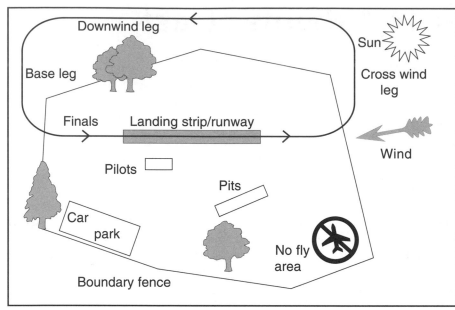

Figure 14.2 A circuit at a typical club flying field. Many clubs have mown strips, a few lucky ones have tarmac runways.

With modern radio, you are unlikely to reach the limit of radio range before your model is so small that you cannot see to control it. Nevertheless, establishing the ground range of your set is essential and you should do it before the first flight of a new model and at regular intervals thereafter. A typical range of at least 40 paces until the servos start to twitch, with the tranny aerial down is normal, but check the actual distance for your own set so that you will immediately know if the performance has changed dramatically. You should carry out range checks when you are sure no-one else has their transmitter on.

Finally, do familiarise yourself with your flying field layout. Learn where there are any obstacles or no fly areas and familiarise yourself with the take off/landing area and where pilots stand while flying. Make sure you understand what you are going to learn or practice before each flight. Do not try to continue for longer and do try to relax between flights after a debriefing by your instructor.

Air speed and ground speed

You need to understand the difference between air speed and ground speed. Air speed is the speed the model passes through the air. The faster the air speed, the greater the drag generated by the model, and the lower the wing angle of attack necessary to generate the required lift.

Ground speed, on the other hand, is the speed the model moves over the ground. In still wind conditions, ground speed is the same as air speed. When a wind is blowing, a model flying into the wind will have a ground speed lower than

---

Tips

Learn your club's field rules and obey them.

Check your frequency is clear before turning on your transmitter.

Don't start your engine if someone is about to make a maiden flight of a complex model.

Don't waste your instructor's time. Be ready when he/she wants to get you airborne.

Move off the strip immediately after take off or landing.

Take care if you have to walk across the landing path.

Don't fly low over the pit area or any person.

Don't fly for too long. Someone else may want to get airborne on your frequency.

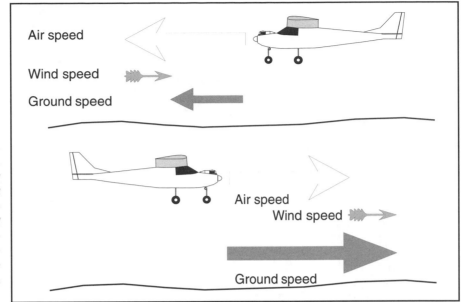

Figure 14.3. The relationship between air speed and ground speed depends on the wind speed and whether the model is flying into wind, cross wind or down wind.

its air speed and vice versa when flying downwind. This makes it difficult to estimate the air speed of a model if there is any wind, and also how it is possible for slow flying models to appear to hover stationary when heading into a strong wind.

Checks

In the RAF in the 1950s, the checks were said to consist of 'kick the tyres and light the fires'. The high accident rate reflected this. Today, check lists are religiously used to ensure that everything is set correctly before committing either to start engines or take off. The same should apply to your models if you are to avoid unnecessary damage.

When you unload your model, secure the wing in place, having first connected your aileron servo if you have a removable wing fitted with ailerons. Check the model for obvious signs of physical damage and ensure the control surfaces are still firmly attached to the fuselage and the control rods/snakes/wires are without undue slop.

Remember, it is vital to ensure your frequency is clear before turning on your transmitter. Most clubs run some sort of peg board system, and you should thoroughly familiarise yourself with this system.

So, your frequency peg is on the board. Extend the aerial, switch on your transmitter and then your receiver (never the other way round as anyone else transmitting may drive your servos beyond their normal limits.) Check on your transmitter display/meter that the voltage/RF output is within limits. Then select the correct model, if you use a computerised tranny, and set the rate and any other switches, such as coupled ailerons/rudders, to the desired positions. You have filled your fuel tank, haven't you and replaced any bungs/put the pipes back on their nipples. Your wing is firmly in place and all hatched closed securely.

You are now ready to start. Check behind the model to ensure that there are no loose items or other models in the slipstream. With the model restrained, connect your glow plug lead and start up. Do keep out of the line of the rotating prop and be very careful not to put your hand/fingers into the prop disc.

Check the engine at full power, idle and mid range, adjusting the main and slow running needles as required. Certainly for the first flight

ICARUS, LAD, NOT TOO CLOSE TO THE SUN OR YOUR WINGS WILL MELT!

of the day, or after any needle valve adjustments, get someone to hold the model vertically up and check the engine still runs smoothly at full power. OK? Throttle back and once the model is on the ground, check all the controls for full and free movement in the correct sense. Right, right down is a good memory jogger when checking ailerons. Always stand behind the model when doing these checks to avoid mistakes.

Now you're ready to taxi, but before take off, a set of final checks:

- Meter reading OK on the transmitter.
- Aerial fully extended.
- Controls full and free movement.
- Computer set to correct model and rate switches set.

Do all the controls move in a logical sense? Pilots think so, you may not. The elevator stick is pushed away from you to lower the nose and towards you to raise it. The aileron stick is moved to the side towards which you want the aircraft to roll. The throttle moves forward to open it

and go fast, backwards to throttle back and reduce speed. The rudder is the control some people find unnatural. Move it to the left to yaw left. Those who sail full sized boats put the tiller left to turn right! You soon get used to it. Also remember the greater the stick movement the greater the control deflection.

Basic flying

When learning to fly, most pilots experience the problem of getting tense on the controls. If you drive a car, remember your first outings, white knuckles clasping the steering wheel. You must relax and stroke the controls. Be gentle, avoid over-controlling and worst of all, when things start to go wrong in the air, try not to freeze on the controls. The other key factor is that you must never, ever take your eyes off your model when it is airborne.

In the early phases of learning, plenty of height gives you time to recover from any mistake, but it also makes it harder to see small changes in the model's attitude. It also emphasises the importance of not flying the model too far from you. The model should spend most of its time within a circle of 250 metres (yards) around you. It is important to fly your model upwind from you, but not into sun. The problem with flying downwind is that if you accidentally turn the wrong way, the model quickly gets beyond the range of easy visual control. In similar circumstances upwind, at least the model is blown back towards you. A moderate breeze will blow your model downwind at a rate of 10 metres per second (33 ft/sec)! You also must comply with any restrictions imposed by your flying site. It helps to think about where in the air you will fly the model before you ever get airborne.

Flying into sun is difficult to avoid in the early stages of learning to fly. Wearing sun glasses and a peaked cap can help to minimise the problems when your model ends up close to the sun. If you do actually fly through the sun, close one eye, so that you are not temporarily blinded when you come out the other side.

The directional controls of your aircraft, aileron and rudder, will reverse when your model is flying towards you. The habit of applying the control in the wrong direction is a difficulty which only practice can help you to overcome. If you are a full sized pilot as well, you may find this apparent control reversal particularly difficult to master.

There are three tips which may help. First, move the stick towards the low wing to raise it, second, only make a small control deflection and if the model turns/rolls the wrong way, a quick reversal of control deflection is easy. Third, try looking over your shoulder at the model so that the reversal does not occur. However you approach this problem, you will suddenly find you are not thinking about it and putting on the correct control automatically.

Taxying

Taxying may appear a manoeuvre hardly worth mentioning, but there are some invaluable lessons

Figure 14.4 Open the throttle gently to start the model taxying out to the take off point.

you can learn. First, it takes more power to start a model moving than to keep it rolling, so that once the model starts to move, close the throttle slightly. Second, particularly if the model is a tail dragger, hold on full up elevator to avoid nosing over or, if the model has a noseleg, to avoid putting too much strain on this component.

For most people with most transmitter configurations, steering involves using the left thumb and it takes time to get used to this. You must avoid at all cost the danger of reaching take off speed and unintentionally getting airborne. Smooth movements of the controls, trying to find the correct stick deflection for any particular turn radius is an important lesson. Avoid any tendency to keep blipping the stick to one side.

Before you start to move out of the pits area, check that no-one else is about to, or has just started taxying. It is ill-mannered to blast your throttle open when there is another model parked behind yours, or another person for that matter. You will commit them to a blast of dusty, oily slipstream.

This is your first opportunity for real to check how your engine responds to stick movements when the model is on the move. Many models tend to weathercock into wind and this tendency

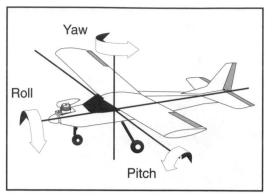

Figure 14.5 *A model yaws, rolls or pitches when inputs are provided by rudder, ailerons or elevator.*

may require fairly coarse use of rudder. Getting used to steering the model on the ground, and controlling its speed, is a great way to gain some initial experience and build confidence in handling the model. Practise taxying towards yourself and make sure you learn instinctively how to turn the model the correct way. If you've driven R/C cars or boats, this should present no problem.

Models with steerable noselegs are probably the easiest to handle, followed by those with fixed ones. While tail draggers are the hardest, and may be prone to ground looping, they do have other advantages which offset this initial snag. Regardless, time well spent on this exercise will bring rapid rewards.

Effects of controls

It is worth discussing the relative merits of transmitter modes 1 and 2. These modes are illustrated in Figure 7.9. The proponents of mode 1 say it is much easier to make delicate control movements if elevator and aileron are

---

Tip

When learning to fly:
- Fly regularly
- Plan what you are going to do before each flight
- Get a debrief from your instructor after each flight
- Try to relax when you are in control

---

on different sticks. The mode 2 supporters say that having elevators and ailerons on the same stick is just like a full sized aircraft. In fact, there is no right or wrong way. What is important is that you feel comfortable with your selection. Regardless, you should also use the same mode as the person who is trying to teach you to fly.

Left-handers must either learn to fly right-handed, or fly a mirror image of mode 1 or 2. The former is quite practical as I myself, a life-long left-hander, fly normal mode 2. Left-handers flying this mode also have the advantage that hand launching is easy. The left hand throws the model while the right hand holds the elevator/aileron stick.

Once airborne, the first thing to learn is how moving the main controls affects the model. All the sticks except the throttle are spring loaded to the central position. The primary effects of the controls are:

- The elevator pitches the nose of the model up and down.
- The ailerons roll the model left and right about its lateral axis.
- The rudder yaws the nose of the model left and right.
- Opening the throttle causes the model to increase speed and vice versa.

There are, however, secondary effects as well.

1. The secondary effect of elevator is to alter the speed of the model; nose up and the speed starts to reduce and vice versa nose down.
2. The ailerons, having started the model rolling, cause it to yaw in the same direction.
3. The rudder, having induced a yaw, will then try to roll the model.
4. The secondary affect of the throttle is that as speed increases, the model starts to climb and vice versa.

You will find that the greater the control deflection, the greater the resulting effect. In addition, the primary controls become increasingly more effective as speed is increased. Note also that controls in the prop wash, like rudder and

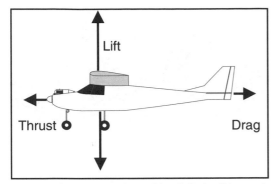

Figure 14.6. In straight and level flight, lift equals weight and thrust equals drag.

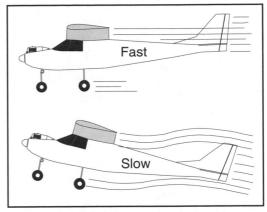

Figure 14.7 The attitude of a model depends on whether it is flying fast or slowly.

elevator, become less effective with the throttle closed. You should try these effects for yourself. When moving the throttle, do so slowly, as slamming it open risks causing your engine to falter or even stop.

Trims are fitted to all four of the primary flight controls, usually inside and below each stick. You must learn to move them without hesitation when you are flying. Their purpose is to avoid you having to hold your sticks off centre during normal flight, apart from the throttle, where the aim of the trim is to allow you to shut down the engine after it has landed safely.

Trim

The trim of any model changes depending on its airspeed and the amount of fuel it has used. Warps can also alter trim; a particular problem if you store your model in a damp garage or shed. The trims on the transmitter are there for you to use to neutralise any stick forces and make flying more comfortable. You must learn to feel for the trims and not look down to find them.

Straight and level

Well, at least you won't have a problem with this! Don't be too sure. First, you can't fly straight and level for very long before your model flies out of controllable range. Twenty seconds at typical trainer speeds is about all that is possible before you have to start a turn.

In straight and level flight, lift is equal to the weight of the aircraft and thrust is balanced by the drag produced by the airframe. The wings are level and the aircraft is not altering its heading, nor gaining or losing height. You must judge the correct pitch attitude of the aircraft, and the look of the airframe when the wings are truly horizontal. The faster the aircraft is flying, the more nose down will be its attitude for straight and level flight, and vice versa.

The main problem is not the straight bit, although that does involve keeping the wings level. It is the level bit! A one degree change in pitch attitude quickly results in a climb or descent, and that small change is hard to detect when you are in the early stages of learning to fly. Figure 14.8 overleaf shows the problem.

Fortunately, you quickly come to recognise small pitch variations and make correspondingly small elevator movements. A few degrees of roll hardly turns a model at all, though it is important you can instantly recognise the wings' level position, even though with dihedral, neither wing is actually parallel to the ground.

The position of the elevator trim in straight and level flight will depend on the position of the throttle. The faster the aircraft is flying, the more down trim you will need.

Level turns

There are a number of ways of entering a turn. Most common is to apply aileron in the direction

Figure 14.8 No, they are not three identical photographs! Top left is the model flying straight and level, bottom left the model has a one degree nose up attitude and, top right, a one degree nose down attitude. It needs an experienced eye to detect these small changes of attitude which will put the model into a climb or descent.

Steep turns

Steep turns are usually practised with an angle of bank of around 60°. You enter them in the same way as a normal turn, but they require more up elevator to maintain height as well as an increase in power to maintain air speed. A tight turning circle is the result of a steep turn. Maintaining a constant angle of bank without gaining or losing height are the skills you must acquire when practising steep turns. At a later stage, you will have to master turns at even

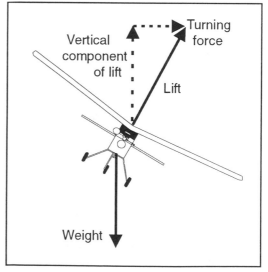

Figure 14.9 In a level turn, lift must increase so that its vertical component equals the weight.

of the turn (rudder if ailerons are not fitted) until the model has around 30° of bank on, then neutralise the ailerons and apply a little up elevator to avoid losing height. Most learners find feeding in exactly the right amount of up elevator to keep the model in level flight one of the most difficult parts of this exercise.

Figure 14.9 shows why a model needs to generate more lift than in straight and level flight. The use of up elevator increases the wing's angle of attack slightly, increasing the lift it generates. It is the horizontal component of the lift which produces the turning force.

Up to about 30° angle of bank, this is fine, but at greater angles, the increased lift also generates more drag, and an increase in power is required if speed is not to reduce in the turn.

If the model is set up correctly as a trainer, the wings will maintain a constant angle of bank. Rolling out of the turn involves the use of opposite aileron to level the wings, remembering at the same time to release the back pressure on the elevator stick. Do not forget that when the model is coming towards you, the aileron controls are effectively reversed.

It is a good idea to practise level figures of eight by completing a 360° turn in one direction and then rolling straight into a similar turn in the opposite direction.

steeper angles of bank. At the highest angles of bank, over 80°, the very large amounts of up elevator and full power necessary to maintain a level turn generate large amounts of positive 'G'. If you pull back hard enough on the elevator, particularly with a jerky movement, it is likely your model will rapidly flick into a spin. If you are flying fast enough, you may overstress the wings and break them in two!

Climbing and descending

Climbing requires the application of power, usually full power and positioning the nose of the model above the horizon. Too steep a nose up attitude causes a loss of speed and then a stall. Too low a nose attitude, on the other hand, produces a sluggish rate of climb. Try to learn the ideal nose up attitude for your model.

Do not muddle a steady climb with the zoom climb, where excess speed is traded for height when the nose of the model is pulled up, as for example in the entry to a loop.

Descending, likewise, calls for you to lower the nose, usually with a reduction of power or the throttle completely closed. Too steep a nose down position results in a rapid increase of speed, trying to zoom the model out of the ensuing dive. Again, try to maintain the same speed as you would in straight and level flight at half throttle.

Gliding

Gliding, either with the engine throttled right back or after it has cut, uses the lift and drag to balance the weight of the model and give it forward speed. The faster the glide, the quicker the model descends, but this does not mean that it does not glide as far.

Full sized practice, theoretical calculation and modellers' practical experience all show that you achieve the minimum rate of descent at a speed just a little above the stalling speed, whereas you obtain the maximum distance covered for a given loss of height at a somewhat faster speed than for the minimum descent rate. The actual glide angles are very dependent on the design of the model, a biplane with a radial

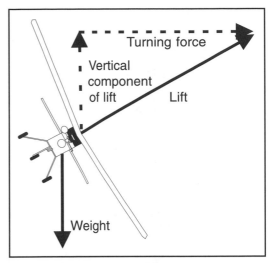

Figure 14.10 *This model is turning sharply at a high bank angle. To stop losing height, increase lift by using up elevator to hold the wing at a high angle of attack.*

cowl having a much worse glide performance than a sleek monoplane.

Climbing and descending turns

Turns during a climb or descent are slightly different from level ones. To establish a climbing turn, you must lower the nose of your model slightly as you feed in bank before easing on some up elevator. The rate of climb will reduce. Likewise in a descending turn, you must lower the nose slightly and the rate of descent will increase.

Spiral dives

A spiral dive is a manoeuvre which normally results from an over-steep turn where the nose drops and the model starts to descend quite rapidly. Pulling back on the elevator will only increase the rate of turn and descent. Recovery is simple, but needs to become an automatic reaction. First roll the wings level and then use elevator to pull the model out of the dive.

Stalling and spinning

When a model flies too slowly, the wing loses its ability to produce sufficient lift. In straight and level flight, when the wing reaches

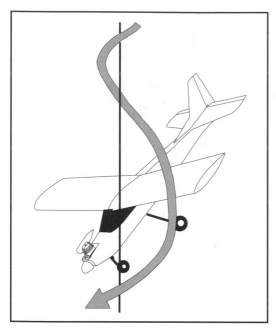

Figure 14.11 In a spin, the model's wings are stalled and the aircraft rotates about a vertical axis.

its stalling angle of attack, there is a sudden loss of lift and the model pitches nose down and loses a significant amount of height. On some models, though rarely on trainers, one wing will stall before the other causing the model to roll at the instant of the stall. If uncorrected, the model will then enter a spin.

A stall occurs when the flow of air over the wing of a model breaks down at a high angle of attack, resulting in a sudden loss of lift.

A spin can follow a stall, when one wing stalls before the other producing a continuous

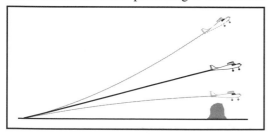

Figure 14.12 The climb after take off must be steep enough to clear any obstacles, but not so steep that the model stalls immediately if the engine falters.

rotation during the stall. In a normal spin, the nose of the model will point downwards at quite a steep angle. Some models enter a flat spin, with the fuselage near horizontal during the spin.

You must learn to recognise a stall and make a rapid recovery. The most likely time for an unintentional stall to occur is during the final approach to landing, when the speed of the model is low and the wing angle of attack high. Unfortunately, models do not normally provide their pilots with any indication of their air speed, and their ground speed is not a good indication as it varies both with wind speed and the direction the model is flying relative to the wind.

You can practise stalling by closing the throttle and maintaining straight and level flight with increasing up elevator until the model stalls and starts to lose height. Recovery from a stall involves easing forward on the elevator, applying full power and, as speed increases, pulling out of the ensuing dive and throttling back.

If a wing drops, trying to pick it up with aileron will only aggravate the situation and may put the model into a spin. Wait until you have unstalled the wings before trying to level them.

You can enter a spin on most models by applying full rudder at the stall. Some models, particularly trainers are so stable they are reluctant to enter a spin. Most models will recover from a spin if you release the controls. Some require you to close the throttle, apply full rudder opposing the direction of the spin and then apply down elevator, again pulling out of the ensuing dive and feeding on power to return to straight and level flight.

Take offs

The take off can prove a surprisingly difficult manoeuvre to master. Before lining up on the strip, look around, particularly into wind to ensure that no-one is coming into land. If they are, remember that they have absolute right of way over you. Also note the direction of the wind. Line up facing directly into wind or facing down the take off strip and carry out the pre-take off checks:

Figure 14.13 Gently open the throttle, with up elevator to stop a nose over, keeping straight with rudder.

- Meter reading OK on the transmitter.
- Aerial fully extended.
- Controls full and free movement.
- Computer set to correct model and rate switches correctly positioned.

Gently open the throttle fully, keeping straight with rudder. With a tail dragger, use up elevator initially to avoid nosing over, releasing it as speed increases and letting the tail rise. With a normally rotating tractor engine, a model tends to swing left, so be prepared to feed in right rudder.

As the model reaches take off speed, gentle back pressure will ease the model into a steady climb. Trim out the aircraft in pitch and roll. If you are unlucky enough to experience a wing drop just after lift off, react with rudder since trying to pick up the wing with aileron may simply cause the wing tip to stall and induce a cartwheel into the ground. Remember that the take off run will be longer and the ground speed higher at take off if there is little or no wind blowing down the strip.

Do not climb too steeply as your air speed will remain low, making it almost impossible to recover from an engine failure at this point. By now the model will be moving away from you quite rapidly, so make a gentle climbing turn back towards the strip. If at any stage you lose control during the take off run, close the throttle and steer the model to a stop with rudder.

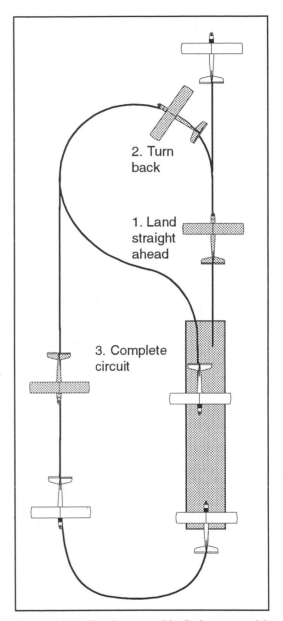

Figure 14.14 The three possible flight pattern following an engine failure after take off.

Engine failure after take off

An engine failure straight after take off is one of the hardest emergencies to handle and therefore regular practice is a good idea. There are basically three possible scenarios shown above:

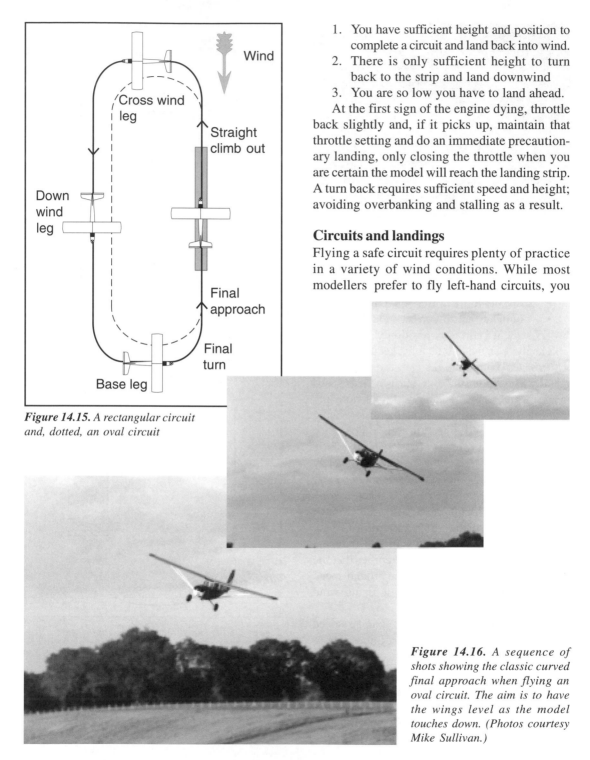

Figure 14.15. A rectangular circuit and, dotted, an oval circuit

1. You have sufficient height and position to complete a circuit and land back into wind.
2. There is only sufficient height to turn back to the strip and land downwind
3. You are so low you have to land ahead.

At the first sign of the engine dying, throttle back slightly and, if it picks up, maintain that throttle setting and do an immediate precautionary landing, only closing the throttle when you are certain the model will reach the landing strip. A turn back requires sufficient speed and height; avoiding overbanking and stalling as a result.

Circuits and landings

Flying a safe circuit requires plenty of practice in a variety of wind conditions. While most modellers prefer to fly left-hand circuits, you

Figure 14.16. A sequence of shots showing the classic curved final approach when flying an oval circuit. The aim is to have the wings level as the model touches down. (Photos courtesy Mike Sullivan.)

184

JUST A LITTLE BIT HIGHER ON FINALS NEXT TIME, BLOGGS!

must practise right-hand ones regularly to avoid becoming 'handed'.

Learn the basic rectangular pattern first. Oval circuits come later. Climbing after take off and with the aircraft safely trimmed out, make a gentle climbing turn to the left through an angle of ninety degrees. Fly for about 100 metres (yards) levelling out at a height of around thirty metres (100 ft) and throttling back to roughly half power. Trim the model again and make a level turn through a further ninety degrees so the model is flying downwind, parallel to the take off direction and about 100 metres from the landing area. When some 100 metres beyond the touchdown point, turn again through ninety degrees, throttling back to idle or just above to establish the model in a glide. Call "landing" to warn other fliers. Just before reaching the extended centre line of the runway, make a gentle descending turn to line up the model with the landing strip.

Remember that on finals, elevator controls the air speed of your model and power controls the rate of descent. Keep asking yourself if your model is high, low, or just right. If high, throttle right back, if low, put on some power. In both cases, adjust the pitch angle of the model to maintain the air speed. As the model reaches a height of about three metres (10 ft), close the

Figure 14.17 On finals, keep thinking "Am I high, low or just right" and apply or reduce power to adjust the flight path if necessary.

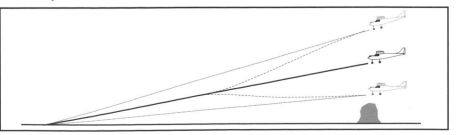

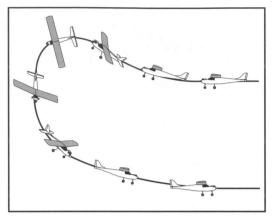

Figure 14.18 *While the wing over is not an aerobatic manoeuvre, learning to do it is a first step to more advanced aerobatics.*

throttle and gently ease back on the elevator, hopefully reducing the rate of descent of the model to zero as the wheels touch the ground.

This does take plenty of practice. If you over-flare, check forward on the elevator to stop the climb and try to flare again. If you've got too much of a climb, or if you touch down and bounce into the air, open the throttle fully, establish a safe climb and try another circuit. You should also go round again if you mess up your final approach.

The time spent on each leg of the circuit depends on the wind speed and direction. For example, you should turn earlier onto your base leg and expect a steeper final approach if the wind is strong.

Basic aerobatics

Aerobatics are manoeuvres which help to build pilot confidence and get you used to recognising and recovering from unusual attitudes.

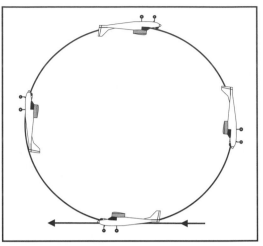

Figure 14.19 *The loop is the easiest aerobatic manoeuvre and most trainers can perform it successfully from level flight with full power.*

However, particularly in the early stages, make sure you have plenty of height before you start any manoeuvre.

The wing over

If you can manage a wing over, you are well equipped to start learning basic aerobatics. The wing over starts from straight and level flight with a reasonable speed and amount of power. It involves pulling the nose up about 30° above the horizon, starting to roll and at the same time releasing the back pressure on the elevator. As the nose drops below the horizon, ease off the bank and pull out of the ensuing dive.

The loop

The aim of the loop is to fly a perfect circle in the vertical plane. This is not as simple as it looks since the air speed of the model will vary around the loop as speed is traded for height. A

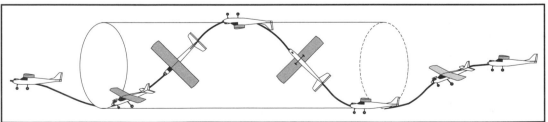

Figure 14.20 *The barrel roll needs co-ordination of control in pitch and roll.*

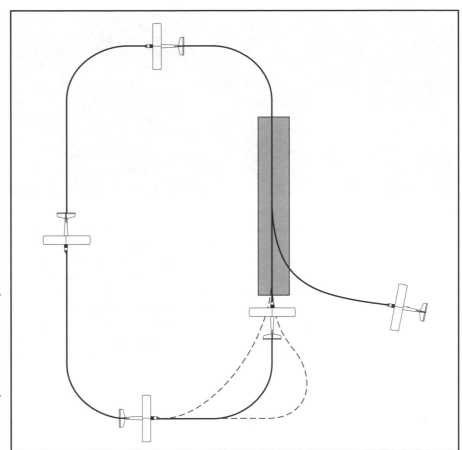

Figure 14.21 If you are carrying out a forced landing, glide overhead the strip, then join the circuit pattern, cutting off or extending the final turn if too low or too high.

loop requires full power and for some models a slight descent prior to entry to build up speed. A smooth pull back on the elevator initiates the loop, and as speed reduces towards the top, you will need more up elevator. Once over the top, a reduction in elevator and throttling back will help to maintain the shape of the manoeuvre.

The barrel roll

A barrel roll starts from a diving turn. You pull up rolling in the opposite direction, into what is in effect a rolling loop. Alter your control deflections to maintain a standard rate of roll and pitch and use the throttle to try to keep a fairly constant air speed.

Unusual attitudes

It is common to panic in the early stages of learning to fly if you find your model in an unusual attitude; pointing vertically upwards with the air speed rapidly reducing. This is why your instructor should put your model into a variety of difficult attitudes and get you to recover to straight and level flight. The key rules are to centralise the control and let the model build up speed with full power if flying slowly. Close the throttle if in a dive, roll the wings level and then use elevator to bring the model back to level flight at the same time setting cruising power.

Forced landing without power.

Having looked at the engine failure after take off, the engine may falter or fail when flying at height and you will be 'dead stick'. Again, throttling back slightly may help the engine to pick up due to the increased suction through

Figure 14.22 The Balsacraft International Hi-boy kit includes instructions on how to fly the model.

the carburettor. Assuming, however, that the engine has died, turn back towards the strip and fly to the overhead. Then circle down until you can safely fly a gliding circuit.

If too high on finals, a snaking pattern helps to lose height, as will diving off height or even better, side slipping. If too low, anticipate the turn onto finals and cut off the corner.

Flying the Hi-boy

If you have built a Hi-boy, the following is an abridged extract from the manufacturer's instructions for flying the model. It is written for those who have no choice but to learn to fly alone.

Choose a reasonable day, without a strong or blustery wind. Run through the pre flight checks. Check all controls respond as they should including the motor.

When satisfied, and assuming the ground is suitable for take offs, release the model into wind and let it gather speed. If it doesn't unstick on its own, apply a gentle touch of up elevator to get it away. If you have to hand launch the model, either you or a helper should run into wind with the model held high. Launch firmly and slightly downwards. Don't throw it like a javelin; it should virtually fly out of your hand.

Let the model climb away, allowing the power do the lifting, not the elevator. Keep the model flying straight into wind until you have 100 metres (300 ft) altitude, then throttle back to about half throttle to maintain that height.

The ideal flight pattern for the early flights is an oblong course, all upwind of you. When the model is well upwind gently apply rudder and as the model begins to turn, ease on a little up elevator to keep the nose up. Between the two you will find you can control the turn. Do not overdo the stick movements. Now flying downwind towards you, and faster of course, turn the model back upwind again before it passes you, and repeat the whole operation again. After about 15 minutes or so of this, get set for the most difficult manoeuvre of all; landing.

Ease back on the power until the model begins to lose height. Fly the same pattern as before. If you feel the model is flying quite fast and losing height quickly, apply a couple of notches of up trim to slow it down. If this is the case perhaps the centre of gravity is too far forward. Try to judge how much height is lost on each leg. In an ideal world the model should be coming towards you about 15 metres (50ft) up and 50 metres (yards) to one side of you.

This time let the model pass you by 100 metres or so, before making the final turn into wind and back towards you. Then it's just a case of keeping the wings level until touchdown. If you misjudge the turning point and the model passes you still quite high up, open the throttle, climb away and try again. Never apply down elevator to shorten the distance you may have to walk to recover the model. It's better to walk 250 metres to pick up a model than 50 to gather up the bits!

Figure 14.23 The Flair Cub lifts off safely at last, but slightly starboard wing low. It is a docile model to fly.

If you are going to teach yourself to fly you may find it helps avoid disorientation if, when the model is flying towards you, you turn your back on it so that it is always over your shoulder. When facing the model, the controls will appear to be reversed as it comes towards you, so that when you push the stick to your left, the model turns to your right.

Mistakes will happen when the model is coming towards you. Try to imagine that your transmitter stick is propping up the wing that drops. For example, the wing on your right drops, so you move the stick to the right to prop the wing up. You may find it helps.

Flying the Cub

If you have built the Cub, the following instructions from the manufacturer start by saying that it is impossible to learn how to fly by reading a few words and no-one should consider it a reasonable option, though a few just may learn by trial and error but most soon become disenchanted with this approach.

The best advice is to join the local club; there is usually one within a reasonable distance. There you will meet people who are well versed in flying and who are usually only too pleased to pass on their knowledge. Your kit supplier should be able to put you in touch with the club.

There are a few things you can do for yourself however, before you ever get near a flying field.

Double check the following items:
1. The balance point or centre of gravity is in the correct position.
2. All the hinges and control runs are secure.
3. When you push the transmitter throttle stick forward, the throttle opens and the servo does not 'stall' at either end of its travel.
4. When you pull the elevator stick back the elevator goes up and the movement each way is correct and unimpeded.
5. When you push the rudder stick to the left the rudder goes left and the movement each way is correct and unimpeded.

It all sounds obvious, but I have seen many sad faces over the years when I have refused to trim out a new creation because of unsafe hinging or control runs. It is also a good idea, but not always practical due to the noise, to run in your engine if it is new and set the throttle for reliable tick over and power before attempting to fly. Give the model a range check with the engine running.

With the Cub facing into wind and up elevator held in, open the throttle. When the model is at a slow walking pace, release the elevator to neutral. After a short time the tail will lift and the model will accelerate to flying speed. During this ground roll it will probably be necessary to apply a small

Figure 14.24 Some limited maintenance can take place at the flying field. This sports MiG 21 is Nexus Plan RC 1472. (Photo courtesy Bill Burkinshaw.)

amount of right rudder to make the model track straight. It will not be long (especially with a 0.40 motor) before flying speed is reached and a hint of up elevator will have it flying.

If you are a beginner, fly high enough to give you thinking time if things start going wrong, but not so high that you cannot see which way it is going. Only execute gentle turns at first, these will only require a small amount of up elevator, if any, to maintain altitude. When landing you will find that your Cub possesses a remarkable glide for a power model! Quite a long approach is required.

Essential maintenance

Your model, like any other piece of machinery, requires regular servicing. This is important as you are dealing with a flying machine. Any failure in the air can have catastrophic results. Maintenance should concentrate on three main areas:

- The airframe.
- The engine and its fuel system.
- The radio and its control linkages.

Each of these three sub-systems requires checking on a regular basis. Checks fall into four broad categories.

Before every flight

- Meter reading OK on the transmitter.
- Aerial fully extended.
- Controls full and free movement.
- Computer set to correct model and rate switches correctly positioned.

Daily

Check the airframe and its control surfaces for obvious signs of damage. Examine the prop and change it if it shows any signs of damage. Make sure you charge the radio batteries as required.

Clean down the model at the end of the flying session carefully removing any oily exhaust residue. A mixture of water and washing-up liquid sprayed on the model is very effective for this task.

Weekly

Check the control surfaces are securely attached to the airframe, the control horns are secure and the clevises are in good condition and closed over the horns. Ensure that the servos are firmly attached to their mounts and that the engine and silencer are still securely bolted in place. Unscrew any fuel filters you use and clean out any debris before screwing them tightly back together again. Check the condition of any elastic bands for holding on the wings, discarding any which show signs of perishing.

Annual or after any major crash

Check the radio system, or have it checked for worn or frayed leads, not forgetting the receiver aerial,

Pilot	Transmitter failure	Clunk weight came off
Disorientation	Receiver failure	Problems with fuel flow
Flew into sun	Flat battery in Tx or Rx	Ran out of fuel
Heavy landing	Flew too long	Prop failure or came off
Flew too far away	Forgot to charge them	Mechanical failure
Radio	Charger problem	**Model**
Someone else transmitting	Battery capacity problem	Control linkage failure
on your frequency	Servo failure	Loose radio equipment
Plug or crystal came out	Mechanical	Hinge failure
Wiring fracture	Electronic	Structural failure
Switch failure	**Engine**	Control flutter
Black wire	Problems with mixture	

Table 14.1 It is important to try to discover why your model crashed.

battery condition and potential black lead on both the transmitter and airborne battery packs. Do the servos operate smoothly with no jitter at neutral and no chipped or broken gear teeth? Clean the transmitter and the airborne equipment. Also, carry out a range check.

Check the engine for wear of the main bearings and for loss of compression. Clean cooling fins with a proprietary cleaner if very dirty. Replace the glow plug. It may look alright but it will not last for ever. Check for oily gunge or other dirt in the fuel tank and the condition of the rubber bung or O-ring seal. Replace if worn or perished and also replace all silicon fuel pipes. Clean out the carburettor by pumping through clean fuel.

Crashes and crash repairs

Everybody crashes their model from time to time. The more experienced and careful you are, the less often these traumatic occasions occur, but sooner or later, they always will. Immediately after a crash, try to discover the cause. The most common reasons are pilot error and poor construction/maintenance of the model. In the first group come crashes caused by disorientation and flying the model too far away, particularly downwind. It can be tough to admit that it's your fault, so do try to be honest with yourself.

In the second category, radio failure is the least likely but most often blamed. A common

problem is the engine stopping either at the worst possible moment or when the model is too far away to reach the strip. Airframe failures are not unusual, particularly the control connections.

What is essential is that no-one touches the wreckage until you have done some basic investigation into the cause of failure. If you have made a mistake as the pilot, admit it and put all the remains in a black bin liner. Remember to turn off the radio. Pull the engine out of the ground carefully without turning the prop and sucking dirt inside the engine.

If it is not pilot error, try to decide exactly what you think happened during the last few seconds of the flight. If the engine cut, is there still fuel in the tank? There may not be if the tank has split on impact. Is the clunk weight still in place?

If you think you had a control failure, try to decide if the damage was a result of the crash or occurred before impact and was the cause of the accident. Lastly, is the radio still working? It is remarkably robust and usually survives, though the battery or some servos may have become unplugged. Was this the cause or the effect of the crash?

When you get home, a full check of the radio will show if it still works. Regardless, if the accident was a bad one, the airborne part of the radio will need a complete checkout, and manufacturers prefer to have your transmitter as well.

Chapter 15 Once you're solo

So, you have gone solo, can carry out a competent take off, circuit and landing as well as doing a basic loop and barrel roll. Where next?

Advanced aerobatics

Most pilots like to explore the performance limits of their model, and there is no better way than by learning advanced aerobatics. Some of these will demand a more advanced model than your basic trainer, ideally a low-wing model. You can start by practising inverted flight. Roll upside down and apply sufficient down elevator to keep level. Your ailerons will work as normal but your elevator function becomes inverted; push forward to raise the nose.

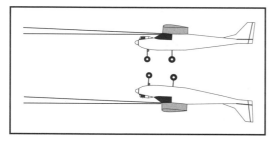

Figure 15.1 The change from upright to inverted flight involves pushing the nose up, when inverted, with down elevator.

Slow roll

A good slow roll is one of the most difficult manoeuvres to perform properly. You must do it slowly, keeping the rate of roll constant without gaining or losing height. Looking at the manoeuvre in detail, from straight and level flight, start the model slowly rolling with aileron. As the model approaches the ninety degree position, you will require some top rudder to stop the nose dropping. This rudder, in opposition to the aileron, means an increased aileron deflection to maintain the roll rate. As the model moves towards the inverted position, neutralise the rudder and consequently reduce the aileron deflection while, at the same time, introducing down elevator to keep the model level. On models with symmetrical aerofoils and a zero/zero set up, you may not need this down elevator.

The second half of the roll is a repeat of the first except that in this half, the top rudder tries to increase the rate of roll so reduce the aileron during the third quarter of the roll. Trying to co-ordinate the inputs of aileron, rudder and elevator demands endless practice to produce a top class slow roll. Most beginners start with a fast aileron roll, which is a good way of getting

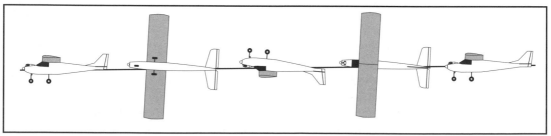

Figure 15.2 A good slow roll requires lots of control co-ordination and a slow but constant rate of roll.

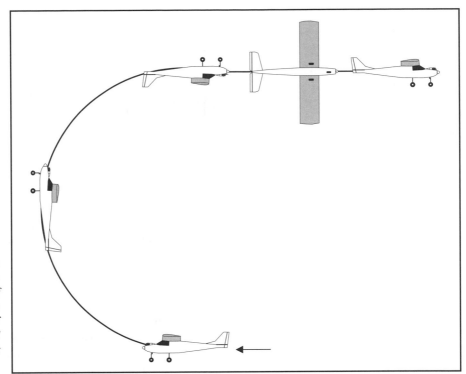

Figure 15.3 A roll off the top needs plenty of speed on entry and full power if you are to avoid barrelling out at the top.

used to the changing attitude of the model, but is miles away from a slow roll.

Hesitation roll

Paradoxically, a hesitation roll is easier to perform than a slow roll. The two most common versions are the four point and the eight point ones. The manoeuvre requires a high rate of roll, which then stops dead every forty-five or ninety degrees, with the appropriate rudder and elevator inputs as these cardinal points are reached. Items which require practice are stopping the roll crisply at each cardinal point and the amount of each of the three primary control inputs needed at each point. Yes, you do need aileron at the 90° and 270° points to counteract the effect of the top rudder.

Flick roll

A successful flick roll requires you to fly the model above the straight and level stalling speed. A rapid input of full up elevator combined with

full rudder should pull the model rapidly into an attitude where one wing is stalled. The model will roll very rapidly in what is the start of a spin. Centralising the controls should stop the roll within half a turn, but judging the right moment so that, say, the aircraft ends up wings level, can be tricky.

Roll off the top

A roll off the top consists of the first half of a loop, followed by the second half of a slow roll. Neither manoeuvre is that hard on its own. The problem is that the speed at the top of the loop is inevitably low, making it hard to achieve the roll from inverted to upright without barrelling out.

Vertical roll

A successful vertical roll demands plenty of speed at entry and a good power to weight ratio to pull the aircraft through the manoeuvre. It starts with the first quarter of a loop, checking to hold the model truly vertical. Then use ailerons

193

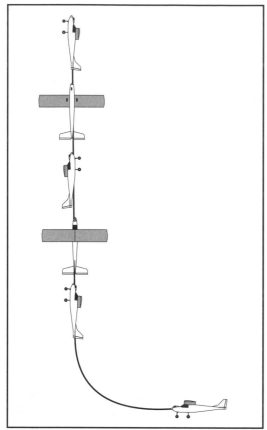

Figure 15.4 *Enter a vertical roll at high speed and full power if you want to complete a full 360° turn.*

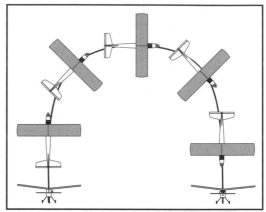

Figure 15.5 *A proper stall turn uses rudder and slip stream to turn the model below the straight and level stalling speed.*

a stall turn gets the aircraft ready for the next manoeuvre.

Derry turn

The Derry turn was named after the de Havilland test pilot killed at Farnborough in the prototype Sea Vixen. John Derry found there were two ways of rolling from a turn in one direction to one in the opposite direction. The first and obvious way was to roll through wings level to the required angle of bank in the opposite direction.

The alternative was to increase the bank and roll through the inverted position until the required angle of bank in the opposite direction was reached. This pretty manoeuvre needs some

to roll at a constant rate, increasing aileron deflection as the speed decays. Counteract any adverse yaw with rudder. At the end of the roll,

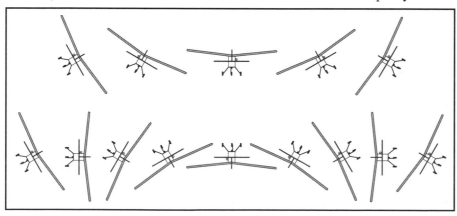

Figure 15.6 *Top; The normal way to change from a right-hand turn to a left-hand one. Bottom; A Derry turn from a left-hand to a right-hand turn via the inverted.*

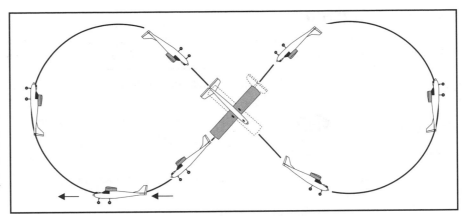

Figure 15.7 The Cuban 8 is a manoeuvre which is easy to fly once you have mastered a roll off the top.

practice, particularly in feeding from up elevator in the turn to down elevator as the model passes through the inverted.

Stall turn

The stall turn is a delightful way of turning a model through 180°. Pull the aircraft from level flight through the first quarter of a loop and hold it climbing vertically. As the speed reduces to zero, kick in full rudder and close the throttle. As the model yaws through 180°, stop any roll with aileron. A dab of opposite rudder will stop the model pointing vertically down so that you

can then ease it out of the ensuing dive back to straight and level flight.

Cuban 8

A Cuban 8 follows the shape of an eight on its side, in the vertical plane. You can either pull up into a forty-five degree climb, roll the aircraft inverted and pull through, repeating for the second half of the eight or alternatively pull through three-quarters of a loop until descending inverted at forty-five degrees nose down, roll upright and pull out of the dive straight into the second three-quarter loop and roll.

.. NOW THATS WHAT I CALL A CUBAN EIGHT !

Before a first flight

Alright, you've gone solo and have become proficient in flying. You can do basic aerobatics and you've probably got your BMFA 'A' certificate. You've just completed a new model and decided that you are going to undertake the first

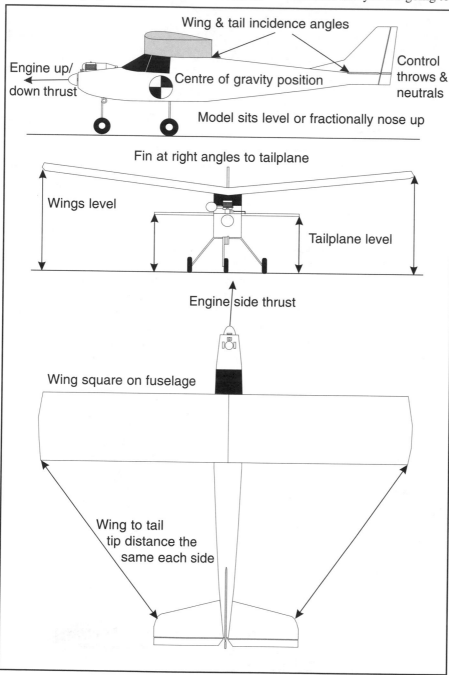

Figure 15.8 Before the first flight of any new model, you must make a number of checks.

I'M TRYING TO FIND THE CENTRE OF GRAVITY...
... I'M TOLD THAT IT'S IMPORTANT!!

flight yourself. Before the maiden flight of any new model, it is vital to make a number of checks to minimise the risk of problems.

Balance

The most important single factor in ensuring the safe first flight of a new model is to locate the centre of gravity in the correct position. This will be marked on the plan. If for any reason this is not so, contact the kit supplier/plan designer to find out the right position. **Too far back and the model will be uncontrollable, even by the most experienced pilot, reacting so rapidly to any control input that a crash is only seconds away from lift off/launch.**

Have I caught your eye? Read the highlighted sentence again and be sure that it never happens to one of your models. Too far forward and the model may refuse to take off or sink into the ground after launch despite full up elevator. In less severe cases, you may need lots of up elevator for level flight, with a sluggish response in the pitching plane.

Of the two, a centre of gravity that is too far forward is an inconvenience; too far back is fatal.

Ballasting the model to achieve the correct centre of gravity may increase the wing loading, but without the ballast, the chances of a successful first flight are low.

Many people forget to balance a model laterally as well. A small amount of weight in the wing tip, if required, can avoid lateral balance problems such as crooked loops.

Rigging

It is all too easy to end up with the wing or tail not parallel or at right angles to each other. Carefully check the rigging of any new model in all three dimensions. In addition, ensure the wing and tail incidences are correct and the angle the model sits on the ground is right. Finally, check the up/down and side thrust of the engine and the controls at neutral are in line with their main surfaces.

Checking the weight

Once the model is complete, make a final check of the all-up weight. Kitchen scales are ideal for smaller models, normally coping with up to 2.5 kg (5½lb). Above this weight, a spring balance or bathroom scales both offer a capability up to maximum likely weights. This check will confirm how close your model is to the weight quoted by the designer. It is worth remembering that if the weight is over 7kg (15.4lb), a fail safe and a CAA exemption certificate are legal requirements, not that your early models should be anywhere near this limit.

Control throws
Check all controls move in the correct sense, with aileron the most likely to be accidentally connected up in reverse. The amount of movement required should be as indicated on the plan. Don't forget the prop wash over some controls and their likely change of effectiveness if the engine stops halfway through a flight.

The use of rates
Probably the best way to overcome the difficulty in achieving the right control throws is to use the rate switches now fitted to most transmitters. A large throw with the ability to reduce it after take off if the control proves too effective can both calm your nerves and prevent catastrophe on that heart-stopping first flight.

Choosing the propeller
To find the best propeller to suit your new model you should look at the list of engine manufacturer's recommended prop sizes. There is normally a range of diameters and pitches. The question is which one is right for your model. Think about what type of model you have built to get an idea of how fast it will fly. In order of increasing top speed are typically:
- Biplanes.
- High-wing trainers.
- Low-wing trainers.
- Aerobatic models.
- Pylon racers.

The faster your model is likely to fly, the coarser pitch of prop you need. The exception is a model with a large radial cowl, where sufficient prop diameter is the key criteria.

The best take off and climb performance is achieved at the cost of top speed. A fine pitch propeller, say 10cm (4in) pitch, will provide a better take off performance than a coarser pitch prop.

A final important point is that a large prop turning at low revs is much more efficient and quieter than a small one turning at high speed.

Taxying trials
Opening up the motor and taxying your brand new model around the flying field can give a first indication of some of the handling characteristics. It will also show if your mainwheels are pointing straight forward.

For a tail dragger in particular, it will immediately highlight any tendency to nose over or ground loop, either of which may suggest a change in location of the mainwheels before the first flight. It will also give some indication of the effectiveness of the rudder and the elevator.

The first flight of a new model
If possible, try to choose a day for the first flight when the weather is fine and there is a light to moderate breeze blowing down the strip, if your flying field boasts such a thing. It is also preferable that no-one else is flying at the time, since this will make it easier to hear and subsequently deal with any engine cut.

Controllability
From the pilot's point of view, variation in the centre of gravity position is apparent from the amount of stick movement necessary to displace the aircraft from its trimmed attitude. With a forward centre of gravity, your elevator stick movements will be fairly large.

With an aft position, stick movements must be much more gentle. Level flight may be impossible to maintain. The centre of gravity is in roughly the right position when you can use the elevator to change the attitude of the model slightly, centralise it and the aircraft remains in this new attitude.

Take off	Swing direction	Use of rates	Elevator
	Length of run		Aileron
Stability in	Pitch	Trims	Elevator
	Roll		Aileron
	Yaw		Rudder
Control in	Pitch	Motor	Peak power OK
	Roll		Idling OK
	Yaw		Side/up/down thrust

Table 15.1 Factors you should review after the first flight of a new model.

If you have the misfortune to experience flutter in flight, close the throttle immediately, level the model and land. Any delay is likely to lead to a catastrophic structural failure, should this not already have occurred. Chapter 8 gives details of how to avoid a recurrence of flutter.

Stall characteristics

Establish the stall characteristics of a new model early in your flight test programme. The inability to enter a stall may indicate the centre of gravity is too far forward or simply a lack of elevator power. The type of stall, sudden and sharp or just a mushy descent will depend on the aerofoil section used, the wing planform and the degree of longitudinal stability.

A sudden wing drop at the stall may indicate an unmatched pair of wings, an aircraft which is poorly rigged, a lack of lateral balance or one which has a low margin of stability. It may also result in the model entering a spin.

Spinning and spin recovery

Eventually, try to enter a spin and then recover. Entry should be possible with full up elevator, full rudder and the engine at tick-over, unless the model is very stable. Recovery by releasing the controls is usually effective, but you may need opposite rudder and down elevator on a relatively unstable design. In such cases, you may find a burst of power to increase the slipstream over the controls helps.

The first landing

This is where the adrenaline starts pumping. Assuming you have tried a stall, you will have a warning of any unpleasant vices, as well as an indication of the stalling speed. Keep the speed above the stall and plan to land in the middle of the strip. Hold off just above the ground and then lower the model to a safe touchdown.

Assessing flight performance

Once safely back on the ground, nerves take over. While you relax and congratulate yourself, run through the following points in your mind.

What changes to make

After making an assessment, and only then, consider making changes to the centre of gravity and control neutrals/throws before undertaking a second flight. For many aircraft, it takes several flights to try a full range of manoeuvres and get all the characteristics sorted out. The basic rule is only to make one change at a time to correct any particular problem. Otherwise, it is very difficult to establish which change affected the improvement.

Side and down thrust

If the elevator or rudder trims need adjusting with throttle changes, alter the thrust line of the engine. Adding down thrust to an upright or inverted motor presents no problem using washers. Side thrust changes mean modifying the engine bearer plate or bearers themselves. The latter is very difficult. Alterations to side-winder engines are, of course, the opposite in such a procedure (i.e. washers for side thrust). If using a radial mount, it's plain sailing; washers in the appropriate corners will do the trick.

Control neutrals and throws

If, when you land your model, you find that the trims on your transmitter are not central, you

Figure 15.9.
Near the end of a
successful first
flight. This model
is beautifully
positioned for
touchdown.

should lengthen or shorten the control connection until you achieve the control position when you landed but with the trims at neutral.

It may be that any or all of the controls are either too sensitive or not responsive enough. Increasing or decreasing the throws is a straight-forward remedy.

Centre of gravity position

Over-sensitivity in the pitching plane usually means that the centre of gravity is too far aft. A reluctance to lift off and the need for plenty of up elevator suggests the centre of gravity is too far forward. Use lead ballast in the nose or tail to shift the centre of gravity some 3mm (1/8") at a time and then fly the model again to see if you have improved the situation.

Recovering the model

Always, write your name and address on every model you build. It's only too easy to have a flyaway, particularly if your model is stable, as every trainer should be, and you forget to turn on the radio. Radio failure can also cause a flyaway, and with a cruising speed downwind of some 80kph (50mph) and a full tank, the model can easily travel over fifteen kilometres (ten miles).

The other way to lose a model is to fly into the top of a tree. It is easily done, as distance judgement is difficult, even for experienced pilots.

So, your model is caught in the top of a tree. There are several ways of getting it down. The best, if the tree is suitable, is for an accomplished climber with a line to lower the model safely to the ground. You may need a ladder to start the climb. The next alternative is a fishing line with a lead weight on the end. This is swung in a vertical circle and released at the appropriate moment to carry it over the model. With this line, you can haul up a stronger one and then use it to shake the branch and dislodge your model. An arrow is equally suitable if you or a friend are an archer.

Lost model alarm

An electronic lost model alarm, plugged into any spare channel, will emit a piercing noise when your transmitter is off. This is a boon when searching for a model which you have accidentally landed in a wood or field with a tall crop.

Chapter 16 Getting more advanced

Controls for advanced models

Some designs employ additional control surfaces, such as flaps or airbrakes to improve performance. Variations in the design of existing controls may occur, such as the use of all-moving tailplanes instead of elevators. You can mix two control functions together to provide elevons, flapperons, V or butterfly tails. Retractable undercarriages may replace fixed ones.

When flying a model equipped with airbrakes, flaps or retracts, the change of trim when you operate these is hard to predict. Particularly with flaps, raising them can cause your model to sink rapidly unless you raise the nose to increase the angle of attack of the wing.

Airbrakes

Airbrakes are commonly fitted to gliders to allow them to increase their rate of descent when coming in to land. They are less commonly employed on powered aircraft. They are usually found fitted to the wing at about one-third chord or at the trailing edge. Split rudders provide a similar function.

Figure 16.2 overleaf shows two of the more popular types of wing-mounted airbrakes. The first uses plates which hinge out of the wings. The second features a scissors mechanism to lift the airbrake. You can make the airbrakes themselves from balsa sheet or ply, but you must make them sufficiently stiff not to distort when deployed in the airstream. Alternatively, you can purchase ready-made plastic airbrakes.

When using a split rudder as an airbrake, you will need two mixed channels for correct operation. Two rudders are built, usually from sheet balsa, and hinged side by side at the rear of the fin. They operate in unison for the rudder function and in opposite directions to give an airbrake effect. There is not much room for hinging and it is essential that the rudders do not foul each other when working together in rudder mode.

Figure 16.1 This Wot 4 has trailing edge airbrakes fitted to the inboard sections of the wing.

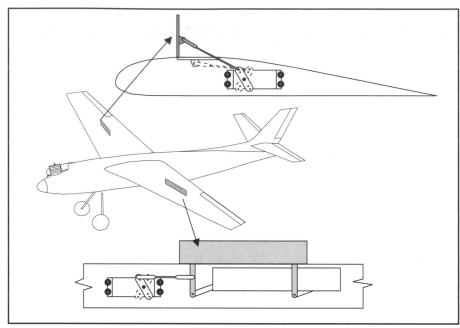

Figure 16.2 It is normal to mount airbrakes in the outer section of the wing. Two popular solutions involve either hinging up the airbrake (top sketch) or a scissors mechanism (lower diagram).

Airbrakes are still a fairly unusual item on any powered aircraft, apart from scale jet models, but they can prove necessary with any high-powered low drag design, as well as providing some interest during construction.

Spoilers as ailerons

The construction of spoilers for use as ailerons is exactly the same as for wing-mounted airbrakes, although they are usually located further outboard. Naturally they are connected up so that only one deploys at a time.

Flaps

The use of flaps can add to the enjoyment of flying and allow you to carry out realistic STOL (short take off and landing) manoeuvres. Flaps primarily increase lift, reducing the stalling speed of a model and enabling it to fly more slowly than is otherwise possible. Flaps are no more difficult to build and install than ailerons.

Flaps are fitted to the inboard section of the trailing edge of each wing. They move in unison to alter the camber of the wing, increasing

Figure 16.3 This model of an Armstrong Whitworth Whitley is fitted with split flaps. It is also a model which would make an ideal first scale twin.

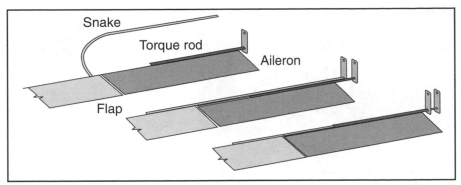

Figure 16.4 If you use outboard ailerons with inboard flaps, there are several ways of organising the control connections.

lift and also increasing drag. They are particularly useful in reducing take off and landing runs, as well as in allowing a steeper approach to landing. Sometimes the flap function is provided by drooping strip ailerons, using a mixing function on the ailerons and flaps (flapperons).

You can construct simple flaps and hinge them in a very similar way to ailerons. There is only one possible problem and that concerns the use of torque rods for both flaps and ailerons. In this case, a concentric tube-based system is usually the best. The alternative is to use snakes to the outboard ailerons or to use strip ailerons with a mixed aileron/flap function.

Split flaps must be thin to recess smoothly into the under surface of the wing. The use of ply or liteply, possibly with thin reinforcing strips to prevent warping, provides an easy solution.

All-moving tails

All-moving tails are usually made in two halves joined with a pair of steel rods, one acting as the pivot and the other the actuating arm. The tail must be securely attached to the fuselage or fin. Exactly the same rules apply for an all-moving fin.

Elevons

The construction of elevons is virtually identical to that of elevators and ailerons. The use of elevons, however, requires a mixer, now

Figure 16.5 A scale Folland Gnat ready for take off with 30° flaps selected. (Photo courtesy Rupert Weiss.)

Figure 16.6 The Bernhard B2 features an all-moving tailplane as well as an all-moving fin. (Photo courtesy Alex Stalley.)

Figure 16.7 *There is little choice but to use elevons on this type of flying wing to control pitch and roll.*

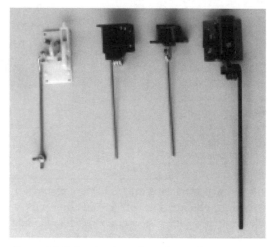

Figure 16.8 *A selection of mechanical retract units requiring a powerful retract servo for operation.*

a common option on most transmitters. For those without this facility, an on-board electronic or mechanical mixer is what you need. Both of these items are easily obtained from model shops.

Retracts

A retractable undercarriage makes most models look better in the air and allows them to fly faster by reducing drag. The additional complexity and the need for a smooth surface for take off and landing, as well as the ability to land accurately, make retracts the domain of the scale modeller and the competitive aerobatics flier.

Retracts are either operated by compressed air, a powerful retract servo or, occasionally by an electric motor driving a long rod and moving nut. Retracts require a good solid wood block mounting, roomy wheel wells to allow for unexpected fore and aft bending of

a leg on take off or landing, some springing to absorb landing impacts and easy access for maintenance.

Pusher engines

A pusher engine has snags and advantages. There is a lack of exhaust goo over the airframe. However, there is no prop wash over the controls on take off/landing and a risk of the prop touching the ground during these manoeuvres, when the nose of the model is high. A typical installation is shown in Figure 9.17.

Scale and semi-scale modelling

Most people consider flying scale model aircraft as the ultimate challenge. Certainly, as experience is gained, you may well feel the urge to build

Figure 16.9 The pilot calls 'Finals three greens' Only the size of the prop gives away this as a model of the Mustang. (Photo courtesy Mike Sullivan.)

models which look more like the real thing. You can go the whole hog and build a model where you replicate every single rivet or stitch attaching a fabric covering to the wing. Particularly when starting in scale, there is a lot of attraction to a semi-scale model. Semi-scale means that after a single glance at the model, everyone will say that is a Spitfire, Hurricane or whatever it is. However, many compromises will allow you to complete a model more quickly which will also prove easier to fly.

There is nothing fundamentally different about a scale model, but there are a number of important issues. First, adequate detail and a scale finish is likely to make the model heavier than the equivalent sports model. It will also take significantly longer to build.

Second, should the model crash, there is more work in repair. Finally, for a faithful scale model, there may be a number of difficulties such as the need for a fully enclosed engine and silencer, a small tail area or sharply tapered wing planform, all of which may endow the model with less than perfect flight handling characteristics.

Most people will try to replicate flaps and retracts when they are fitted to the original aeroplane, while cockpit detail and a credible flight crew are considered essential ingredients.

Figure 16.10 The magnificent air operated retracting noseleg on Richard Crapp's Northrop Black Widow.

Figure 16.11 A de Havilland Tiger Moth taxies out. Evocative of the 1930s era, this aircraft is high on the priority list of many modellers.

Figure 16.12 At last you can build the model of your dreams, a Supermarine Spitfire complete with retracts, flaps and fully cowled engine. (Photo courtesy D.B. Sport & Scale.)

Various categories are worthy of consideration. Do you prefer military or civil aircraft? Is your interest in the period before 1914, the First World War, the inter-war period, the Second World War, post-war propeller aircraft or post-war jets? Do you have the flying site and skills to fly a model fitted with retract? Are you tempted by a multi-engined model?

You must choose an aircraft you wish to model and then overcome the hurdles that scale modelling presents. A visit to a museum to see the real thing is a great advantage and you should take plenty of photographs. The sense of satisfaction when your model gets airborne is fantastic.

Model jets

One of the most exciting forms of scale modelling is building and flying jets. There are plenty of kits and plans for near scale jets with tractor or pusher propellers which vanish into near invisibility once the model is in the air. They fly fast and well, providing a convincing replica of a jet.

There is, however, something missing when viewed from close up on the ground. The prop is always visible, and often the engine/silencer combination as well.

While the ultimate is to power such a model with a turbojet, such engines are still very expensive. A somewhat cheaper solution is to use

Figure 16.13 This early full size World War I Fokker Eindekker was spotted at the Farnborough airshow.

Figure 16.14 In this near scale model of the Northrop Tigershark only the prop gives away the fact that it is conventionally powered, since the engine and silencer are hidden within the jet pipe.

a ducted fan driven by a specially designed racing engine. Turning at 20,000 rpm and more, ducted fans can be powered by anything from a 0.25 (4cc) producing more than 750 watts (one horsepower) to 0.90 (15cc) in the 4 kilowatts (five horsepower) class.

Although there are some plans for built-up balsa wood models, the vast majority are assembled from glass fibre and foam wing kits. Almost invariably being scale models, retracts, airbrakes and flaps are a must and these models are neither cheap to build or fly. Furthermore, the inevitable vibration associated with a high revving engine will not help the life of the items of the airborne radio. However, do not be put off. The rewards of flying such models make it a well worthwhile branch of the hobby.

Ducted fan engines

The relative inefficiency of a ducted fan installation and the need to fly a model jet at a reasonably fast speed means that ducted fan engines have to produce a great deal of power for their size, making them into the racing motors of the hobby. Some engines produce as much power as 470 watts (350 bhp) per litre. This is up to Formula One motor racing standards! You must install such engines really securely and

Figure 16.15 What could be better than a 1950s North American F86 Sabre, the outstanding fighter of the Korean War. (Photo courtesy Jim Fox.)

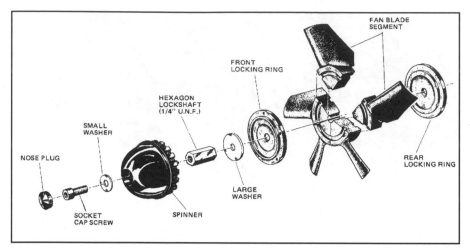

Figure 16.16 The Chart MM ducted fan unit suits 0.40/0.45cu in (6.5/7.5cc) engines and comes complete with ring and stator components. (Photo courtesy Chart.)

glow plug life tends to be relatively short due to the high revs. Their consumption of high nitro content fuel is prodigious, demanding large tanks, often in pairs to fit into available space.

Ducted fan models

While many people have happily started their ducted fan careers flying a Hawk built from balsa and ply, the vast majority choose the fibre glass kit route. While there are some spectacular non-scale ducted fan models, such as the Aggressor, which are designed with outright speed and aerobatic capability in mind, for the majority, the ability to produce a true scale model of a jet aircraft is the main attraction. Glass fibre kits offer superb detail moulded into the airframe

which is strong yet relatively light. Internal space is one of the key factors in these models. As well as the radio and engine, you need space for the air intake ducts, jet pipe and retracts. Many full size prototypes feature twin intake ducts on the sides of the fuselage, leaving space in the forward section for the radio. Others, like the F16 with its characteristic underside air intake, still have a spacious forward fuselage. You can even build and fly models with nose intakes like the MiG 15, the F86 Sabre and F100 Super Sabre without difficulty.

Turbojet engines

Many dream about owning a turbojet, but few are prepared to stand the expense, particularly

Figure 16.17 The fan units are clearly visible in this shot of Chris Gold's magnificent four engined Concorde.

as flying it means a significant chance of having a crash. A few people build their own motors to published designs, and the same is true of piston engines. However, prices are reducing, and turbojets revving in the region of 100,000 rpm are now on the market for £1,250. Turbojets are generally powered either by propane or a liquid fuel such as kerosene or even vehicle diesel fuel. They require great care if you are to operate them safely. There are three risk areas.

The first is that over-revving the engine can lead to the rotor exploding, with catastrophic results. The second is that these engines operate at high temperatures and use large quantities of volatile fuel. Fire is always a risk and safety measures, including a suitable fire extinguisher, are essential. Finally, almost by definition, any turbojet powered model is likely to be comparatively large and fly fast. You need to be a very experienced pilot to fly a jet, particularly as the damage they can cause on impact is very significant.

Turbojet models

Most ducted fan kits can be converted to turbojet operation and a number of manufacturers offer a jet conversion kit for their designs. The main

Figure 16.18 This superb MiG 29 flies as well as it looks. (Photo courtesy Jim Fox.)

requirements of conversion are to cope with the enormous fuel consumption and to provide adequate heat insulation between the jet pipe and the fuselage body.

Figure 16.19 The real thing. This model turbojet is the Weston UK Scorpion giving roughly 44 newtons (10lb) of thrust at 100,000 rpm.

Figure 16.20 It sits ready for another run of its turbojet engine. This is a model of the de Havilland 108 Swallow, the first British aircraft to fly faster than sound.

Vintage

The construction and flying of designs which date from before 1950 is the basis of vintage flying. Most of these models are modified to allow you to fit some degree of radio control. The obsessional will also fit vintage engines, though the availability of replica engines can help in this area.

Vintage models are invariably builders' models, involving complex wooden structures for all the main components of the airframe. Some kits are available, though the majority of modellers in this area rely on plans which can still be purchased from Nexus Special Interests.

Vintage models fly slowly and sedately. They would be suitable for the beginner were it not for the complexity involved in building them and the difficulty of repair in the case of an accident. They are, nevertheless, particularly well suited to learners who are happy to spend plenty of time at the building board.

Snow and water

Flying off snow requires you to build skis and have them ready to fit before any snow falls as, in the UK, snow rarely lasts more than a few days. You can fit floats to most trainers if you end up wanting to fly off water.

Figure 16.21 The Junior 60 is a classic vintage design, in this case powered by a PAW diesel engine.

Figure 16.22 These floats, fitted to a Flair Cub, are foam cored veneer and provide excellent buoyancy. (Photo courtesy Flair.)

Skis

A pair of skis is easily produced from a few pieces of thin plywood. Ideally, the skis will plug in as a replacement for a conventional undercarriage. You can make them roughly 200mm long per kilogram of weight (4" per lb). Coat them well with paint or varnish and fuel proofer. Rubbing some candle wax on the underside before take off will certainly help your model to slip more easily over the snow.

Floats

While you can fit skis at a moment's notice, flying off water requires considerably more

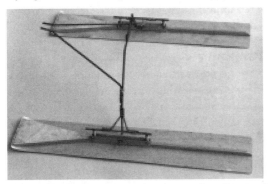

Figure 16.23 If you are going to try skis on one of your models, you must complete them well before the arrival of snow.

forethought. You should build the model using waterproof glue. Neither the normal PVA nor cyanos fall into this category. You can fit floats to most models and purchase a pair to suit your size of model.

Learning to fly off water involves some different skills. First, of course, it is usually impossible to stand behind the model during take off and the landing may be some distance away from where you are standing. Secondly, the model will try to weathercock into any wind and will also continually drift downwind and downstream if its speed is low before take off and after landing.

Figure 16.24 In a steep turn, this Catalina amphibian shows off its hull shape and retracts.

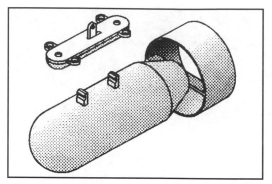

Figure 16.25 A bomb you can fill with flour and drop from its release mechanism. (Picture courtesy Flair.)

Next, it is essential that you can rely on your engine not to cut, as you cannot just walk over and fetch the model back. You will have to learn how to get the model up onto its step before take off. There are also a number of nautical terms you will come across such as bow, stern, beam and freeboard. You can, of course, also build a flying boat from scratch.

Payload carrying

You can get added fun from carrying anything from a camera to a parachutist in your latest model. The issues to face are first that any additional load will increase the all-up weight of the model and its wing loading. Thus, the most desirable characteristics of the model are that it should be reasonably large and have a low wing loading.

Still camera

The two main options for locating a still camera in a model are to fit it looking out of the side of the fuselage, or to put it in the nose of a pusher design. It is essential to insulate the camera from engine vibration and damage should the model crash.

The ideal camera is one with an automatic wind on, which allows you to take more than one photograph each flight. Automatic exposure control is most desirable though auto focus is not essential as most pictures will be taken at the maximum focal distance of the camera. These are now reasonably affordable as well as being quite compact and lightweight. You can attach a servo to the camera with double-sided tape so that the servo arm triggers the shutter.

Video camera

Modern lightweight video cameras can provide thrilling pictures, providing you are prepared to put such a valuable piece of equipment in the air. You will need a relatively vibration-free model with an adequate space to carry your camera. As with a fixed camera, you can point it sideways, but if you want it in the nose, you will almost certainly be looking at a pusher configuration.

Bombs

Bombs can be home-made, or purchased as ready-made items from companies such as Balsacraft International/SLEC. You can fill a hollow two-piece bomb with flour or talcum powder to give a realistic puff of smoke on impact. Do not, under any circumstances, think about using explosives. It is both dangerous and illegal. You should connect the mount under the fuselage or wings to a servo for release.

Toffees

Providing there is room in the fuselage, you can carry a substantial number of sweets in a toffee bomber. It is more fun for the children on the receiving end, and safer for them, if a small streamer of ribbon is tied to each sweet. You will have to build a servo-operated hatch to release your payload.

Parachutists

Action Man is probably the most popular figure in R/C parachuting circles and you can dress him in a realistic outfit. You can easily make a parachute from a suitable circle of coloured nylon and some thin nylon chord, not forgetting to make a hole in the centre to provide a stable descent. Carefully fold the chute and tuck it between the parachutist and the underside of the fuselage, retaining it in place with an elastic band connected to a servo-operated release.

Figure 16.26 You can try to copy Nick Chambers, who indulges in a bit of hovering with his fun flier. (Photo courtesy Parc-Amber.)

Fun fliers

This class of model is designed to complete manoeuvres which are outrageously beyond the capability of any full size aircraft. The key characteristics of these models are:

* Low aspect ratio wing.
* Low wing loading.
* Large tail surfaces.
* Short fuselage.
* Large control surfaces with large throws.
* Relatively low power engine.

They can turn on a dime, hover and carry out any aerobatic manoeuvre you care to name.

Pylon racing

For many, the competitive urge to race leads them quickly to pylon racing. There are several classes, some better suited to beginners than others. From Quiet 500 via Club 20 and Sport 40 to the fastest F3D class run under FAI rules, there are classes to suit your experience and pocket. Whichever class you enter you will require

Figure 16.27 The Shark 40 is a sport 40 pylon racing model and is well streamlined for best top speed. (Photo courtesy Flair.)

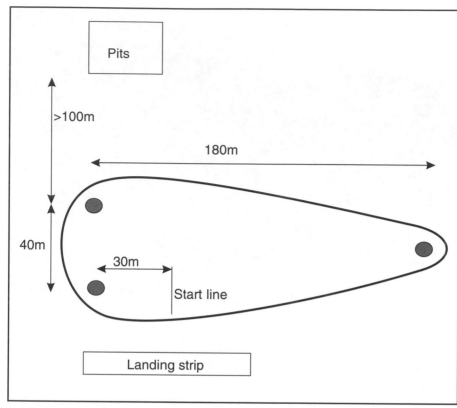

Figure 16.28 A pylon racing course is a triangular shape with the positions carefully defined.

a fast model matched to a racing engine. The engine must be of a particular make and out of the box in some classes, highly tuned in others.

Races are normally run for ten laps with severe penalties for cutting any of the three pylons laid out in a triangular course 180 metres long and 40 metres wide.

Rules governing models include such areas as fuselage and wing sizes, size of engine, type of prop and fuel, aircraft configuration and use of landing gear. You will need a hard hat, alternative radio crystals, some cash to cover entry fees and to pre-enter the event. Racing is highly competitive but great fun.

Figure 16.29 A trio of Regal Eagles, 1930s style racers, largely built from a kit of card and foam board. (Photo courtesy Paper Aviation.)

Figure 16.30 Saphir 40 is a classic competitive aerobatic model. (Photo courtesy Malcolm Corbin.)

Aerobatic pattern flying

The ability to fly an advanced sequence of aerobatic manoeuvres requires endless practice of the required schedule in the right type of model. It also requires a high level of skill and reactions.

A low-wing aerobatic model will feature a symmetrical wing and a zero/zero set up; that is no side or down thrust for the engine and the wing and tailplane both set at zero angle of incidence. A powerful engine, allied to a reasonable weight is essential to pull the model through a range of vertical aerobatic manoeuvres. You will have to spend quite a lot of time setting up the model to fly perfectly. Competitions are held each year with a high standard at the national level, less so at the club events.

Exhibition flying

Before you fly for a money paying public, you need a BMFA 'B' certificate, a reliable, well-proven model and plenty of flying experience. You also need to understand that under no circumstances may you ever fly over the crowd. If you get into difficulties, you must be prepared to fly your model into the ground, regardless of the damage it may incur, rather than risk landing in the crowd. Add to this the natural nerves that apply when performing in public and you will see why you need plenty of experience as well as plenty of practice flying your chosen model.

The event where you are going to fly may be anything from a fete or school open day to one of the major modelling shows. It goes without

Figure 16.31 You need to understand the aerobatic symbols: 1. Take off. 2. Pull vertical ¼ roll one way, ¾ roll opposite, push, 2/4 points down, pull to level. 3. Pull 45° 4/8 pt, ½ square loop to level, 4. 4 point roll. 5. ½ loop, roll off top to inverted.

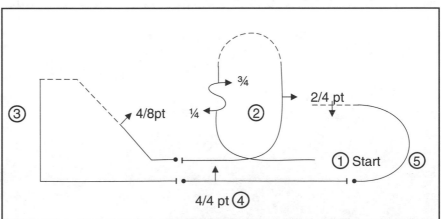

Figure 16.32 Preparation for an exhibition or competition flying requires an immaculate model and lots of practice. (Photo courtesy Malcolm Corbin.)

saying that there must be adequate crowd and transmitter control. You will need to practise a 'schedule' for several weeks before the event and ensure that you can fly it in either direction from where you stand. Never be tempted to add any unpractised manoeuvres on the day.

Make sure you arrive in plenty of time with everything you need. Regular performers have lists to ensure that nothing vital is left at home. If, and only if the weather is suitable, then you should make a final and careful check of your model before you are cleared to start your engine on time for your part of the programme. Safely airborne, complete your schedule, land and switch off. You can then analyse what went right and possibly, what was less than perfect.

Competitions

For many people, it's not the winning that matters, rather just taking part. Competing offers a number of advantages to the participants. It tends to improve the construction and flying ability of all who attend, both by watching what other people are doing and learning from chatting to them. Competitions are friendly events where like-minded people can while away a happy day. Travelling to and from competitions can be a pain. On the other hand the chance to travel to new venues can be a joy, all of its own.

Club competitions

Most clubs run competitions and these often include ones for near beginners. Contests include spot landing, timed landings from throttle closed, limbo, best finish, best scale model, most improved beginner and so on. It is important you realise that competition gets the adrenaline flowing and may make you take unreasonable risks with your model, ending up with a dustbin liner crash. On the other hand, competing will improve your ability, whether in building or flying, and can provide a great deal of pleasure both for competitors and spectators.

National competitions

Anyone with a B certificate can enter the nationals. You don't have to be an ace. In fact, it

Figure 16.33 The Loaded Dice aircraft of Terry Westrop, who has been four times National and British Aerobatic Champion.

is one of the best ways of improving the quality of your flying and your ability to win awards. It is always daunting to be the newcomer at your first nationals, but you will find many of the experts featured in articles in the modelling press are pleasant approachable people who are only too anxious to help you.

You should carefully study the rules as you can always use them to gain the maximum marks on the one hand, while on the other neglecting to meet them in any respect is likely to lose you marks.

Be prepared to show your insurance and B certificates and expect to have to leave your transmitter in the pound except when your turn comes to fly. Then, you will have only a short time to start up and get airborne.

Make sure you know exactly what manoeuvres you are going to carry out and that your caller and yourself have had plenty of practice. It is easy to become disorientated at a strange flying field and end up flying your manoeuvres not directly in front of the judges. This will always lose you marks. Hopefully you will not end up with the lowest score on your first attempt and will quickly find you improve as you compete in more and more events.

International competitions

To attend a competition such as Top Gun as a spectator can be thrilling. To attend as a competitor requires a climb up the competition ladder until an invitation drops through the front door. To represent your country at an international contest will involve you in a national fly off against intense competition.

All international competitions involve significant travel and the expense of accommodation unless you can take your own tent or caravan. The standards are high, even for the national qualifying events, and to get to the top requires exceptional dedication and practice.

Figure 16.34 A twin-engined model like this B26 presents many challenges both in terms of building and flying.

Chapter 17 Gliders

Gliders have a number of special appeals; their quietness, the struggle against gravity, learning to read the weather and achieve the desired flight performance. Many gliders are fitted with airbrakes to allow you to vary their rate of descent. The two main types of gliding are slope soaring and thermal soaring. As the titles suggest, the former takes place on top of a hill with the wind blowing at right angles to the side of the hill. The latter involves finding areas of rising air caused by the heat of the sun.

There are two main differences when building gliders as opposed to powered models. First high aspect ratio wings generally take longer to assemble and second, the space for radio equipment in the fuselage is invariably limited to maintain a streamlined shape.

Thermal gliders

Thermals are typically generated by corn fields, areas of tarmac and the roofs of buildings. On suitable days this thermal activity results in 'cotton wool' clumps of cumulus cloud outlined against a blue sky.

To climb in a thermal, a glider needs to be efficient in terms of generating lift and minimising drag. Thus, high aspect ratio wings between 12:1 and 20:1 are normal. Fuselages are well streamlined, and both of these factors reduce drag.

The main concern with thermal gliders is to get them to sufficient height to allow you time to find a thermal. The main methods involve the use of a tow line, either pulled by a friend or a winch, a length of bungee rubber included in the tow line,

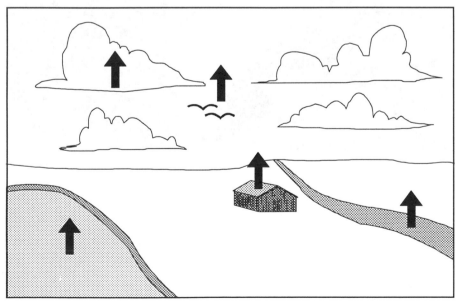

Figure 17.1 Learn where thermals are generated and watch the birds. Where they are circling, you too will find thermal lift. You will also find lift over cornfields, tarmac, barn roofs and where there is cumulus cloud.

Figure 17.2 A classic thermal glider. This is Flair's Sunrise which spans 2500mm (98.5").

or the use of a small internal combustion or electric motor.

Bungee

The use of bungee or Hi Start is ideal if you fly alone. The height at release is normally less than with a hand tow because most of the bungee part of the line un-tensions before the tow ring will slide off the hook, unless you manoeuvre fairly violently to release the hook from the model.

If you use an R/C releasable tow hook, such as that illustrated in Figure 17.4 overleaf, you can usually release your model under tension to gain more height. It is possible to stretch your bungee a lot during the launch, providing the wind is sufficiently strong and you can fly your glider fast, weaving from side to side and using the inertia of the model.

To make up your bungee line you will need:
1. 100 metres (yards) of nylon, monofilament line with a breaking strain of 20–25kg

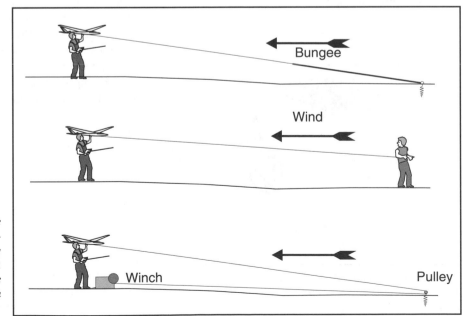

Figure 17.3 The three main methods of launching a thermal glider. You can choose the one which suits you.

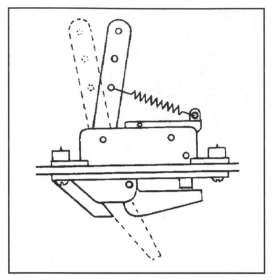

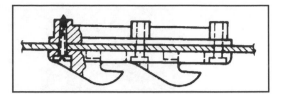

Figure 17.5 A two position hook allows you to alter the position to match the wind. (Picture courtesy Chart.)

Figure 17.4 A classic design of servo-operated release hook. (Picture courtesy Chart.)

(40–50lb) The line should be two to four times the length of the unstretched bungee, depending on the size of your flying site.

2. 30 metres of cotton covered or surgical bungee. Surgical bungee has three advantages over cotton covered ones.
   • More controllable elasticity.
   • Suitable for a wider range of glider weights and sizes.
   • Easier to repair.

Look after your bungee to obtain a long life. Do not expose it to excess heat in use or when stored. Over-stretching quickly ruins bungee, particularly cotton covered types. Store your bungee clean and dust it with talcum powder, when dry.

3. A pennant or a drogue parachute to attach to the top end of the line. A chute is preferable and you should attach both ends of it so it becomes part of the tow line. Attach the top of the chute some 500 mm (18") from the ring. When you pull the line tight, the chute is held closed until you release the glider from the line, when it will open and gently lower the line directly into wind, ready for the next launch.

4. A fishing swivel of 25kg (50lb) breaking strain mounted between the drogue chute and the tow line will stop the line getting twisted during post-flight recovery.

5. A large diameter reel to store the bungee and line when you are not using it.

6. A tethering stake which screws into the ground to secure the end of the bungee.

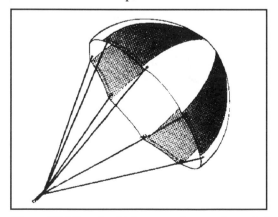

Figure 17.6 You should fit a parachute to the end of any tow line to lower it safely to earth after glider release. (Picture courtesy Chart.)

Hand tow

Nylon monofilament fishing line is the material almost always used for tow lines. A length of 100 metres (yards) with a breaking strain of around 20kg (50lb) is ideal. You will need a helper who will run with the tow line to pull your model to height. This is a skilled task requiring a team effort as running speed will depend on the model, the wind speed and the way you are flying the model on the tow line.

Positioning of the tow hook on your model is always something of a compromise, as the

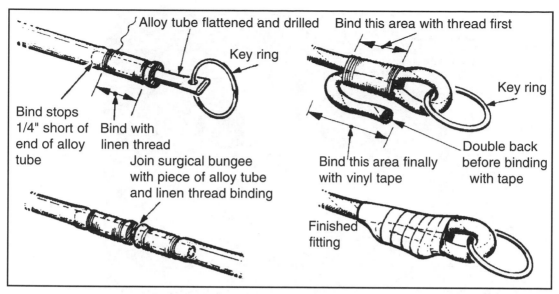

Alloy tube flattened and drilled   Bind this area with thread first

Key ring

Key ring

Bind stops
1/4" short of
end of alloy
tube

Bind with
linen thread

Join surgical bungee
with piece of alloy tube
and linen thread binding

Bind this area finally
with vinyl tape

Double back
before binding
with tape

Finished
fitting

Figure 17.7 End and joint fittings for surgical bungee (left) and cotton covered bungee (right). (Pictures courtesy Chart.)

ideal position depends on the wind strength. An adjustable hook is an optimum solution.

Winch

There have, over the years, been many designs of electric winch published in the modelling press. All use a geared motor driving a drum which reels in the tow line. You normally regulate the speed of the winch with a foot controller. A pulley, securely staked in the ground at the upwind end of the field, allows you to place the winch right beside you at the launch point and control the speed of winching with your foot.

Bungee launching your glider

Securely fix the elastic end of your bungee line to the ground, near the upwind extremity of your flying site and lay out your line directly downwind.

The amount you stretch your bungee depends on the strength of the wind and the weight of your model. A light model in a strong wind only needs slight tension as once launched, the wind will stretch the bungee. Avoid stretching bungee more than twice its length.

You should raise the nose of your model some 15° above the horizontal, wings level, as initial

acceleration is fast. The model will maintain any bank, veering it to one side. Control corrections for this may seem ineffective. Use small amounts of up elevator as a normal straight launch proceeds to keep your glider climbing. You have finally reached the top of the launch when your model stops climbing. You should release it immediately, otherwise the bungee will start to drag your model down.

Flying a large model in windy conditions, fitted with a releasable tow hook, you can achieve very high launches by releasing the bungee under tension. With care in light winds, by weaving your model either side of the wind direction, you can maintain considerable line tension. The climb occurs as you steer your model diagonally across the wind. Repeating this manoeuvre helps you climb to maximum height.

Piston engine power

The two popular layouts for powered gliders are with the engine and fuel tank in a removable pod above the wing or with these items in the nose of the model emulating the full size Fournier RF4 motor glider. The detractors complain about the noise of the motor and the dirt from the

Figure 17.8 The Rookie is a 2 channel powered glider suitable for small diesel engines. The two versions span 1727mm (68") and 2184mm (86"). (Photo courtesy D.B. Sport & Scale.)

exhaust which seems to get all over the glider. The advocates point out that you only need a relatively short motor run and that you avoid the hassle of a tow line. It is often the only solution when a mixture of thermal soaring and powered flying take place from the same site.

Electric power

The attraction of electric power for a glider is that it does not make the model either dirty or noisy. This means that the use of existing flying sites is not threatened by electric gliders.

The penalty is that the model has to carry the heavy battery and not so heavy motor for the whole flight. The use of a folding prop means that there is little increase in drag once the power is turned off. You can, however, use the motor when landing to adjust the glide path. There is more information on electric power in Chapter 10.

Glider towing

For experienced fliers, the joy of using a powered model to tow up a glider, mimicking full size practice, is hard to beat. You will have to find an agreeable powered flier and ensure:

1. The towing model is large and stable, can fly slowly and cope with the extra weight and drag of your glider.
2. You have a suitable tow line comprising some 50 metres (150ft) of normal monofilament with R/C release mechanisms on both models. Normally, the glider will release first, and the powered model will then drop the line on the flying strip.
3. You have agreed how the tow will proceed, preferably in wide steady circuits, keeping the tow line taut.
4. You have both planned what to do in emergencies including:
   - Engine failure of the towing model.
   - Glider control problems from turbulence or the towing aircraft's slipstream.
   - Towing aircraft control problems due to the glider getting well out of position.
   - Failure of the tow line release system.

Slope soaring

Slope soarers use orographic uplift; the lift caused by the wind striking the side of a hillside at right angles and being forced upwards. Gliders

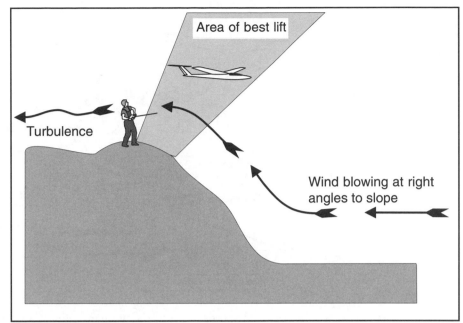

Figure 17.9 *The ideal slope should rise smoothly at an angle between 45° and 60° degrees.*

designed for use on a slope usually have a much lower aspect ratio than thermal soarers as manoeuvrability is essential if you are to keep the model in the lifting area.

They also usually have to land on the rough ground found on top of suitable hills. This has led to many high-wing designs with T or V tails to keep these vulnerable parts away from the ground.

Slope soaring requires some wind, blowing at right angles to the slope. This means that while north/south running ridges face into the prevailing westerly wind in the UK, slopes running in other directions may be suitable on certain days, depending on the direction of the wind. The ability of a slope soarer to fly will depend on the wind speed and the design of the model, particularly its wing loading. Most slope

Figure 17.10 *A typical slope soaring site somewhere in England. (Photo courtesy Malcolm Corbin.)*

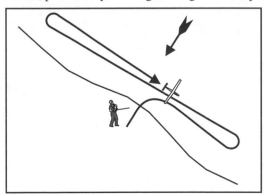

Figure 17.11 *Once you have flown out into lift, tacking back and forth along the slope will keep you in lift.*

WE DO THIS FOR FUN, SON!

soarer designers quote a range of wind speeds for flying their models.

Standing on top of a ridge is rarely warm, so good protective clothing is essential and, because of the remoteness of the locations, some refreshments as well. Ridges also get used by full sized gliders and hang gliders so take care to avoid conflicts in the air. Remember it is only your model, but it is also someone else's life. Keep well clear of any full size aircraft.

To start soaring, launch your model off the slope into wind, climb and turn to fly parallel to

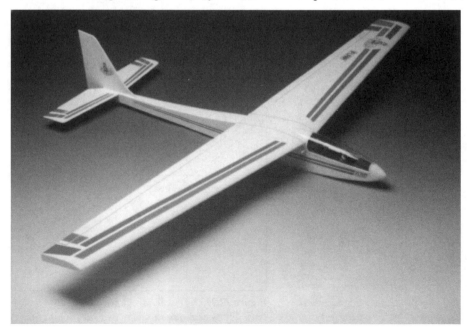

Figure 17.12 The *Fledgling is a basic slope soaring trainer which you can fly with 2 or 3 channels. Spanning 1800mm (71"), a 2535mm (100") wing conversion kit allows you to try thermal soaring with the same basic model. (Photo courtesy Flair.)*

224

Figure 17.13 A selection of the PSS models produced by Howard Metcale. He is holding an F15 Eagle and from left to right are a Tornado, F4 Phantom and Focke Wulf Ta 152.

the ridge keeping in the area of lift. Turn through 180 degrees away from the ridge and fly back along it. This process, unsurprisingly, is called tacking and is shown in Figure 17.11. The area where the lift is strongest is shown in Figure 17.9. Behind this area, you are likely to experience some degree of turbulence, requiring care during landing.

Power scale soarers

Power scale soarers, usually abbreviated to PSS, are not powered models at all, but rather scale or semi-scale models of powered full size aircraft. There are many superb models flying from slope soaring sites in the UK every year, including such unlikely subjects as the Boeing B52 bomber, the BAe Nimrod and the Boeing 747 Jumbo jet. Constructed by dedicated aficionados, usually from foam, these massive models have a superb performance and the Boeing models feature knock-off engine pods to reduce the risk of damage when landing.

Coming more down to earth, there are kits and plans for most modern jet fighters and many older ones, not to mention civilian executive jets. Piston-engined aircraft are equally suitable and anything from a Spitfire to a Piper Cub will fly

off the slope. Often, the wing span is increased a little to improve flight performance without completely ruining the look of the model. Most of these models are straightforward to build but do

Figure 17.14 Not a typical PSS model, this Edgley Optica is scratch-built and spans just over 1600mm (64"). (Photo courtesy Colin Moynihan.)

Figure 17.15 The Stiletto is a high performance 1520mm (60") pylon racer using a foam wing and ply/balsa fuselage. It uses 3 channels and weighs around one kilogram (2¼lb). (Photo courtesy Phoenix Model Products.)

require a reasonable wind over the slope to cope with their higher than average wing loadings.

Other classes of glider

There is a range of competitive classes, both for thermal and slope soarers and, of course, you can always try your hand at building and flying a scale or vintage glider. There are also several flying wings which perform well.

At the competitive end, pylon racing is popular among slope soaring pilots as indeed are aerobatics. There are regular competitions in both areas at club, regional and national levels.

You will find much more information about the whole subject of gliding in George Stringwell's superb book, *A Complete Guide to Radio Control Gliders* (see page 243).

Figure 17.16 This magnificent scratch-built PSS Learjet spans some 2300mm (90"). (Photo courtesy Colin Moynihan.)

Chapter 18 Autogyros and helicopters

Rotary wing aircraft are very different from fixed wing ones. They rely on the lift generated by spinning their wings, rather than using the forward motion of a fixed wing through the air. In the full size world, the helicopter is totally dominant because of its ability to make truly vertical take offs and landings, a characteristic not shared by the autogyro.

In the model world, the helicopter is also much more popular, but this does not mean that an autogyro does not make an attractive model to fly.

Autogyros

An autogyro may look, at first glance, very similar to a helicopter, but the way in which it flies is entirely different; the common factor being the use of rotating wings in both types of machine. An autogyro is an aeroplane where the fixed wing is replaced by a freely rotating horizontal rotor. Unlike a helicopter, the engine does not drive the rotor in flight, but instead drives a propeller to provide forward motion. A helicopter doing an auto rotation landing is flying like an autogyro with the throttle closed. Because the

Figure 18.1 Al's Autogyro is fitted with a pair of simple contrarotating rotors without any articulation. As a result, it can safely be flown using only rudder, elevator and throttle controls.

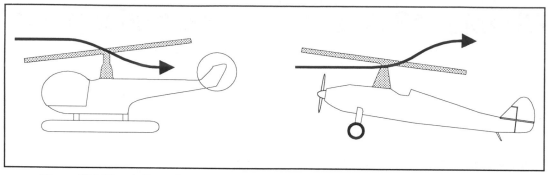

Figure 18.2 The air flows down through a helicopter rotor but up through that of an autogyro.

rotor is not engine driven, there is no torque to balance and therefore no need for a tail rotor. In fact, a basic autogyro can be controlled simply by the use of conventional elevator and rudder tail surfaces. More advanced models use cyclic control for pitch and roll.

The full size autogyro was the brainchild of Juan de la Cierva. In the 1920s he was worried by the high accident rate caused when conventional aircraft stalled. He determined to build an unstallable aeroplane and devised the autogyro, which, with its rotating wings, could not be stalled.

Due to the rearward tilt of the rotor, the air flows up through it providing the lift, which can be resolved into two components. One is parallel to the rotor shaft and the other, at right angles,

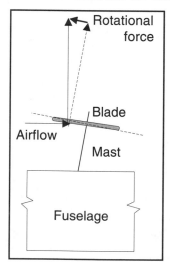

Figure 18.3 The lift generated by the blades of an autogyro resolves into two components, one parallel to the rotor shaft, which supports the model and the other at right angles to the shaft, which causes the blades to rotate.

provides the force which rotates the rotor. The arrangement is shown in Figure 18.3.

An autogyro is a STOL (short take off and landing) aircraft. It has no vertical capability. Cierva's early experiments were dogged by an uncontrollable roll as the aircraft accelerated into forward flight. The reason for this is that the forward-going blade experiences the rotational speed of the blade plus the forward speed of the autogyro, while the rearward moving blade has the two velocities subtracted. This is shown in Figure 18.4.

Cierva overcame this problem with the teeter head, Figure 18.5, which allows the forward-going blade to rise as it advances, reducing its effective angle of attack, and the rearward moving blade to descend, increasing its angle of attack. Thus it is possible for both blades to produce equal amounts of lift by balancing out the velocity and angle of attack differences. Having successfully developed a practical autogyro, which first flew in 1923 and was the world's first rotating wing aircraft, Cierva went on to develop his craft into a thoroughly practical flying machine.

The autogyro might have become a winner but development came to an abrupt end as a result of the outbreak of the Second World War and the success achieved by Igor Sikorsky in developing, building and flying the first practical helicopter. Sadly Cierva himself was killed in a fixed wing aircraft accident, when the pilot stalled coming in to land.

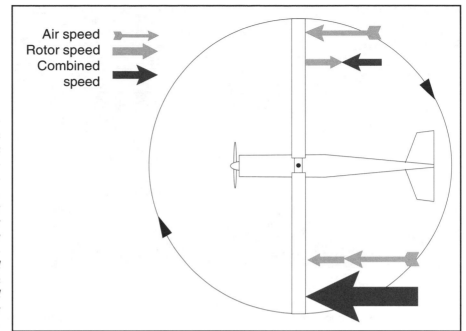

Air speed
Rotor speed
Combined
speed

Figure 18.4 Uncontrolled roll in an autogyro, or a helicopter, results from its forward airspeed. The advancing blade produces more lift as its forward rotational speed combines with airspeed and vice versa for the retreating blade.

Today, the main use of autogyros is in the leisure market, where flying it as a fun machine is a reward in itself. Its shortcomings include its inability to take off or land vertically (jump starts are possible where the rotor is spun up by the engine before take off), its high drag and therefore poor fuel consumption and its paramount need to avoid any sort of manoeuvre involving the slightest degree of negative 'g'.

However, it can fly very slowly, can approach steeply and make very short landings and is mechanically simpler than a helicopter. Some autogyros spin up the rotor on the ground for very short take off performance using a clutched connection from the engine. The inertia of the rotor blades in flight can be used to achieve very short landings.

There are only a few R/C autogyros that you can build. Eric Smurthwaite produced a successful machine called Chippewa 4 as far back as 1972, which featured quite a complex home-built rotor head and also required ailerons to prevent uncontrollable roll. The commercially available Robbe autogyro features a fixed-pitch helicopter head with cyclic control for pitch and roll, although for some the £300 price tag may prove a drawback. Nexus Plan RC 1234 is a twin rotor autogyro model called Gyrace, with the rotors themselves mounted at the tips of a substantial stub wing. It is also available as a kit from D.B. Sport & Scale. Al's Autogyro, Nexus Plan RC 1695, features contra-rotating rotor blades, mounted one above the other on a single shaft. The use of blade dihedral allows control of the

Figure 18.5 The use of a teeter head stops uncontrolled roll. The forward-going blade moves up, reducing its angle of attack and lift, while those of the retreating blade increase, thus matching the blade lift produced despite the different airflow speeds.

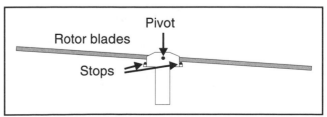

Pivot
Rotor blades
Stops

Figure 18.6 The unique DB Autogyro has twin contra-rotating rotor heads attached to the end of stub wings. (Photo courtesy D.B. Sport & Scale.)

autogyro using conventional rudder and elevator. This means it is possible to use a fixed rotor head with no servo connections for cyclic or collective pitch change. With an all-up weight of 2¼ kg (5lb), Al's Autogyro flies happily on a 0.50 four stroke or 0.40 two stroke.

The use of contrasting colours on the top and bottom halves of R/C autogyros helps solve the orientation problems, though you should not fly them too far away from yourself. An autogyro requires no more maintenance than a fixed wing aeroplane and is usually no more difficult to build.

Flying an autogyro

An autogyro in flight is like a fixed wing model but there are some distinct differences. Apart

from anything else, the drag produced by the rotor means that a more powerful motor is necessary than the size and weight would suggest. Facing the model into wind, the rotor or rotors can be spun up by hand, though if there is any significant wind, they will spin up by themselves. In any case, once the model is released and accelerates, the rotors will quickly speed up.

A tail dragger rapidly gets its tail up. Raise the nose and the model will take off. The climb will appear steep as the forward velocity will be low. The nose-up attitude may initially seem dangerously high. Once you have reached a safe altitude, throttle back and remember to watch the orientation. The approach also needs to be nose high and a short burst of power will help to get a perfect flare with a very short landing

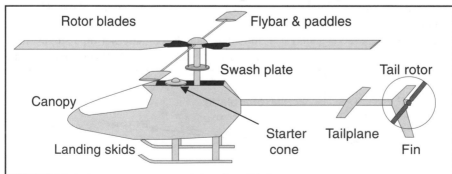

Figure 18.7 The main parts of a helicopter are very different to those of a fixed wing model.

run. With any significant wind, a near vertical landing is quite possible. Should the engine cut in flight, you must react immediately by getting the nose down into a steep dive to maintain rotor speed for the ensuing landing. During this manoeuvre, and every other with an autogyro, you must keep positive 'g' on the model. Rolls and wing overs are thus non-starters.

Helicopters

The popularity of R/C helicopters has increased since they first became a practical proposition, following the outstanding success of Dieter Schlüter in Germany in 1969. Since then, a large number of kits have been launched on the market, many originating from the Far East. More and more modellers have learned to fly R/C helicopters in their search for something different.

While it is quite possible to learn to fly from scratch on a helicopter, a majority of people graduate to them from fixed wing flying. Many of the skills learned are appropriate to both areas of the hobby, including installation and use of R/C equipment, starting and operating I/C motors, not to mention safety awareness. It is worth mentioning that electric R/C helicopters are beginning to make their mark on the hobby, though mostly in the hands of experienced helicopter fliers.

Of all radio controlled models, there is general agreement that the helicopter is the hardest to fly. However, you should not let this put you off giving it a try. The advantage of an R/C helicopter is that you can learn at your own speed. First you can learn to hover, then progress to forward flight knowing you can always slow down to the hover and land. Once you can fly a

Figure 18.8 You will inevitably find a fair degree of mechanical complexity in any R/C helicopter. In this view of a Morley F1 Carbon, the engine, silencer and cooling fan are clearly visible, as are the radio, gyro and connections to the swash plate and fly bar. (Photo courtesy Morley Helicopters.)

Figure 18.9 The standard Morley Maverick helicopter is an ideal trainer. It is competitively priced and readily available. The Maverick can be upgraded to XR specification as experience builds allowing you to learn to master aerobatic flying or to fit a scale bodyshell. (Photo courtesy Morley Helicopters.)

circuit, then rolls, loops and other aerobatics are possible.

Building an R/C helicopter basically involves model engineering assembly, bolting together pre-formed metal and plastic parts as well as complete sub-assemblies, rather than cutting out and gluing together wooden parts. There is a minimum of covering, just the rotor blades, while self-adhesive colour trim is restricted to the area around the cockpit canopy and tail boom. All this can be done on the proverbial kitchen table in a few evenings.

As an R/C helicopter involves the initial outlay of several hundred pounds, you should select a model which will take you through the initial training and last as your skills develop. Assuming you are going to fly at a club, as with your radio, check to see which makes of helicopter are the most popular.

All helicopters, both full size and model, are aerodynamically unstable. They do not fly themselves and require constant pilot inputs. In this respect they are not like fixed wing models which have a degree of stability built in. A fixed wing trainer, left to its own devices, will normally return to straight and level flight.

You must fly a helicopter almost all the time involving continuous stick inputs from both hands. Landings are very challenging for the novice and sooner or later you will damage your model. In addition, moving parts are subject to wear

and tear and will need replacing from time to time.

It is thus important to consider local support as you will certainly have to purchase replacement parts rather than make them yourself. The range of helicopters which your local model shop supports is a good starting point. Maintenance and repair account for much of the cost of flying an R/C helicopter.

Particularly when learning, purchasing replacement parts can prove expensive. It is therefore sensible to check prices of the commonly used spares such as rotor blades, main shaft, tail boom, feathering spindle and fly bar before making your initial purchase decision.

Model helicopters are fascinating and provide an exciting and absorbing hobby. The various different types of machines have their own merits and compromises. There are a number of books covering all aspects of model helicopters. *Radio Controlled Helicopters* by Nick Papillon (see page 243) is a worthwhile investment to obtain a basic understanding of how helicopters work and how to build and fly one. Compile as much information as possible about the various models before making an informed purchase.

Helicopter control functions

The way the controls are used on a helicopter is, unsurprisingly, different from a fixed wing model. You still need four basic channels to fly

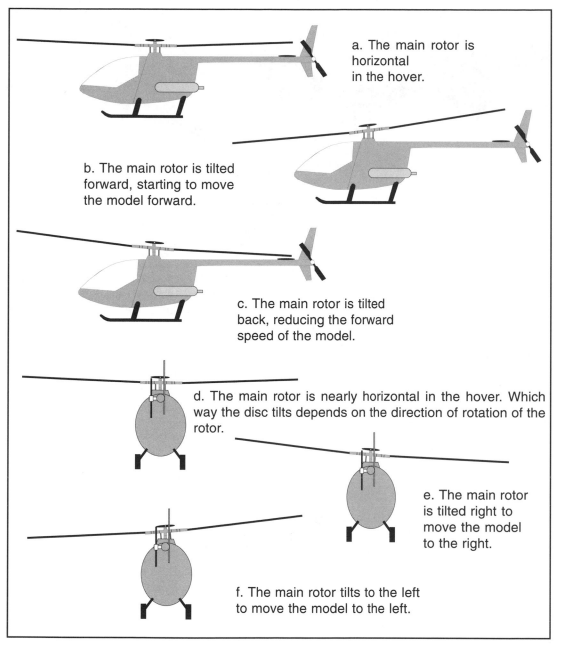

a. The main rotor is horizontal in the hover.

b. The main rotor is tilted forward, starting to move the model forward.

c. The main rotor is tilted back, reducing the forward speed of the model.

d. The main rotor is nearly horizontal in the hover. Which way the disc tilts depends on the direction of rotation of the rotor.

e. The main rotor is tilted right to move the model to the right.

f. The main rotor tilts to the left to move the model to the left.

Figure 18.10 *An R/C helicopter flies in exactly the same way as a full size one. The rotation of the main rotor, operating at a positive pitch, produces the lift. The tail rotor produces side thrust at the rear to counteract the torque of the main rotor and to yaw the model. By tilting the main rotor disc forward (b), the model will move forwards and vice versa when the disc is tilted back (c). In the same way, tilting the disc sideways will move the model sideways (e) and (f). In the hover, the side thrust of the tail rotor is balanced by a slight sideways tilt of the main rotor.*

Figure 18.11 *The pitch of the tail rotor blades can be varied to control the helicopter in yaw. (Photo courtesy Morley Helicopters.)*

a helicopter though these control five separate functions.

Collective pitch and throttle

These two functions cause the helicopter rise or descend by adjusting the angle of attack of the blades in unison, providing more or less lift as collective pitch is altered. The change in lift also results in a corresponding change in drag, calling for an alteration of engine power. This is why collective pitch and throttle are both controlled by the throttle stick on the transmitter. When the throttle is opened, blade pitch is increased at the same time and the rotor speed remains constant.

There is still the odd fixed-pitch helicopter where the amount of lift is controlled solely by the speed of the main blades, in turn a function of the throttle setting. While such systems are

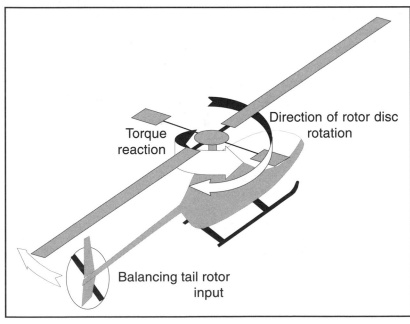

Figure 18.12 *The torque resulting from the main rotor rotation is balanced either by pilot or gyro inputs to the tail rotor. Most Far East helicopter main rotors revolve clockwise, while most of those designed in Europe turn counter-clockwise.*

Figure 18.13 The main rotor head showing the main shaft, fly bar and swash plate. (Photo courtesy Morley Helicopters.)

simpler in mechanical terms, the time lag in increasing or decreasing rotor rpm means that they tend to be harder to fly than systems with collective pitch control.

Cyclic control in roll and pitch

Cyclic control independently alters the angle of each blade as it moves around the rotor disc, thus tilting it to provide two functions; a rolling or pitching force. Cyclic pitch is controlled by the conventional elevator and aileron sticks on the transmitter.

Fore/aft cyclic (equivalent to the elevator function on a fixed wing model) controls the forward and backward movement of the helicopter by altering the pitch differentially on the leading and trailing rotor blades.

Left/right cyclic (equivalent to the aileron function on a fixed wing model) controls the left and right movement of the helicopter by altering the pitch differentially on the left and right rotor blades.

Tail rotor

The last function is the tail rotor which balances out the torque produced by the rotation of the main rotor and is used to yaw the helicopter, pointing it in the desired direction.

It is controlled by the rudder stick, which alters the pitch of the tail rotor blades in a collective sense, producing a positive or negative force depending which way the model is yawed. Every time you change the throttle setting, you must also alter the tail rotor pitch to avoid unwanted yaw.

Specialist helicopter items

You should be able to recognise a number of items found on virtually all R/C helicopters and understand what they do.

Gyros

It is normal to find a gyro electronically connected to the tail rotor to avoid the need for continuous control inputs. The gyro senses any yaw and automatically feeds a correcting signal to the tail. However, any control input by the pilot overcomes the gyro output. You can adjust the sensitivity of the gyro to suit yourself and your model, either by a ground adjustment or, on more advanced gyros, from the transmitter.

Swash plate

The swash plate allows servos fixed to the airframe to transfer their movements to the rotating rotor head. It consists of a pair of discs, free to articulate in two axes at right angles to the main shaft. One disc rotates with the shaft while the other is held stationary by a fixed drag link. On most models, both discs are moved up and down the shaft to alter collective pitch.

Fly bar

With a main rotor turning at some 1,000 – 1,500 rpm it has a fair degree of gyroscopic rigidity which makes it all but impossible for a normal

IT TURNS AT THE SAME SPEED AS MY TAIL ROTOR !

R/C servo to tilt. There is also a need to provide some stability in roll and pitch for what is basically an unstable machine.

It was the invention of fly bar systems by Bell and Hiller which eased the problems of control in full sized helicopters. Variations of the Hiller system are used on R/C models and comprise a pair of control paddles which help to improve the stability of the model and also provide the control inputs to the rotor blades. It is the paddles themselves which are moved by the cyclic servos and the paddles in turn control the main rotor.

Helicopter radios

With a helicopter radio, a number of specialist options are available. Most important is the provision of much more accurate control and mixing of the relationship between pitch and throttle. This ensures that the engine speed, and consequently rotor speed, remain constant throughout the flight.

Collective pitch/tail rotor mixing helps to prevent the helicopter yawing with changes in throttle setting. Switched features include

'throttle hold' which sets the throttle to a fixed position while still allowing the throttle stick to control collective pitch for practice auto rotation (engine off) landings. 'Idle up' increases the potential to do aerobatics by allowing alteration of collective pitch without changing the throttle setting.

Cyclic and Collective Pitch Mixing (CCPM)

A helicopter swash plate slides up and down the main shaft to change the collective pitch and is tilted to change the cyclic pitch of the rotor blades. Mechanical CCPM between the servos and the swash plate is usually accomplished by a complex series of levers, bell cranks and pivot arms.

The alternatives are to use the facilities of a computerised transmitter, or an electronic CCPM mixer, to provide the necessary mixing of functions to the servos. The swash plate still rises, falls and tilts for collective and cyclic pitch, but is controlled via short, straight links directly clustered around the mast directly below the swash plate. This eliminates the need for complex linkages between the servos and swash plate, avoiding flex, slop and interaction.

Figure 18.14 The *Concept 30 is typical of the latest generation of Far East helicopters.*

Types of helicopter

The most practical helicopter for the learning phase is a pod and boom model, with exposed mechanics and a simple canopy. Scale helicopters are more vulnerable to damage, as they usually have an all-enclosing body shell. They also take longer to construct and require a fair amount of building experience. Maintenance on these machines usually involves removing the mechanics from the body shell.

If you are determined from the start to fly a scale model then some pod and boom models can have a scale body fitted once you have the necessary flying skills. Most model helicopters are capable of aerobatics if suitably set up. However, for scale or aerobatic flying, bottom of the range models usually require upgrading and a more powerful engine.

Helicopter engine sizes

There are three main groupings of model helicopters based on engine size. The smallest is the 30 size, powered by a two stroke glow plug engine of around 5cc (0.30 cu in) capacity. The 40/50 size is the mid range, while the largest and most expensive models are the 60 size, powered by 10cc (0.60 cu in) motors. A few models of even larger size and greater engine

capacity are built and flown by some dedicated enthusiasts.

Basic entry level helicopters, such as the Hirobo Shuttle, Kyosho Concept 30 and Nexus 30 appeal to the beginner because of their low initial cost. However, these small models are very light and can be difficult to handle in any sort of wind.

The larger and heavier 40/50 size helicopters provide better stability in windy weather and their size makes them easier to see at distance. Their airframes are more robust making them less prone to crash damage. They usually include long-lasting ball-raced moving parts, an auto rotation unit and wide impact-absorbing undercarriage. These larger models are slightly more expensive than the 30 size, but you will discover the advantage of these benefits as you progress from the learning phase to scale or aerobatics.

It is unusual to learn on a 60 sized or larger model, mainly due to their increased cost and complexity. However, a larger model does carry the benefits of extra stability and visibility.

Apart from the first helicopter described, the Kyosho Concept 30, the range of machines detailed below is that of a British company, Morley Helicopters. It serves to indicate the type of specification of a range of typical R/C helicopters.

Figure 18.15 The very attractive Hughes 500 body for Maverick or Maverick XR mechanics allows you to transform your basic training model to a scale one.

Concept 30

The Kyosho Concept 30 SR-T is representative of the smallest class of R/C helicopter and is often offered as a complete package including radio, engine and gyro. It is custom-designed for beginners, is a durable model and comes at an affordable price.

The use of a long main shaft increases its stability and reduces the chance of a tail boom strike on a hard landing. An integral clutch and gear drive simplifies construction, while starting is by a rearward pointing cone.

It has a main rotor diameter of 1200mm (47.2") and an overall length of 1031mm (40.6"). It weighs some 2½kg (5½ lb.) and can be powered by a 4.5 – 6cc (0.28 – 0.36 cu in) engine. It needs a five channel helicopter radio to provide the required control functions.

The SR-X version of the Concept is the same size as the SR-T but requires at least a 5.5cc (0.32 cu in) engine. It incorporates much mechanical redesign and simplification of the cyclic controls, with ball races replacing oilite bearings to reduce friction. The model also has an improved tail rotor drive and control system. It is fully aerobatic and scale bodies are available to convert the Concept into a Hughes 300 or 500, Jet Ranger or Bell 222.

The Maverick

The Morley Maverick is designed for the novice flyer and is rugged, stable and easy to fly. It requires an engine of 6.5 – 8.5cc (40 – 53cu in) and features a direct starting cone above the canopy. You can also set it up for a full range of aerobatics. It includes an auto rotation unit, 10 mm hardened steel main shaft, one-piece steel clutch, 22 precision ball and roller race bearings, impact resistant undercarriage and efficient two-stage gearing. Its control system uses no control bell cranks but only requires a basic four channel radio with five servos. It has a main rotor diameter of 1250mm (49") and a body length of 1150mm (45").

The Maverick XR is an upgraded version of the basic model with a larger 1325mm (52") rotor diameter and wide chord blades. These changes increase hovering and straight line running stability allowing it to perform smooth aerobatics. A longer tail boom provides increased tail power and a pair of support struts keep the tail rigid. The airframe's upper and lower main frames are made from multi-directional, multi-laminated carbon fibre. These are lighter, stronger and stiffer than the original alloy items and are able to withstand severe impacts. The XR needs a high power engine such as the O.S.

Figure 18.16 To fly any helicopter inverted close to the ground requires much skill and plenty of practice. This Morley F1 Carbon is a 60 size model, custom-made for this type of aerobatic manoeuvre.

46-50 FSRH or Rossi 53H to exploit its full capabilities.

All the upgraded parts in the XR kit can be added to a standard Maverick if required and a range of performance enhancing and other optional items is available for both versions.

Hughes 500E

The Hughes 500E body conversion kit allows you to produce a scale helicopter from the basic Maverick mechanics. The kit includes a one-piece glass fibre fuselage, transparent canopy, tail fins, and other ancillary items as well as a new tail drive. The fuselage fits the standard or XR Maverick mechanics after removing the tail boom, undercarriage and canopy. The forward raked mast increases speed and the powerful rotor head provides great manoeuvrability. Overall body length is 1170mm (45"), the model stands 480mm (19") high with a flying weight only marginally heavier than a standard Maverick.

The F1 Carbon

The Morley F1 Carbon is a 60 class super-sports performance R/C helicopter. The combination of a high strength, light weight, carbon fibre composite airframe with robust dynamic components endows the F1 with aerobatic performance matched to high reliability and simple maintenance. The electronic cyclic/collective pitch mixing (CCPM) on the F1 provides a simple, durable and accurate control system that eliminates complex linkages, bell cranks and costly bearings. The F1 has a 1500 mm (59") rotor diameter with an airframe length of 1350mm (53").

Maintenance checks

Success in flying an R/C helicopter provides great satisfaction, but is only possible if you undertake regular maintenance of the model. The following checklist will help you fly safely.

General

During your last flying session with the model, were there any strange noises or odd behaviour such as a short or long tank run? Had the trims changed?

Main blades

Check the blades for stress cracks, particularly if they are covered with heat-shrink or self-adhesive covering. Twist each blade along its length and look for ripples which may indicate a crack underneath. Check the roots of glass fibre, epoxy or carbon fibre blades for stress cracks.

Linkages and ball joints

Look for bent or damaged push rods and check for freedom of movement. Check ball joints are neither too loose or tight and ensure they cannot pop off.

Figure 18.17 The pilot of this Maverick is an accomplished flier. Plenty of practice is necessary to achieve this level of skill in the hover.

Radio installation

Check the receiver and battery are secure, examine wires for chafing and ensure all plugs are firmly located. Carefully exercise servos by hand to check for gear problems. Check servo mountings for loose or missing screws, damaged or perished grommets and cracked or broken lugs. Check the gyro for secure mounting and noise while running, noting run-down time to a stop.

Engine and tank

Check for oil leaks, loose carburettor and security of mountings. Check pipework for security and leaks, check tank for leaks and correct clunk weight operation.

Gears and belts

Check for backlash and lubricate metal gears as required. Lubrication requires judicious use of light machine grease, which must be kept well away from the clutch. Check belts for tension, side and tooth wear.

Canopy, frames and chassis

Check the canopy for stress cracks and examine the condition of grommets if used. Inspect internally for oil splash which may indicate a leak. Check that the metal frames are not bent and glass fibre, nylon and plastic parts are free from cracks, which can be hairline and difficult to see. Carbon fibre frames are generally trouble-free.

Tailplane/fin and boom

Check for hairline cracks, then ensure parts are tight and cannot rotate on the boom. Ensure the boom is firmly clamped in the chassis and has not moved forwards or backwards. Examine the tail rotor blades looking for splits or bad nicks caused by contact with the ground.

Screws

Check all screws are tight. Always use thread-locking compounds, such as Loctite, so that vibration does not loosen bolted together parts.

Flying a helicopter

There are several basic problems you face with your first helicopter. The first is that you will find it difficult to use all four controls at the same time, especially as every control has an effect on every other one. This requires a high degree of eye to hand co-ordination. The other difficulty is how to set up your model so that it will fly satisfactorily when you don't know how to fly yourself. The easy answer is to get an experienced helicopter pilot to help you set it up.

You must carefully balance your blades about the centre of rotation and ensure the centre of gravity of each blade is the same distance from the root. The classic method of balancing is to use self-adhesive tape wrapped around the tips of the blades, with different colours for the two blades.

These differently coloured tapes will allow you to set up the blade tracking. This involves spinning up the main rotor with the engine and checking by eye that the plane of rotation of the two blades coincides. If they do not, the colour of the tracking tape will indicate which blade is running high and which low. A slight adjustment to the length of the control rods to the blades, reducing the angle of attack of the high running blade and increasing that of the low running blade will quickly get the tracking right.

You should initially set the collective pitch to zero degrees with the throttle closed, four degrees at mid throttle and ten degrees at full power. Later you may wish to incorporate some negative pitch when the throttle is closed. A tail rotor gyro is indispensable during the early learning phase, so do fit one. Then it is just a question of perseverance and practice.

Starting the engine of most helicopters is done via a top or rearward facing cone and a normal starter, though some need a belt drive. The throttle must be set at idle to prevent the clutch engaging as soon as the engine fires. It is normal practice to hold the main rotor firmly while using the starter. When setting up the motor, the mixture at full power must be on the rich side, as a lean engine cut in flight can be terminal. The idle must be set so that the clutch disengages fully.

Choose a day with only a light breeze blowing. With the model on the ground facing into wind, stand behind it and open the throttle to spin up the rotor until the model starts to get light on its skids. You will quickly learn that each time the

Figure 18.18 A pair of floats strapped to the skids will make landing without tipping over much easier. (Photo courtesy Rupert Weiss.)

collective pitch and engine rpm change, the model starts to yaw until you feed in a corrective tail rotor change. This is where a gyro proves invaluable. It is one thing less for you to concentrate on when learning to hover. Remember that while the nose responds to rudder inputs as you would expect, if you are watching the tail, the control function will appear to be reversed.

You will be able to observe the response to the various control inputs when hovering just off the ground and learn to make corrections instinctively. You will also discover that it is much easier to hover out of ground effect, that is when the height of the helicopter exceeds roughly the rotor diameter.

Progress will be slow but steady and you should soon be able to take off, hover and then land again. Fitting a wide-based training undercarriage, such as a pair of floats, improves stability and reduces the risk of the model tipping over in the event of an awkward touchdown.

Remember, especially if you have flown fixed wing models, that if things start to go a little wrong once airborne, what you must not do is close the throttle. Such an action will cause the model to fall out of the sky. Just gently reduce power to a controlled landing.

Advancing to the full helicopter repertoire will take plenty of practice. From the hover, it takes nerve the first time you push the cyclic lever forward to get the model moving away

Figure 18.19 The V22 Osprey is the ultimate in R/C vertical take off models.

from you. As it starts to move forward, it will momentarily start to descend as some of the lift is now providing the forward motion. As the model accelerates, transitional lift will then produce a climb until you throttle back. Use your roll control, co-ordinated with the tail rotor to turn the model and fly it in a circuit around you.

Now for the difficult part. As the model comes towards you, with the roll and yaw controls operating in the opposite sense to that you have got used to in the hover, pull back on the cyclic stick and at the same time feed on power as the model slows down to the hover. Then gently throttle back and land. The sky is yours! You can learn to do auto rotation landings, aerobatics or start to fly scale models.

Figure 18.20 Jim Morley's Osprey in flight represents the achievement of a lifetime.

One of the many fascinations of flying a model helicopter is the fact that you never stop learning. Whether you fly just for the fun of it or for the thrill of a competition, there will always be new developments or new challenges and manoeuvres to maintain the interest.

Advanced vertical take off/landing

While many modellers are happy to live with the challenge of flying a variety of sports, scale and aerobatic helicopters, for some the desire for a new challenge leads them to even greater achievements.

One man alone, Jim Morley, has built and successfully flown a scale Fairy Rotodyne, Chinook twin-rotor helicopter and, by far the most ambitious of all, an Osprey tilt-rotor aircraft. The latter is the achievement of a lifetime and for development difficulties, mechanical complexity and sheer perseverance will take a lot of beating.

While not a rotary wing model, there have been several reports of a successful ducted fan Harrier VTOL aircraft and several builders have achieved success in terms of a hovering model. However, to date there has only been a single report from Canada of vertical take off, transition to forward flight and back again for a vertical landing.

Appendix A Bibliography, specialist organisations and list of useful addresses

Books

Aeronautics for Modellers Alasdair Sutherland (Traplet Publications, 1995)

Airbrushing and Spray Painting Manual Ian Peacock (Nexus Special Interests, 1987)

Basic R/C Flying David Boddington (Nexus Special Interests, 1989)

Building & Flying Radio Controlled Model Aircraft David Boddington (Nexus Special Interests, 1996)

Building from Plans David Boddington (Nexus Special Interests, 1989)

A Complete Guide to Radio Control Gliders George Stringwell (Nexus Special Interests, 1997)

Covering Model Aircraft Ian Peacock (Nexus Special Interests, 1989)

Ducted Fans for Model Jets David James (Nexus Special Interests, 1989)

Fly Electric Dave Chinery (Nexus Special Interests, 1995)

Flying Model Helicopters Dave Day (Nexus Special Interests, 1986)

Flying Radio Control Aerobatics Charles Allison & Andy Nicholls (Nexus Special Interests, 1990)

The Glassfibre Handbook R.H. Warring (Nexus Special Interests, 1989)

Introducing Radio Control Model Aircraft Bill Burkinshaw (Nexus Special Interests, 1995)

Introduction to Electric Flight Ian Peacock (Nexus Special Interests, 1988)

Model Aircraft Aerodynamics Martin Simons (Nexus Special Interests, 1994)

Model Airplane Building Sketch by Sketch Peter Holland (Nexus Special Interests, 1997)

Model Flight Martin Simons (Nexus Special Interests, 1988)

Operating Four-Stroke Engines Brian Winch (Nexus Special Interests, 1990)

Operating R/C Engines David Boddington & Brian Winch (Nexus Special Interests, 1989)

Painting and Finishing Models Ian Peacock (Nexus Special Interests, 1987)

Radio Control Foam Modelling David Thomas (Nexus Special Interests, 1989)

Radio Control Primer David Boddington (Nexus Special Interests, 1996)

Radio Controlled Helicopters Nick Papillon (Nexus Special Interests, 1996)

Radio Controlled Model Aircraft Adrian Vale (Traplet Publications, 1996)

R/C Aircraft Q & A Book Peter Smoothy (Nexus Special Interests, 1989)

R/C Sports Aircraft from Scratch Alex Weiss (Nexus Special Interests, 1996)

R/C Vintage Model Aeroplanes Peter Russell (Nexus Special Interests, 1989)

Scale Construction Duncan Hutson (Traplet Publications, 1997)

Magazines

Aviation Modeller
Electric Flight International
Model Helicopter World
Radio Modeller

RC Jet International
RCM&E
RC Model World
RC Scale Aircraft

RC Scale International
Rotorsport
Quiet Flight International
Silent Flight

Specialist organisations

Associations exist for those interested in many specialised areas of radio controlled flying. Membership helps develop your skills as well as introducing you to like-minded people.

British Association of Radio Controlled Soarers
36, Windmill Ave., Wokingham,
Berks., RG11 2XD.

British Electric Flight Association
123, Lane End Rd., High Wycombe,
Bucks., HP12 4HF.

British Miniature Pylon Racing Association
20, Calvin Close, Camberley,
Surrey, GU15 1DN.

British Model Flying Association
Chacksfield House, 31, St Andrews Rd.,
Leicester, LE2 8RE.

British Radio Control Helicopter Association
7, Kiln Way, Badger's Dean, Grays,
Essex, RM17 5JE.

British Water Plane Association
The Hollies, 48, New St., Kenilworth,
Warks., CV8 2EZ.

GB Radio Control Aerobatic Association
84, Holymoor Rd., Holymoorside,
Chesterfield, S42 7DX.

Jet Modellers' Association
8, Crediton Close, Wigston,
Leics., LE18 2QZ.

Large Model Association
61, Moscow Rd.,
London, W2 4JS.

Northern Ireland Association of Aeromodellers
28, Colston Ave., Holywood, Co. Down,
N. Ireland.

Scottish Aeromodellers' Association
66, Well Rd., Glenrothes,
Fife, KY2 5PN.

Society of Antique Modellers
Vine House, 22, Hollins La., Marple Bridge,
Stockport, Cheshire, SK6 5BB.

Sport 40 Association
82, Hermitage Rd., St. Johns, Woking,
Surrey, GU21 1TQ.

List of useful addresses

AGC Sales Ltd
London Rd., Hemel Hempstead,
Herts., HP3 9ST.

Airplanes Etc
9, Orwell Ct.,Wickford,
Essex, SS1 8YJ.

Balsacraft International Ltd
Norwich Rd. Industrial Estate, Watton,
Norfolk, IP25 6DR.

D.B. Sport & Scale
24, Pine Copse Close, Durston,
Northampton, NN5 6NF.

Enya U.K Sales
80, Church St., Frodsham, Via Warrington,
Cheshire, WA6 6QU.

Flair Products
Holdcroft Works, Blunsdon,
Wilts., SN2 4AH.

Hoot Model Making & Tooling
155, Merton Rd., Bearsted, Maidstone,
Kent, ME15 8LS.

Howard Metcalfe Models
Brook Cottage, Wintershill, Durley,
Southampton, SO32 2AH.

Irvine
New Southgate,
London, N11 1JL.

Jim Fox Models
16, Old Village Rd., Little Weighton,
E Yorks., HU20 3US.

Litesold
97-99, Gloucester Rd, Croydon,
Surrey, CR0 2DN.

MacGregor Industries
Canal Estate, Langley,
Slough, SL3 6EQ.

MainLink Systems
1, Blunham Rd., Moggerhanger,
Bedford, MK44 3RD.

Morley Helicopters Ltd.
West Entrance, Fairoaks Airport, Chobham,
Woking, Surrey, GU24 8HX.

Nexus Special Interests
Nexus House, Boundary Way, Hemel
Hempstead, Herts. HP2 7ST.

Newman Precision Aeros
39, West Rd., Westcliff on Sea,
Essex, SS0 9AU.

Paper Aviation
85 Paines La, Pinner,
Middx. HA5 3BX.

The Parc-Amber Co Ltd.
48a, Fairlight Ave., Telscombe Cliffs,
Peacehaven, E Sussex, BN10 7BS.

Perma-Grit Tools
The White House, Pointon, Sleaford,
Lincs., NG34 0LX.

Pettipher's Plastics
Unit 3, Gun Lane Business Centre,
Gun Lane, Strood, Kent, ME2 4UD.

Phoenix Model Products
14, Orbec Ave., Kingsteignton,
Newton Abbot, Devon, TQ12 3ED.

Ripmax plc.
Ripmax Corner, Green St.,
Enfield, EN3 7SJ.

SMC
1 & 2, Teville Gate, Worthing,
W. Sussex, BN11 1UA.

Tigre Engines World Electronics
12, Smith St., Watford,
Herts., WD1 8AA.

Traplet Publications Ltd.
Severn Drive, Upton upon Severn,
Worcs., WR8 0JL.

Tru-Flite Technology Ltd.
Draymonds Lodge, 1, Kings Meadow,
Crudwell, Malmesbury, Wilts., SN 16 9EK.

Unitracts International
87-89 Farleight Rd., Warlingham,
Surrey, CR6 9JE

Vortex Plastics
73, Stonehill Ave, Birstall,
Leicester, LE4 4JF.

Weston UK
84-88, London Rd., Teynham,
Nr Sttingbourne, Kent ME9 9QH.

Appendix B Glossary of terms

ABS A plastic used for moulding fuselages and other components.

Adverse yaw The effect of aileron drag causing the opposite turn to that demanded.

Aerofoil The cross sectional shape of a wing.

Ailerons Moveable surfaces at the trailing edge of wings giving control about the roll axis.

Airbrakes Controls used to increase drag.

All-moving tail A tailplane, the whole of which moves to give an elevator effect.

Angle of attack The angle between the chord line of an aerofoil and the airflow.

Angle of incidence The angle between an aerofoil's chord line and the fore/aft datum line of the fuselage.

Aspect ratio The ratio of the span to the average chord of a wing.

Ballast Weight carried to adjust the position of the centre of gravity of a model.

BEC Battery elimination circuit.

Bell crank A device for transferring control linkages through a sharp angle.

Butterfly tail Tail surfaces set in the form of a V to provide both the fin and tailplane functions.

Cabane struts An arrangement of struts for supporting a parasol wing or the top wing of a biplane or tri-plane above a fuselage

Camber Curvature in the line equidistant between the upper and lower surfaces of an aerofoil.

Canard A model with a foreplane in front of the wing. Also the forward winglets either on a delta or an otherwise conventional model.

Cap strip A thin strip glued to the top and bottom of a wing rib to form an I section.

Carbon fibre A very strong composite material.

Centre of gravity The balance point or the point through which the total weight of a model acts.

Centre of pressure The point through which the lift of a flying surface acts. Its position varies with angle of attack.

Chopped strand mat A material used in GRP consisting of random direction, non-woven fibres.

Chord The width of an aerofoil, wing or tail surface from leading to trailing edge.

Clevis An adjustable connection between any control surface and its linkage.

Closed loop A control linkage using thin wire to both sides of a control surface in a push/pull mode.

Dead stick The call by a powered flier after experiencing an engine failure.

Dihedral The angle by which a wing is inclined upwards from the lateral axis.

Doubler A reinforcing thickness of wood laminated onto a flat component e.g. a fuselage side.

Dowel A cylindrical section of wood or metal.

Drag The total retarding force which occurs when a flying model moves through the air.

Elevator A control surface hinged to a tailplane and used for control in the pitch axis.

Elevons Surfaces combining the functions of elevators and ailerons.

Epoxy A two part adhesive or laminating resin.

Expanded polystyrene White (or blue) polystyrene foam used mainly for making wing cores.

Fin The fixed vertical tail surface of a model.

Fibreglass See GRP

Flaps Wing-mounted surfaces producing extra lift and drag depending on their deflection angle.

Flaperons Wing-mounted control surfaces combining the functions of flaps and ailerons.

Flutter Continuous vibration of flying or control surfaces, usually occurring at high speed and resulting in structural failure.

Former A fuselage cross sectional member.

GRP Glass reinforced plastic. A material made from glass fibres laminated with a resin to form a structure or provide reinforcement.

Heat-shrink fabric Plastic covering material with built-in colouring, heat-sensitive adhesive and a textured woven finish.

Heat-shrink film Plastic covering material with built-in colouring, heat-sensitive adhesive and a high gloss finish.

Horn Structure projecting from a control surface to provide leverage for the control linkage.

Incidence The angle between an aerofoil's chord line and the fore/aft datum line of the fuselage.

Induced drag That part of total drag caused by a wing producing lift.

Kevlar A high strength organic fibre used as a composite material.

Lateral axis The axis about which a model rolls.

Leading edge The first part of a wing to meet the airflow.

Lift The upward force produced by a wing which supports a model and balances its weight in straight and level flight.

Longeron A strip of wood used as a lengthwise fuselage constructional member.

Longitudinal axis The axis about which a model pitches or loops.

Mixer An electronic or mechanical device which mixes two control functions together to operate one pair of surfaces e.g. elevons, flaperons.

Mylar A flexible plastic material used to make heat-shrink materials and hinges.

Nicad Nickel cadmium rechargeable battery.

Pitch Movement about a model's longitudinal axis.

Polyboard A material comprising a sandwich of expanded polystyrene between two layers of card.

Polyester resin Two part resin used to make GRP laminates.

Polyhedral A dihedral layout with an additional amount added to the outer panels of a wing.

PRTM Please read the manual.

Push rod A rigid control link from a servo to a control surface.

PVA glue A slow drying, flexible glue used for general wood construction.

Pylon mounting An engine mounted above the fuselage on a streamlined pylon.

Rib A chordwise constructional member in a wing which replicates the aerofoil section.

Roll Movement about the lateral axis of a model.

Rotation The positive nose-up movement of a model on the take off run just prior to lift off.

Rovings Material used in GRP construction where the fibres are orientated in one direction.

Rudder The control surface which controls yaw.

Ruddervators Control surfaces on V tail models combining the functions of rudder and elevator.

Semi-symmetrical An aerofoil with a little camber and convex upper and lower surfaces.

Slop Undesirable free movement in any control linkage.

Snake A type of control link comprising a Bowden cable or plastic rod in a plastic tube.

Span The wing tip to wing tip size of a model.

Spin An automatic, continuous rotation which occurs when one wing stalls before the other.

Spar A major component which lies along the span of a wing.

Spoiler A control for reducing lift by spoiling the airflow over part of a wing's upper surface.

Stall At a model's lowest straight and level speed, the stall is a marked by loss of lift, increase in drag and loss of height. Stalling speed is affected by manoeuvring and using high lift devices.

Straight and level flight Flight in a constant direction, neither climbing nor descending.

Stringer A secondary longitudinal member running part or the whole length of the fuselage.

Symmetrical section An aerofoil without camber.

Tailplane The horizontal stabilising surface of a model.

Tip The outboard end of wing or tailplane.

Tip stall A wing drop caused by a stall on the outboard portion of only one wing.

Trailing edge The rear edge of any flying surface.

Veneer Thin wood sheet used to skin foam wings.

Washout A built-in twist in a wing where the tip is at a lower angle of incidence than the root.

Web A structural part between two others, typically spars, to increase strength.

Wing area The span of a wing multiplied by the mean chord.

Wing loading The weight of a model divided by its wing area.

Wing thickness The maximum thickness of a wing, divided by the chord at that point, as a percentage.

Yaw Movement about the directional axis of a model.